The First Black President

The First Black President

Barack Obama, Race, Politics, and the American Dream

Johnny Bernard Hill, PhD

First published in 2009 by PALGRAVE MACMILLAN® in the United States –
a division of St. Martin's Press LLC, 175 Fifth Avenue, New York, NY
10010.

Where this book is distributed in the UK, Europe and the rest of the world,
this is by Palgrave Macmillan, a division of Macmillan Publishers Limited,
registered in England, company number 785998, of Houndmills, Basingstoke,
Hampshire RG21 6XS.

Palgrave Macmillan is the global academic imprint of the above companies
and has companies and representatives throughout the world.

Palgrave® and Macmillan® are registered trademarks in the United States, the
United Kingdom, Europe and other countries.

ISBN: 978-0-2306-1861-9

Library of Congress Cataloging-in-Publication Data.

Hill, Johnny Bernard.
    The first Black president : Barack Obama, race, politics, and the
American dream / Johnny Bernard Hill.
        p. cm.
    ISBN 978-0-230-61861-9 (alk. paper)
    1. Obama, Barack—Political and social views. 2. Obama, Barack—
Influence. 3. United States—Race relations—Political aspects. 4. United
States—Race relations—Government policy. 5. United States—Social
conditions—21st century. 6. African Americans—Race identity—Political
aspects. 7. African Americans—Social conditions—21st century. I. Title.
    E908.H55 2009
    973.932092—dc22   2009009522

A catalogue record of the book is available from the British Library.

Design by Macmillan Publishing Solutions

First edition: November 2009

D-10-9-8-7-6-5-4-3

Printed in the United States of America.

Dedicated to:

My children: Regan and Jonathan

Nieces and nephews: Ashley, Alex, Alexis, Brandon, Kenyatta, André, Keiara, Courtney, Travis, Catrice, Aaliyah, Malik, Miles, Lauren and Tariq, and Deante

Dare to Dream!

Contents

Acknowledgments

Since Barack Obama announced his historic bid for the presidency of the United States in Springfield, Illinois, in 2007, I have thought very carefully about what it means to reflect on the historical and social aspects of the moment. Without the support of many friends, colleagues, and relatives, I highly doubt this project would have moved beyond mere speculation. Through their urging, I was both encouraged and empowered to lay down these tentative thoughts on race in America and how Obama may come to our aid in these reflections.

At every stage of the campaign, Scott Williamson, my close friend and colleague at Louisville Seminary, was an important conversation partner. He was incredibly instrumental in helping me think through various aspects of the project, the audience, and sources. I also wish to thank my colleagues at Louisville Seminary who have provided a continuous source of strength and encouragement throughout.

My deepest thanks and appreciation go to my beloved family. To my sisters (Gina, Leanette, Sherri, Joyce, Melissa, Teresa, and Cheryl), I say thank you for lending your ear and hearing my constant bickering and pontification about the issues raised in this book. My friend Michael Cook, who is now in a doctoral program in counseling at Columbia Seminary in Atlanta, Georgia, was a calm voice and affirming personality at many points of frustration during this project. For that, I am eternally grateful. Finally, my wife, Trinia, has been a steady rock and faithful partner who has been central to making this book a reality. Additionally, I found myself constantly reflecting on the lives of my beautiful children, Jonathan and Regan, in writing the book with the hope and expectation that their lives might be a little better and brighter than previous generations because of Obama's presidency. They will not know of a world without a black president, which holds tremendous possibilities for how they envision the world and their lives into the future. For them, I say with the sincerest of simplicity—I love you and dare to dream.

Introduction

Away back in the days of bondage they thought to see in one divine event the end of all doubt and disappointments; few men ever worshipped Freedom with half such unquestioning faith as did the American Negro for two centuries. To him, so far as he thought and dreamed, slavery was indeed the sum of all villainies, the cause of all sorrow, the root of all prejudices; Emancipation was the key to a promised land of sweeter beauty than ever stretched before the eyes of wearied Israelites. In song and exhortation swelled one refrain— Liberty; in his tears and curses the God he implored had Freedom in his right hand. At last it came, suddenly, fearfully, like a dream. With one wild carnival of blood and passion came the message in his own plaintive cadence—
"Shout, O children! Shout, you're free!
For God has bought your liberty!"[1]

Obama and the American Dream

Barack Obama, in so many ways, is an expression of the fulfillment of the American dream. His presidency also marks a decisive moment in the grand story of the black freedom struggle in America. With tears in his eyes, John Lewis, the pioneering civil rights leader, who walked with King and other freedom fighters, swelled with pride as millions gathered to witness Obama's inauguration on January 20, 2009. The world was also watching. All around the globe, many are following the developments of an Obama administration with painful expectancy. With the hopeful idealism of Obama comes the promise and possibility of what America might become and what the world hopes America would be. With the election of Obama, America has experienced nothing short of a political and cultural revolution. This idea may very well be a stretch for some observers, such as Vincent Hutchings, political science professor at the University of Michigan. Hutchings has argued that the demographic changes that took place over the last decade reflected a kind of geographic diversity and contributed to Obama's success in the primaries and later in the election. Hutchings also asserts that in terms of attitudes toward governmental programs, blacks and whites essentially share common divisions and commitments as a part of society in general. However, in terms of race, make no mistake. Obama's election was no small feat. Generations from now, historians and political theorists will be toiling over the events of 2008 and the January 20 inauguration, where millions poured into Washington, D.C., to witness the grand occasion. Many questions will be asked, but one unavoidable question is what would America be without its black sons and daughters? What would the American dream be without the black freedom struggle that gives it intelligibility?

If Obama's presidency means anything, it marks a grand achievement in the unfolding historical American struggle for freedom and human dignity. This book is about understanding these very questions, to contribute to the beginnings of what will become a long and enduring conversation of what the nation, and subsequently the world, has experienced with the election of America's first black president—Barack Obama. Just days before clinching the Democratic nomination for president from Hillary Clinton, I walked into the local Borders bookstore to purchase my own paperback copies of David Mendall's *Obama from Promise to Power* and Obama's *The Audacity of Hope*. While checking out, standing before me was a graying near-retirement white woman. As she was scanning the books, she paused to tell me a story of her experience with Obama. She had read his book *Dreams from My Father* some years earlier. "As I read the book I said to myself, this is our president," she gasped. With a sense of controlled emotion, she said, "I get chills just thinking about it." She continued on about how his background as a global citizen and labor activist was exactly what the nation needed during this time of war and economic crisis. Thinking about what the woman said, I walked out of the store damn near baffled. In all my years, I have never seen any white woman, especially in the south, excited about a black politician or any other black public figure. Perhaps there was something about Obama that, like Martin Luther King, Jr., appealed to something so fundamentally human within us all that causes us to look at race in new and intriguing ways.

Indeed, the eager words of the checkout lady would make very little sense and probably wouldn't even deserve a second thought were it not for America's painfully divisive racial past and present. Were it not for slavery, Jim Crow, black men in prison, and Jena Six, Obama's candidacy or political leadership in general wouldn't mean very much at all. Organizations such as COFO (Council of Federated Organizations), SCLC (Southern Christian Leadership Conference), FOR (Fellowship of Reconciliation), SNCC (Student Nonviolent Coordinating Committee), NAACP (National Association for the Advancement of Colored People), and the MFDP (Mississippi Freedom Democratic Party), and countless others all worked tirelessly to create the conditions under which an Obama presidency could be possible.[2] For instance, Harold Washington's historic win as the first African American mayor of Chicago in 1983, the 1988 presidential campaign of Jesse Jackson, and Al Sharpton's presidential campaign in 2003 helped pave the road for Obama's victory. It is, in fact, precisely because of America's social, cultural, and economic heritage that Obama's presidency is a moment of celebration, wonder, and consternation. In my lifetime, I can't recall this much activity or excitement around any presidential candidate. I certainly can't remember a time, perhaps since the late sixties, when so many young people have been engaged in the election process. Sitting at the dinner table with my ghetto-fabulous teenage niece whose idols are Jay Z, Beyoncé, and 50 Cent, I nearly choked on the food I was eating when she went on about the latest political tensions between Obama and Clinton during the Democratic primaries in Spring 2008, explaining her views on why Hillary needed to let it go and drop out. This simple feat points to the dramatic way in which Obama's presidency ignited a new generation of black and white youth in their struggle to navigate a culture of intensified violence and materialism.

Since the announcement of Barack Obama's run for president in the shadows of the Lincoln Memorial in Springfield, Illinois, the nation, and for that matter the world, has been astounded by the historical possibilities of the young senator becoming the "first black president" of the United States of America. As an African American man born in 1971, part of the "post–civil rights" generation, I have watched with both inspiration and awe the historical magnitude of what the world is now witnessing on the lands of former slaves and former slave owners. I mean, who could have imagined that in our lifetime, just forty years after the assassination of Martin Luther King, Jr., on the balcony of the Lorraine Hotel in Memphis, Tennessee, we would witness such a momentous occasion? Obama's campaign, inauguration, and presidency speak loudly about the possibilities and limitations of racial progress in the country. Revisiting W. E. B. Du Bois' conversation about the "color line" related to Obama's rise to prominence and what the future holds for all of us is not only timely but necessary as we move forward in a post–Bush/Cheney political narrative.

Setting the Stage: Racial Politics in the Age of Obama

This book offers a critical, yet personal, account of the historical significance of Obama as the first black president of the United States, what it means for the "color line" that Du Bois spoke of more than a century ago, and its implications for racial politics in America and the world. Who would deny the amazingly historic journey of Obama's campaign for president, his warring with Hillary Clinton, and the raging ideological battle between Obama and John McCain? Behind the talking heads of the news networks, inexhaustible political blogs, and print articles about the campaign, many questions rest under the surface about ancient assumptions, feelings, stereotypes, fears, and anxieties concerning racial difference, which have existed for generations. Many blacks have believed, very passionately, that racism hasn't gone anywhere. In fact, some point to the Hurricane Katrina debacle, overcrowded prisons, housing and health disparities, and other social issues as evidence that racism not only still exists, it has become much worse. On the other hand, the masses of white Americans, and many nonblack minority communities, maintain that racism is by and large a thing of the past.

The Obama campaign, and his subsequent election, reveals the depth of misunderstandings harbored by whites and blacks alike when it comes to where the "other" is on race and politics. In this book, I explore the political, historical, and racial dynamics behind Obama's run for president and what it means for each of us in the years, perhaps even decades, ahead. The fact that Obama is now the "first black president" of the United States only makes sense on the backdrop of America's racist past. At the same time, the ways Obama himself views race of mixed racial identity says volumes about who we are as Americans and what it means to possibly inhabit new spaces of meaning and community when it comes to overcoming the pain and suffering of the past. This book is written for individuals who wish to understand the historical contours and meaning of Obama's presidency— that it's not a freak of nature or an anomaly in American racial politics. Rather, it represents a natural development in the historical, political, and cultural saga of America as an experiment with justice, freedom, and liberty. It is my hope that this is the beginning, not the end, of a conversation that leads to meaningful developments toward equality, justice, and freedom in America and the world.

Looking Back to Reach Forward: Confronting Du Bois' Challenge for Our Time

As a point of departure, I employ the ancient wisdom of W. E. B. Du Bois as a necessary conversation partner to understand the provocative landscape of race and politics in light of the Obama presidency and what it means for the future of race in America. Had Du Bois lived to see Obama's inauguration as the first bona fide black president of the United States, he would be as thrilled as he would be ambivalent. The world that Du Bois knew was openly and aggressively racially hostile. It was a world of Jim Crow, lynching, and emphatic black powerlessness. When Du Bois wrote

The Souls of Black Folks in 1903, there were few to no black senators, congressmen, governors, or federal judges. In fact, public black political leadership was nearly unheard of. Blacks were forced into a courageous existence of struggle. Du Bois, at the turn of the century, admonished that the problem of the twentieth century would undoubtedly be the problem of the color line. And, truly, he was dead on. In *The Souls of Black Folks*, with painful and prophetic accuracy, Du Bois' words still holds dramatic meaning for us today in the new era of an Obama presidency. Du Bois wrote:

> "And thus in the Land of the Color-line I saw, as it fell across my baby, the shadow of the Veil.
>
> Within the Veil was he born, said and there within shall he live,—a Negro's son. Holding in that little head-ah, bitterly!—the unbowed pride of a hunted race, clinging with that tiny dimpled hand-ah, wearily!—to a hope not hopeless but hopeful, and seeing with those bring wondering eyes that peer into my soul a land whose freedom is to us a mockery and whose liberty a lie. I saw the shadow of the Veil as it passed over my baby, I saw the cold city towering above the blood-red land. I held my face beside his little cheek, showed him the star-children and the twinkling lights as they began to flash, and stilled with an even-song the unvoiced terror of my life."[3]

In poetic prose, Du Bois was describing what it means to be black in America. His descriptions are not only poignant for today's context but desperately necessary to advance racial understandings and forge ahead in the quest for freedom, justice, equality, and a beloved community at home and abroad. Du Bois was insistent on a bold struggle to help America overcome racism, while always acknowledging the perennial legacy of racial difference—that there are fundamental differences among blacks and whites, as well as other ethnic and cultural groups around the world, differences that ought to be respected, honored and celebrated.

Although America had survived two world wars, the Great Depression, and the Korean War, the plight of black folks in America refused to retreat into the shadows of public indifference. The African American freedom struggle of the 1950s and 1960s was an inevitable eruption of mounting racial oppression and discontent. Out of this context, Du Bois would ask, what does this history of struggle mean for Obama? Having grown up in Hawaii and Indonesia as the son of a Kenyan father and a midwestern Kansas mother, does Obama share in the pain and struggle of most African Americans who have come through the storm of racial injustice in America? Obama's upbringing does not suggest the presence of the kind of generational memory and experience that most blacks in America have encountered through relatives, friends, colleagues, and others whose lives are deeply infused with white bitterness and years of political disappointment. Du Bois' forecast of America's racial climate gives us a necessary glimpse into Obama's presidency and what it means for all of us in this time.

A Brief Word about Perspective

My simple perspective on these historical events is neither unique nor compelling in the one sense. What I do provide, however, is a heartfelt, passionate perspective on a historical moment that, I believe, people across the globe will be pondering for many years to come. Like most black men, I've been through the storm. I've seen my share of struggle and pain. In the southeast Georgia town of Vidalia, where I was born, there was not much cause for optimism concerning race. In the town of a population of around 15,000, black businesses are virtually nonexistent. My father was a sanitation worker and my mother a nursing aide at the city's nursing home. We were poor but dignified. So now, thinking about my own experience, as I think about what Obama as the first black president means for black folks in my small southern hometown, I swell with both pride and enthusiasm. At the same time, I am pessimistically optimistic, because in America, race runs as deep and thick as the Mississippi River.

What I hope to do in these few pages is to talk about Obama's historic campaign and inauguration as the official first black president of the United States of America in light of America's racist past. Of course, in some real sense, all presidential elections are historic. Any time there is a presidential election, the great issues of the world come to bear. The person elected or selected for president carries with them the hopes, dreams, and aspirations of millions. So, on the one hand this election is indeed as historic as all the rest at the very least. On the other hand, there is something uniquely historic about this election, the Obama candidacy for president, and his inauguration. Since the very beginning of his announcement of his presidential bid in Springfield, Illinois, on the steps of the historic backdrop of the Lincoln Memorial, there has been something especially appealing about this election. For many whites, it has sort of a mystical quality to it. It conjures up feelings of a kind of idealistic era, the era of John F. Kennedy, Martin Luther King, Jr., and the Beatles. For many blacks, Obama comes as somewhat of an heir of the King legacy, as someone acutely aware of the deep pain and suffering many blacks feel and having the courage to tell the truth in the face of incredible odds. While some blacks were a bit hesitant to support Obama at first, they quickly came around when they saw that he could not only win over white voters (as was the case in South Carolina of the Democratic primary) but speak eloquently and plainly to the particular challenges affecting black America.

No Easy Road: Blacks and Politics in America

It has always been a struggle for black Americans entering into politics. In 1867, reconstruction acts were passed by Congress granting the first newly freed enslaved Africans voting rights.[4] These new laws paved the way for men like John W. Maynard, who was elected to the House of Representatives in 1868 in Louisiana. Joseph Hayne Rainey was elected to the U.S. House of Representatives in 1870 and was reelected four more terms. The first black U.S. senator was Hiram Revels, representing the state of Mississippi. The historic voting rights gains of the Thirteenth and Fourteenth Amendments and the Civil Rights Act of 1964 during the civil rights movement further opened the door for blacks to participate in the political process. Shirley Chisholm's courageous run for president in the early 1970s served as a forerunner to Jesse Jackson's bid for president in 1988. Without the historical achievements during postreconstruction, the painstaking work of early twentieth-century leaders like Du Bois, Booker T. Washington, A. Phillip Randolf, Mary McLeod Bethune, and Thurgood Marshall, as well as those magnificent freedom fighters of the civil rights movement, what the nation and the world is experiencing now with an Obama presidency would be little more than a hopeful imagination.

In the eyes of many black people, Obama not only has star quality, he has prophetic vision. In a CNN interview just days after Obama had clinched the Democratic nomination, the former head of the SCLC and civil rights pioneer Joseph Lowery shared his enthusiasm by suggesting that Obama (like many other black leaders) may have been "called" by God to lead the nation through this turbulent period. Lowery's comments speak to both the incredible hope and confidence many blacks feel about Obama's candidacy and subsequent rise to power. With dramatic symbolism, Lowery offered the closing benediction during the inauguration, expressing the ways in which Obama's election was a continuum in the unfolding saga of the quest for black freedom in America.

As the reader will pick up in these pages, I offer a word of caution about the tempting "messiah complex" of the black community that would often cast onto its leaders near-superhuman prowess. History has taught us well that viewing human leaders in this way can lead to feelings of debilitating disappointment and social stagnation. We must resist the temptation to place President Obama on a highly deified pedestal. While celebrating his achievement and all that it means for African descendents throughout the world, we must continue to acknowledge his humanity while holding him accountable as a politician in the highest office of the land.

The confidence many blacks feel is based not just on what Obama might *do* as president. Indeed, that's critical. Hopefully, Obama will do something about the many issues facing black America from the overcrowded prisons, deteriorating schools, and housing to joblessness and healthcare. However, many blacks are ecstatic about Obama's presidency for *who* he is, his racial identity, and what he represents within the shadows of America's racist past. This is truly a dangerous orientation. Like all politicians, Obama is beholden to a pervasive systemic political structure that does not have a history of being kind to reformers. From Abraham Lincoln and Dwight Eisenhower to John F. Kennedy, Martin Luther King, Jr., and Shirley Chisholm, historical precedence would say that the political system in America breeds corruption, compromise, and violence. Obama is not naive in this sense. He knows what's at stake and recognizes that compromise is always part of the political reality. This is why many blacks would do well to proceed with caution in their love and adoration of this talented political figure. Unlike his wife, Michelle Obama, and the vast majority of black Americans whose ancestors carry with them the blood of slaves in their veins, Obama became an African American by choice. He chose to identify with the African American experience, its history and culture. He chose to cast his lot among the masses of black Americans who for centuries have labored in the sun of American oppression and suffering. He chose to take on the cloak of the black racial struggle for survival and human dignity. Yet, Obama's experiences have also led him to an entirely different worldview when it comes to race—a worldview much more trusting, optimistic, and enthusiastic about the possibilities of political and racial progress in America.

Most blacks, through generations of struggle and historical memory handed down for many years, have come through the storm. Black folks know all too well that the sting of racism does not easily go away. In fact, it burns deeper and more severe in nuanced ways over time. Growing up in Hawaii and Indonesia, Obama was shielded from many of the insidious structural realities of racism in America. Although he experienced racial language and perhaps even the attitudes of white racist family members, he was protected by his white mother and grandparents from an otherwise treacherous racist world. Certainly racism was present in Hawaii and other parts of the world, but it comes with a different face and intensity in the South and many northern ghettos. Blacks in the South and northern ghettos were naked in the face of public ridicule, rejection, and outright racial violence. Racism was and is a way of life for the overwhelming majority of black people living in America. By and large, Obama experienced a privileged existence compared to most blacks. He attended the finest schools, traveled the world, and was allowed entrance to spaces often reserved for "whites only." Those few blacks who are skeptical about Obama have good reason. His lived journey does not exactly mirror that of most blacks.

In some real sense, though, Obama has shown in his personal narrative signs of genuine committed black leadership. Granted, Obama was raised by a white mother from the midwest and his paternal roots lie in Kenya, but his commitment to supporting laid-off steel workers in Chicago and challenging the seat of Bobby Rush, longtime African American Southside congressman, certainly points to his integrity. Even one of his friends during his time in the state house of Illinois, Donne Trotter, accused Obama as lacking in black authenticity.[5] After losing to Rush, Obama was alienated by many of Rush's old school civil rights–era friends. He was viewed as an outsider and criticized for speaking in condescending ways to black folks in Southside Chicago. Many blacks were more interested in what Obama would do to make their lives better rather than in his impressive resume.

According to the journalist David Mendell, Obama did some serious "soul searching" after the crushing defeat to Rush. He learned quickly and painfully that the suffering endured by many blacks made them profoundly sensitive to light political rhetoric. For years they had heard slick politicians making their rounds to churches, social clubs, restaurants, and even bars to make their case as they attempt to woo the crowds with their fancy rhetoric and empty promises. What they had learned was that politicians had better have more in their corners than in their resumes. Obama's close friend and pastor, Dr. Jeremiah Wright at Trinity United Church of Christ, was exactly the ace in the hole that Obama needed to make an electrifying comeback— quest for U.S. Senate.

Indeed, Obama received tremendous help from the black Church, no doubt due to the support of his controversial pastor. Obama's relationship with Wright of course proved to be not only problematic but downright fatal during his bid for the Democratic presidential nomination. His connections to Wright weren't controversial because Wright had been involved in some kind of terroristic conspiracy, legal allegations, or even just plain bad character. His relationship with Wright was harmful to his political future solely because Wright, like many black folks (including those who attend church every Sunday morning), holds a radically different view of America than many of its predominately European counterparts. Du Bois described these differences in terms of what he called the "veil" between blacks and whites in America. Like two sides of a coin, blacks and whites have experienced different, albeit competing, historical narratives—the one filled with hopes and dreams saturated with tones of manifest destiny, the other with songs of sorrow and suffering, yet struggle and triumph. The Wright controversy also pointed out the complex racial dynamics at play throughout this election.

The question on the minds of many whites throughout the nation was, "can Obama be trusted?" One of the realities that whites have long feared in this country was if blacks gained political power, would they retaliate for the tremendous history of suffering from slavery through segregation and the persistent pain of racism. On the other hand, many blacks wanted to know and still want to know if Obama, like many blacks before him through the history of the black experience, would, to borrow Randall Kennedy's concept, just "sell out."[6] Would Obama, in the ambitious quest for the most powerful political seat in the world, obfuscate his loyalty to the plight of black folks in America? This question still looms. It has yet to be revealed what kind of president Obama will be. He is young. He is gifted. He is black. But whether or not he will courageously hold up the banner of freedom and human dignity as far as the poor and powerless are concerned is truly a mystery within an enigma. One thing is for certain: the world will be watching.

The Promised Land? Seizing the Moment for Real Change

Obama's presidency makes little sense apart from both the image of the American dream as a metaphor for the perceived promise and possibility reflected in American society and the black freedom struggle that has come to define the very heart and soul of American democratic ideals. Throughout the book, I intend to make connections between Obama's presidency and the interrelatedness of race, politics, and the notion of the American dream. The first chapter presents the civil rights movement and Martin Luther King, Jr., as laying the foundations of an Obama presidency a generation later. As Tom Brokaw said just moments after official numbers came in confirming Obama's historic win, it is impossible to understand Obama as a political leader and the meaning of his inauguration and presidency apart from the civil rights movement. It is because of the civil rights movement, with the defeat of Jim Crow and passing of the Voting Rights Bill, that Obama was able to even have a chance to win the election. Furthermore, the civil rights movement established a cultural sea change toward racial inclusivity that continues to have reverberations today. This chapter also offers a comparison of Obama and Martin Luther King, Jr., as a way of getting at the possibilities and limitations of Obama's leadership in our time. Because of King's assassination on the balcony of the Lorraine Hotel in Memphis, Tennessee, on April 4, 1968, we will never know what might have been for race relations in America and uplift of the world's poor. We do know that toward the end of King's life, he set his sights more toward economic issues, recognizing the profound connections between racism and poverty in America and abroad. He introduced the Poor People's Campaign in 1967, attempting to advance what he called a "Bill of Rights" for the poor. Some described this effort as a push for a form of democratic social-ism, in which safeguards that provide minimal shelter, food, healthcare, and education for the poorest among us are built into the economic fabric of global and domestic policy. Civil rights leaders of the time viewed this as somewhat of the unfinished business of the civil rights movement. Obama has demonstrated his commitment to low-income and working-class peo-ple. But would he support the kinds of initiatives King was protesting for toward the end of his life, causes for which he ultimately died?

In Chapter 2, I explore the life of Barack Obama and the current debates around race in America. Obama, without question, has helped us to once again establish a new and vigorous debate about race in America. His own life story, as a person of mixed ancestry yet fully African American, points to the complexity and rapidly changing landscape of racial difference in America. No longer are there clear lines and distinctions between "blacks" and "whites," both linked directly to the history of the slave trade. America is changing. With the expansion and reality of globalization and other changing racial and ethnic demographics in the country, it is now time for Americans to pause and dramatically reassess notions of national identity and how we view race. Because, in many ways, Obama represents these changes, as the first black president and new leader of the free world, bring-ing into conversation his unique experiences with the eloquent insights of Du Bois will broaden our scope and analysis of the situation.

Contrary to some claims that have tried to use Obama's presidency to hail the inauguration of a "postracial" society, race is still perhaps the most urgent problem in our society. In fact, given the ways in which America's influence expands across the globe, the problem of race may very well be one of the greatest global problems of our time. I point to the sharp distinc-tions in Obama's multicultural roots from many other African Americans tracing their lineage to Africa through the slave trade and how it has impacted Obama's obvious sense of optimism about America while fueling the sense of nihilism felt by many in the African American community over prospects for meaningful social change. Evidence of the dramatic differences in white and black America is also addressed, as exposed in the scandal around Obama's longtime pastor, Dr. Jeremiah Wright, during the Democratic primaries and circulating throughout most of the campaign.

In the third chapter, I confront the historical dimensions of race in America and attempt to situate Obama's election as the first black president in the contemporary context of a persistently racially hostile society. Here, I address the question of the implications of the Obama presidency in light of what Derrick Bell calls the "permanence of racism." There will no doubt be a fair amount of jubilation around Obama's presidency from all sectors of society, especially black folks and Africans across the globe. I would be surprised if many in the black community did not swell up with a great sense of pride and awe, of empowerment and hope. But does this mean the activists, idealists, skeptics, and naysayers need to be silenced, to close their suitcases, pack up, and go home? Will an Obama presidency instantly change the realities of overcrowded prisons, a crumbling public educational system, poor housing, and other social ills particularly burdening life in black America? Certainly not. Tavis Smiley's book, *Accountable,* which issues a call to the American people to hold all political leaders responsible for their actions in representing them, is the kind of awareness I am referring to here. My aim in this chapter is to try to make sense of the historical significance of Obama's election in light of the history of racial struggle in America. At the same time, I invoke history as a compelling reminder that an Obama presidency is not the time to grow content with the state of race and racism, but an occasion for renewed and radical action to confront the social, political, and economic legacies of racism.

To do this, I enlist the aid of two leading thinkers, one a historian and the other a philosopher and social critic. John Hope Franklin, a leading historian who chaired Bill Clinton's landmark commission on race in the late 1990s has spent his life chronicling African American history in America and the gripping saga to overcome racism. Franklin provides the historical backdrop of a critical social and political analysis of what the issue of race has looked like in recent years. From the Rodney King beatings to the recent events of Jena Six, Cornel West helps us to uncover the deep roots of race, racism, and white supremacy that permeate the very soul of America. Only by looking at this reality in the raw, for what it is, can we look upon Obama's presidency with a profound sense of hope and possibility for what lies ahead. Without question, Obama's election is a historical event of epic proportions in its own right. However, the plight of many blacks living in America, who feel the bitter sting of racism and economic injustice on a daily basis, deserves the kind of serious attention that goes beyond mere emotional exuberance. The fight for freedom, justice, and equality will continue and must endure.

Chapter 4 looks at some of the broader implications of Obama's presidency across the African diaspora. Black- and brown-skinned peoples, across

Africa, Asia, Latin America, and Pacific Islands alike, looked upon the American presidential campaign with majestic awe. As evidenced in Obama's own life, the African diaspora is now in America, with our neighbors, coworkers, friends, relatives, and lovers. Technologies, mass communication, travel, and global media have now brought the world to our doorsteps. Indeed, the ways in which Americans are now deeply connected to global realities are undeniable. The world is now in America, and America's presence is felt throughout the world. In Obama, many throughout this vast globe see a chance for a more peaceful and brighter future. They see in Obama an expression of their deepest hopes and dreams for a better future for their children and grandchildren. Obama's European tour during his first one hundred days in office is a compelling example of the sort of expectancy that has gripped much of the world since he took charge—a world that America can no longer ignore.

Because of the entrenched interrelatedness of the current global economy, there is nowhere to escape the long-reaching tentacles of U.S. economic and cultural influences. When the financial markets on Wall Street began to freeze up in late September 2008 during the campaign, we saw the shivers that the crisis delivered up the spine of foreign governments all over the world. Particularly affected are countries still attempting to overcome the ravages of colonialism, slavery, and decades of economic neglect and hardship. In places like Kenya (Obama's paternal native land), the Republic of Haiti, Brazil, and parts of Europe, there is a passionate air of expectancy about the possibilities of Obama's leadership of the most powerful nation on earth. The issues of HIV/AIDS, genocide in Darfur, and poverty in developing nations have reached epidemic proportions never before seen in human history.

The growing gap between the more privileged nations of the West and, primarily, developing nations of Asia, Africa, and Latin America is intensifying and seems to be reaching a point of no return. According to a World Health Organization report, entitled "Primary Healthcare Now More Than Ever," blatant health disparities around the world are intensifying like never before. They argue that "of the estimated 136 million women who will give birth this year, around 58 million will receive no medical assistance whatsoever during childbirth and the postpartum period, endangering their lives and that of their infants."[7] How will Obama respond to this cry of desperation? Will he call the wealthiest nations of the world to account and respond in urgent ways to these global crises or simply turn a blind eye and deaf ear to the problems? Indeed, Obama's greatness has already been demonstrated by breaking down the long-held historical racial barriers to become the president, so it is fair to assume he will most likely be attentive to these concerns.

In another sense, the fierce urgency of present realities warrants a more determined effort to transform U. S. and global economic policies in a more equitable direction on behalf of the poor of the world. Obama has characterized himself as a "citizen of the world." So, based on his rhetoric and lived experience, there is evidence that would suggest that Obama is indeed willing. Because of the powerful and systemic forces of greed, white supremacy and Western dominance, and the lusts of empire, the question is also whether he will be able to. In either case, looking at Obama's presidency through the lens of the global African community may shine light on these questions and issues.

Chapters 5 and 6 consider the ways in which Obama, as president, really marks a radical transition in the shape and face of the black community. The black community is no longer a homogeneous body of individuals who could largely trace their roots through the history of slavery in America. The black community is much more fluid, global, multilingual, and interconnected, in ways unimaginable more than a generation ago. As a multiracial, culturally diverse, political figure, Obama's life reflects the ways in which black identity is changing. These changes, as seen with Obama, will have enormous implications in mobilizing for social change in America and abroad. Specifically, in Chapter 5, I show how Obama's presidency causes us to reexamine the nature of black political identity and its connections to the roots of black nationalism in America. Obama walks in the legacy of the history of black nationalism, from Marcus Garvey through the Harlem Renaissance to Du Bois, Malcolm X, and the Pan-Africanism movement. Reflecting on this tradition enhances our ability to understand the historical significance of Obama as the first black president and its impact on the campaign.

Building on the idea that Obama's presidency will have reverberations beyond America's shores and that race in America is in effect about more than America itself, in Chapter 7, I examine the interconnectedness of power and technology in this new age. Few would deny the powerful role technology played in Obama's seizure of political power. From the very beginning, Obama's fund-raising strategy was classically grassroots. With the capacity to raise money online and the dynamic, even superfast, abilities to text message, e-mail, and share information in near real time, Obama was even able to conquer possibly the most powerful political machine of our generation—Bill and Hillary Clinton. The Clintons relied on lifelong friendships, dated campaigning strategies, and old school print and organizational mobilization, while Obama invoked the resources of technology, urging students and young professionals from across the country to text message friends, family members, coworkers, and leaders to give what they had to the political process. Most of Obama's supporters donated less than $200 per gift. By doing this, Obama not only empowered people who were usually marginalized from the political process, he dignified their desire to participate in their own political reality. He was able to give voice to entire legions of Americans who for decades saw no hope of having voice at all. In a strategic sense, by using this grassroots, "bottom up," strategy, Obama was also gaining the allegiance of thousands of foot soldiers who could help organize local communities and establish a fund-raising machine of supporters he could continue to appeal to throughout the campaign, and perhaps into his presidency. Technology has forever changed the political process in America. What impact will technology play in reshaping the politics of race, economics, and global influences in the years to come? I briefly explore these themes and its connections to the abundance of information generated throughout the campaign.

From here, I consider in Chapter 8 the dramatic economic changes that have taken place, Obama's interest in pushing corporate interests out of the political process, the collapse of Wall Street and free-market capitalism, and what all this means for black America. Too often, the concerns of black folks in the mirage of political debates never receive adequate attention. For instance, the fact that the housing foreclosure crisis contributed to the meltdown on Wall Street reflects the dramatic housing and economic disparities in this country. Millions of Americans, particularly black folks, are suffering from the racialized policies and segregated housing communities across the country, which cannot be divorced from the crisis in education. Obama, as a community organizer, is well aware of the interrelatedness of the disastrous *laissez faire* (hands off) economic policies on Wall Street and poor people in local communities struggling to find decent shelter for their children and elderly members. Many Americans benefited greatly from the "high-risk" mortgage-lending practices with little regard for the broader housing crisis in America. Under the Bush administration, many investors saw their portfolios swell as Wall Street had a field day as the kind of cutthroat predatory lending practices became cloaked in adjustable rate mortgages. The housing crisis in America is real and is having dire consequences for poor and working-class black communities. This is an issue directly related to funding for education and high dropout rates among young black males, which consequently contributes to gang activity and high rates of juvenile and adult incarceration. This chapter offers an appraisal of the current economic dilemma in America, its connections to race, and the ways in which Obama's "bottom up" economic commitments may yield some hopeful possibilities for poor black communities.

Chapters 9 and 10 probe the meaning of an Obama administration for Americans and the world in a number of areas. Drawing on the legacy of Martin Luther King, Jr., I look at Obama's influence on global policy. I argue that, on the one hand, by simply being elected president, Obama has changed the face of global politics. Like King, Obama inspired millions of black- and brown-skinned peoples around the world, fueling passionate determination to change the sort of policies that hamper development in their countries and communities. On the other hand, because Obama's administration is so new, I show how Obama must take bold and courageous steps to do politics differently. He has already announced that he favors a dialogical style of diplomacy. Meaning, instead of alienating political enemies, he is more apt to enter into some form of dialogue without "precondition." This is an important shift in the Bush-and-Cheney brand of "punishment" diplomacy, which if employed correctly, could transform international policy configurations in astounding ways.

Chapter 10 offers some tentative reflections on how Obama's presidency could impact each of us by examining a host of policy issues from health care, militarism, education, and housing to incarceration, the legal system, and generally the black family. I conclude that chapter with a brief word about Obama's rhetoric of hope, what it means for the nihilism of many in our time, and an appropriate response. Obama is a human being and historical personality who, like those before him, will be judged not only for what he does but also for what he does not do. There is also a sense in which, like other historical figures, Obama is a reflection of all of us—our hopes and fears, our dreams and nightmares. So, what is our individual and corporate responsibility in light of Obama's presidency and the times in which we now live? What are we called to do and how do we do it? From this perspective, I cast an imaginative vision of what should be on the agenda in this regard and the ways in which history is depending on our individual and collective faithfulness both now and for generations yet unseen.

CHAPTER 1

I Have A Dream! Martin Luther King, Jr., the Civil Rights Movement, and Barack Obama

We shall overcome, we shall overcome, we shall overcome some day; Deep in my heart, I do believe, that we shall overcome some day.[1]

I may not get there with you, but I want you to know tonight that we as a people will get to the promised land; so I'm happy tonight; I'm not worried about anything. Mine eyes have seen the glory of the coming of the Lord.[2]

The idea of the American dream has always been shaped, molded, and purified in the fires of dissonant voices calling the nation to be what it ought to be. Without the Civil Rights Movement, there would be no Barack Obama as we now know him. The mere idea of a black male running for such a high office, in fact the highest office in the land, would only be a distant fantasy without the courageous service of countless freedom fighters, known and unknown, more than a generation ago. If we are to fully understand the magnitude of Obama's presidency and appreciate what his administration means for today and generations to come, delving into the lives and events around the Civil Rights Movement is essential. More than fifty years after the nonviolent protest of the Montgomery Bus Boycott in 1955, persistent questions continue to loom as to the ways in which oppressed peoples are to pursue justice while at the same time attempting to live in peace with one's neighbor. This is not an easy conversation. The postmodern world of the twenty-first century has incited new challenges and problems. These problems now find dramatic expression in increased racial, ethnic, and cultural fragmentation and the insidious prominence of technology situated in everyday human life. Increased cross-continental travel, mass communication, and multinational trade mechanisms have compelled theologians, political scientists, cultural critics, and persons of diverse religious faiths and culture as a whole to think critically about how to forge community in such a world of difference. The Civil Rights Movement was as much about the pursuit of justice as it was about constructing new understandings of how to live with difference and otherness in the world. The same is true for Obama and his presidency. Seeking justice and equality for all and reconciling difference are intertwined. Obama, it seems, was well aware of this. Early on he recognized that he must communicate both his differences and commonalities with all Americans if he was to have a chance of being elected. Obama also understood that the creative resources of the Civil Rights Movement, in generating all the passion and energy of any large-scale social movement, could turn the tables on his chances for victory.

Of course, the world has always reflected a marvelous array of differences and otherness. This is not new. In fact, these various differences have been present in humanity and creation since the dawn of time. However, in present-day culture, differences are intensified within local spaces. Many global conflicts to a large extent are visible in local communities battling to articulate a language of tolerance and mutual social acceptance. The legacy of Martin Luther King, Jr., and other courageous freedom fighters of the Civil Rights Movement offer insight to processing what the Obama presidency means for all Americans, particularly black people, as well as thinking about the broader dimensions of community and justice amid the inescapable realities of racial, cultural, economic, and ethnic differences.

In this chapter, I intend to bring into conversation King's legacy of nonviolence, social justice, and the Civil Rights Movement in general with Obama as the first black president and the critical problems in postmodern culture. Although the Nobel Prize recipient is known around the world for his work in the quest for peace and justice, with only about a generation removed, many still think of King only in terms of the "I have a dream" speech of 1963. The complicated nature of King's thought and context of decision making has virtually gone unnoticed in contemporary literature and mass communique. This is primarily due to the fact that King, like many others before him, has become a larger-than-life iconic figure who spoke prophetically to the tumultuous problems of his time. Like Obama just months ago, some held that King's ideas were considered unreasonable and unreachable for the complexities of today. The waters of skepticism and individual personal autonomy have doused King's fiery vision of nonviolence as an interpersonal or global ethic. But in many ways, King's work is perhaps as relevant, if not more so, today than the social and historical environment of his life. King's vision continues to speak loudly to those committed to justice and nonviolence. His legacy also speaks to a hopeless generation scrabbling to forge vision and hope out of nightmares of poverty, abandonment, and social neglect.

On the monument erected on the grounds of the Lorraine Hotel in Memphis, Tennessee, where King was slain, one reads the words from Genesis 37, "And they said one to another, Behold, this dreamer cometh. Come now therefore, and let us slay him, and cast him into some pit, and we will say, some evil beast hath devoured him: and we shall see what will become of his dreams."[3] These words bring to mind King's provocative and imaginative vision of the beloved community, which still provides creative resources for helping the least, the loss, and the left out. At the beginning of the campaign, Obama employed the language of hope and change as his key slogans. He invoked many of the triumphalistic themes of the Civil Rights Movement and in rhythmic cadence spoke eloquently like the young black preacher from Ebenezer Baptist Church of old. In many ways, King (and Obama as well in many ways) illuminates for us the ways in which our individual dreams and aspirations are best fulfilled through the interconnectedness of the dreams of others. King's legacy allows us to see that the dreams of individuals are wrapped up in the dreams of others—that regardless of our gender, age, race, ethnicity, religious identity, or sexual orientation, human beings share a common humanity and that our destinies are intertwined.

I would agree with Cornel West, the American pragmatic philosopher and Princeton professor, that perhaps the greatest threat to justice and community today is nihilism. It embodies the quivering possibility of giving up on any desire for change that inevitably leads to destruction and mutual annihilation. According to Howard Thurman, the African American mystic and theologian who served as spiritual adviser to King, dreams are the quiet, inward persistence in the heart that enables a person to ride out the storms of life and the monotony of limitless days of dull routine. Important lessons can be gleaned from King's life who, in spite of the desperate conditions of segregation in America, had the audacity to challenge collective evil and indifference.

King and the Ideas that Moved the Nation

Like in Obama's case, one of the most interesting aspects of King's life was his ability to identify with those who suffered most in his social environment. As the son of an African American Baptist preacher in one of the most prominent churches in Atlanta, Georgia, King lived a very privileged life compared to many of his counterparts. He studied at the finest schools—Morehouse College, Crozer Theological Seminary in New Jersey, and Boston University School of Theology. Certainly, he had every reason to pursue any number of possibilities in the academy or church. But he intentionally chose to cast his lot among the marginalized and dispossessed. When he assumed his role as pastor of Dexter Avenue Baptist Church in Montgomery, Alabama, at twenty-six years old, he was well on his way to a very comfortable and prosperous life with his new wife, Coretta Scott King, and daughter, Yolanda.

Part of what it means to recover King's vision of nonviolence and community involves considering anew the ideals that made King and shaped the movement. Martin Luther King, Jr., was born into a southern African American religious tradition that interpreted the Christian faith as the fundamental source of liberation and freedom. In dramatic contrast to American southern white understandings of Christianity as obsessed with religious piety and maintenance of the status quo, King drew on the tradition of his forefathers and foremothers. He was born into a relatively privileged family of preachers and activists. As a child, King experienced a warm, secure, and structured home life. He was the son, grandson, and great-grandson of Baptist preachers. Preaching and church life permeated every facet of King's life. He grew up down the street from his church, Ebenezer Baptist Church, where his father was the esteemed pastor. As the son of a very distinguished and prominent family in Atlanta, Georgia, King had access to the finest dimensions of black southern life, from black-owned shops and stores to the prestigious intellectualism of Morehouse College, Spellman College, and other institutions just minutes away.

It was quite natural that King would continue his education at the all-male Morehouse College where his father had attended school. At Morehouse, King was an average student but did have the opportunity to study the major trends of the day. He studied sociology, English, philosophy, and religion, yet excelled in the area of religious studies under Professor George Kelsey. Under Professor Kelsey, King was introduced to the field of Protestant liberalism, a school of thought that appeared to be sympathetic to the plight of disadvantaged groups. The president of Morehouse College, Benjamin Elijah Mays, was also a tremendous influence on the young King. Mays' and King's father were close friends. In contrast to King's father, who was very Pentecostal and fundamentalist in his religious orientation, Mays gave King a vision of ministry that incorporated serious intellectual and scholarly commitments with deep faith. Mays' commitment to social uplift and education was also very attractive to King as he thought about what to do with his life. In fact, King initially aspired to study law but during his junior year in college announced he would pursue ministry as his life's work.

King left Morehouse College to attend Crozer Theological Seminary in Philadelphia. His experience as a Crozer seminary student was an awakening for King as he became exposed to the works of Walter Rauschenbusch, Edgar S. Brightman, Harold DeWolf, Paul Tillich, Reinhold Niebuhr, and Henry N. Wieman, in addition to classical theological and philosophical voices. It is difficult to determine the greatest influence on King, but the ideas of personalism and the social gospel would unquestionably have a lasting impact on King's thought and work. He would continue to recount and employ the insights from these intellectual strands as he articulated his prophetic call for justice and freedom over the years to come.

Many scholars have pointed out King's intellectual and cultural influences as a way of uncovering the ideas behind the man and the movement. Although many figures stand out, none are perhaps as prominent when it comes to nonviolence in the thought of King as Mohandas K. Gandhi, the Indian lawyer turned revolutionary. As a seminarian student at Crozer Theological Seminary, King was introduced to Gandhi through Mordecai Johnson, who was serving as president of Howard University at the time. Johnson and other African American scholars at Howard University at the time had traveled to India and studied Gandhi's thought very closely. On this occasion, Johnson delivered a fiery lecture on Gandhi's philosophy of nonviolence and its possibilities for social transformation to help the black cause in America.

King also took a class with George W. Davis at Crozer during his first year of seminary where he surveyed great religious figures, including Gandhi.[4] Although King read closely Henry David Thoreau's *Essay on the Duty of Civil Disobedience* in a philosophy class at Morehouse College, it wasn't until his days in seminary that he began to take nonviolence as a method of social change seriously.[5] Even at these early stages in King's formation, he had a strong gravitational pull toward Gandhi's ideas. What was most appealing to King was Gandhi's commitment to both liberation and nonviolence. It was the idea that nonviolence was a way of life and could be used as a strategic weapon of resistance and social transformation. King discovered, through Gandhi, an ethical principle of resistance that was consistent with his beliefs as a follower of Jesus Christ.

King's training translated into his work with organizations like the SCLC that he founded. Like Obama, King was a community organizer par excellence. He understood that taking on the political and economic power structures required a grassroots strategy, appealing to those at the bottom. After the Montgomery Bus Boycott, from 1955 to 1956, King received a shotgun blast at 1:30 a.m. on Sunday morning as a reminder that his effort to bring change in the city would not be forgotten.[6] During church service later that morning, King said to his Dexter Avenue congregation that killing him would do no good because the goals of the bus boycott were much greater than Montgomery. He surmised that his work had just begun, that the ultimate goal was complete equality through integration—integrated schools, buses, public facilities, political access—in all sectors of American society.

With this goal in mind, King recognized the need to establish a more sustainable and far-reaching organizing base. Bayard Rustin and his companion, Stanley D. Levison, introduced the idea to King of using the Montgomery experience to establish the basis of a larger effort for social change in the South. Rustin was pushing King to visit India and Africa to get a sense of the larger global movements taking place around anticolonial struggles and liberation. Sessions were held at the historic Ebenezer Baptist Church in Atlanta, Georgia, on January 10 and 11, 1957, to begin forming the Southern Christian Leadership Conference (SCLC). The SCLC would become perhaps the most important political machine for the black freedom struggle since the founding of the NAACP by W. E. B. Du Bois decades earlier.

Through organizations such as the SCLC, and student groups like the SNCC, Congress of Racial Equality (CORE), and others, King's ideas concerning nonviolence and the beloved community would continue to gain momentum throughout the movement. In a world of incredible violence, particularly among many oppressed and marginalized groups, Gandhi's thought is a refreshing antidote to those whose legitimate discontent leads them to feel they have no alternative but to resort to either violence or nihilism. Gandhi formulated his concept of nonviolence in the tradition of John Ruskin, Leo Tolstoy, Henry David Thoreau, and Jesus and the Sermon on the Mount. He also looked within his own historical and cultural heritage as embodied in the two pillars of his thought—"satyagraha" and "ahimsa." Satyagraha is a Sanskrit term meaning truth-force or soul-force. Gandhi affirmed the reality of another force or power at work in human existence more effective and transformative than physical violence. It was seen in the power of truth-telling and exposing hypocrisy, injustice, and exploitation.

By exposing the lies of dehumanization, the power of satyagraha is invoked. Satyagraha was certainly not passive, in the traditional sense as seen in the Christian pacifist tradition. For Gandhi, it was active, transformative, and deliberate. In fact, it actually required incredible strength, courage, and discipline to practice. Ahimsa articulated the commitment to "nonkilling" or "noninjury." Armed with the power of truth-telling and nonviolence, Gandhi built his philosophy of nonviolence into a powerful social and political method of resistance. Gandhi would, in many ways, become one of the most important figures shaping King's thought and actions.

The idea of nonviolence as a means of bringing about social change was such an integral part of the movement that it deserves some serious attention. King appropriated Gandhi's philosophy of nonviolence to fit the social and political landscape of the American South. Without the use of nonviolence as a means of securing voting rights for blacks to enter into the political process, Barack Obama would not have been able to run an effective political campaign, especially one geared to a grassroots, community-organizing base. Obama's entire campaign was contingent on the capacity of ordinary citizens to participate in the political process, in the caucuses, local Democratic Party headquarters, and statewide efforts. In order to capture the imagination and zeal of many blacks who were more than prepared to fight (violently if necessary) for freedom, King had to show that Gandhi's method, though physically nonviolent, was a powerful and active weapon of protest.

For King, Gandhi's method had four essential characteristics, which made it incredibly relevant for their context. It was indeed a form of resistance: it seeks friendship and understanding, not humiliation and domination, and the attack is focused on evil forces, rather than persons. Lastly, King argued that nonviolent resistance refrains from any form of violence, both physical and internal violence of the spirit. What makes King's conception of nonviolent resistance distinctly Christian was the fact that it was grounded in the love-ethic of Jesus. It was Jesus' love-ethic characterized by his ethical teaching and life that made nonviolence, and the quest for racial justice, for that matter, sensible and ultimately a moral obligation. Indeed, King's conception of nonviolence continues to have major implications for the church and its witness to the world today. Racial, ethnic, and class differences, from the urban ghettos of America to the cultural wars among Jews, Christians, and Muslims across Europe, are indicative of the need to reflect more patiently and critically about King's enduring legacy for what some have called these "postmodern times."

The Civil Rights Movement, Martin Luther King, Jr., and Obama

Already, in many circles parallels are being drawn between King, Obama, and the Civil Rights Movement and Obama's election as the first black president. No one can deny the strong feelings of validation and cultural pride in witnessing Obama's election. Millions, in fact, poured into Washington, D.C., on January 20, 2009, to witness the grand occasion to watch history unfold. But King and Obama are two very different individuals who emerged at two different cultural, political, and historical moments, and who hold contrasting views of America and the world. King was, first and foremost, in his mind, a black Baptist preacher who understood his work in the movement as a calling from God. As a student of Gandhi, he also believed in nonviolent passive resistance.

Although Obama, according to Stephen Mansfield in *The Faith of Barack Obama*, considers himself a man of faith "fashioned from the hard-won truths of Obama's own spiritual journey,"[7] he is not a preacher. Obama has made no claims of divine unction in his speeches or interviews. In his support of increasing troop levels in Afghanistan during the campaign, he also made it quite clear that he was not a pacifist. Obama is a politician. He admits that he was not raised in a religious household. Raised by grandparents, as well as his mother, Obama indicates that religion did not play a very prominent role throughout his youth. His faith journey was a long and thoughtful process that led him to the altar of Trinity United Church of Christ on Chicago's Southside. It was a process of thought. As he reflects, "kneeling beneath that cross on the South Side of Chicago, I felt God's spirit beckoning me. I submitted myself to His will, and dedicated myself to discovering His truth."[8] Both drew on the American school of pragmatism and modern philosophy as a way of thinking through the complexities of politics in America. They both shared a common concern for the poor, the working class, and the marginalized voices of American society and were committed to grassroots organizing in a way that yields revolutionary changes.

I believe King, in particular, was a forerunner of Obama. He, along with other freedom fighters of the Civil Rights Movement, opened the floodgates of opportunity and possibility in America by exposing the demons of American racism to itself. Obama's presidency gives us a fresh opportunity to revisit the meaning and legacy of the Civil Rights Movement and King for today. As I intend to argue throughout the book, our ability as a nation to remember the historical context of Obama's election, especially the Civil Rights Movement and King's vision of the beloved community, will determine the future of race relations in America and abroad for generations to come.

In a much broader sense, the Civil Rights Movement generally covers a broad historical moment bracketed between the Supreme Court decision of *Brown v. Board of Education* in 1954 and the assassination of King on April 4, 1968. Indeed, aspects of the movement go beyond this period, before and after. However, the intensity and wave of grassroots political action was most prominent during these turbulent years of American history. Although King was by and large a seminal leader of the movement, he alone was not the movement. It involved many outstanding organizations (NAACP, SNCC, CORE, SCLC, Black Churches, black sororities and fraternities, etc.) and countless individuals and institutions to help sustain the movement.

I do not wish to make a direct comparison here between King and Obama. In the biblical sense, King would be the prophet, while Obama would be sitting in the seat of the king. King held the prophetic mantle as a religious and spiritual leader of a movement calling America to live up to its own democratic ideals. Obama, on the other hand, is explicitly a politician, who, though inspired by God, recognizes that negotiation and diplomacy are a consequence of the office he holds. King was an absolutist on the question of nonviolence. Obama, as president, has made no such claims and because of his position, he cannot. Nevertheless, examining these figures and their historical movements will yield some fruitful insights for understanding the future of race relations and quest for justice in America.

For this reason, King and the Civil Rights Movement must be a central conversation partner in considering the historical meaning and promise of the Obama administration for promoting real change in America. In an article that appeared in the *Christian Century*, a liberal Protestant journal, King delineated the meaning and objectives for his conception of nonviolence in connection with the pursuit of racial justice.[9] The article was written shortly after the founding meeting of the SCLC, where King was elected its first president. The article was King's prophetic call to black Christians to use nonviolence as a means of liberation and freedom from the shackles of Jim Crow segregation. From 1619, he argued, enslaved Africans were considered a thing to be used, not a person to be respected. Now, he announced, black Americans were claiming their dignity and humanity, and the real question was only a matter of how the battle for freedom would be waged. It would take place through either violence or nonviolence. In either case, oppressed people will have their freedom. Because privileged groups seldom relinquish power and influence without struggle, the inevitability of conflict was a reality. King's message to the black masses was summarized in the following passage:

> If the American Negro and other victims of oppression succumb to the temptation of using violence in the struggle for justice, unborn generations will live in a desolate night of bitterness, and their chief legacy will be an endless reign of chaos.[10]

King's ideas were tested fiercely during the early days of the Montgomery Bus Boycott. Although the movement did not officially take off until Rosa Parks' historic stance by sitting in the "whites only" section of a city bus, the situation had been mounting for quite some time. Jo Ann Robinson, an English professor at Alabama State College, had written to the mayor about the conditions on the city buses over a year earlier in May 1954.[11] Robinson was also president of the Women's Political Council, an activist group in town. Several black women were arrested in March 1955 for not complying with the segregated seating laws. Parks, who was among this courageous group of women leaders in Montgomery, worked as a secretary with the local NAACP. On December 1, 1955, at around 5:30 p.m., when Parks had just left work, she had picked up a heating pad from the corner drugstore across the street from the bus stop. She boarded the bus for the Cleveland Avenue route.

As the historian David J. Garrow chronicled in his Pulitzer Prize–winning work, *Bearing the Cross: Martin Luther King, Jr., and the Southern Christian Leadership Conference*, Parks took an aisle seat next to a black man and two black women in the row immediately behind the rows designated for "whites only."[12] As more passengers boarded the bus, all of the seats became occupied, and the bus driver, J. F. Blake, ordered Parks and her fellow black passengers to move in order for one white man to have the entire row. While the others stood up to allow the white male passenger to sit, Parks remained in her seat. After making repeated demands, the driver called the police. Two officers showed up shortly thereafter and took Parks to police headquarters. E. D. Nixon, a past president of the city's chapter of the NAACP, called a white liberal lawyer in town, Clifford Durr, to see if the association could come up with the $100 bond to bail Parks out of jail.[13] Nixon had known Parks for several years through her involvement with the NAACP and thought she would be ideal as a test case to challenge the system of segregation in Montgomery and subsequently across the south.

Nixon was well connected and had been exposed to many of the progressive ideas found in northern cities like Chicago, New York, Philadelphia, and Detroit. He was a Pullman porter and an active member of the Brotherhood of Sleeping Car Porters, of which A. Philip Randolph served at the helm.[14] Robinson, Nixon, and Durr were all aware of the landmark *Brown v. Board of Education of Topeka* decision handed down on May 17, 1954, which called the "separate but equal" doctrine unconstitutional. They were also cognizant of the racial mode of the city's black residents who were fed up with the ill-treatment of blacks. On March 2, 1955, just months earlier, Claudette Colvin (a fifteen-year-old high-school student) was dragged from a city bus for refusing to give up her seat, then charged with assault and battery. Because Colvin happened to be pregnant at the time, leaders agreed she would be an undesirable candidate for representing the plight of blacks in the city under Jim Crow. Nixon and Robinson helped to organize a meeting of Montgomery's black leadership that Friday while the Women's Political Council (WPC) printed leaflets to be distributed throughout the city. Nixon called Ralph D. Abernathy to help assemble the ministers. It was Abernathy who called up his good friend, and new minister in the city, Martin Luther King, Jr., to attend and E. D. Nixon asked king to host the meeting at his church, Dexter Avenue Baptist Church. It was during this meeting that King reluctantly stepped into the role as head of the Montgomery Improvement Association (MIA) and leader of the new movement.

On December 5, 1955, King delivered his first official speech as the MIA president at Holt Street Baptist Church. There, he echoed what Gary S. Selby called the "rhetoric of freedom," and said: "We are here because of our love for democracy, because of our deep-seated belief that democracy transformed from thin paper to thick action is the greatest form of government on earth."[15] Here is where King and Obama, though emerging from radically different cultural and historical paradigms, share a great deal in common. King and Obama maintained a high regard for the American concept of democracy. Although Obama has pursued the path of politician as the primary space to enact social change, King viewed himself as a revolutionary activist and Baptist preacher. They both, however, would agree with J. William Fulbright's description of democracy when he observed, "in a democracy, dissent is an act of faith."[16]

Obama's entire campaign was an unconventional, albeit revolutionary, movement that was multicultural in character and culturally transformative in scope. As I discuss in the next chapter, Obama was introduced to King and the Civil Rights Movement by his mother, a liberal activist and organizer with midwestern Kansas roots. It was the Civil Rights Movement that provided resources for Obama and others to envision the possibilities of his presidency and its meaning for symbolizing social and political change in America. The Montgomery movement came to a head on February 21, 1956, when nearly every black leader was indicted for violating a state antiboycott statute.

Three months after the end of the boycott, Parks gathered with other leaders to reflect on the movement at Highlander Folk School in Monteagle, Tennessee. Upon reflection, Parks had the following on her mind when she decided to remain in her bus seat:

> Well, in the first place I had been working all day on the job, not feeling too well after spending a hard day working. The job required that I handle and work on clothing that white people would wear, and that accidentally came into my mind. This was what I wanted to know: when, how, would we ever

determine our rights as human beings . . . Just having paid for a seat and riding for only a couple of blocks and then having to stand was too much. These other persons had got on the bus after I did. It meant that I didn't have a right to do anything but get on the bus, give them my fare, and then be pushed wherever they wanted me.[17]

When the movement gained momentum, blacks in Montgomery quickly established car pools, formed the MIA, and made three critical demands to the city: "(1) more driver courtesy toward black passengers, (2) first-come, first-served seating, from front to back for whites and back to front for blacks, and (3) black drivers for routes going to black areas."[18] It was not until later in the boycott, when it was very clear that white city leaders were unwilling to negotiate, that King called the group to not only pursue its demands but dismantle the very foundations of Jim Crow segregation in Montgomery. King delivered the first of many fiery speeches at Holt Street Baptist Church. There, he remembered his studies of the love-ethic of Jesus and the social gospel of Walter Rauchenbusch and proclaimed that God calls Christians to act in all areas of human life. He drew upon the idea that Christian love is radical and transformative, that it seeks justice, fellowship and community, and the alleviation of human suffering. At the height of the protest, King began to receive countless threats on his life and his family. He was faced with the difficult decision as to whether he should continue in his efforts with the campaign. He tells the story of bowing over a cup of coffee one night in agony over the weight of leadership, but recounts that God compelled him to continue in his plight and struggle for freedom and justice. The self-sacrificial character of King's leadership in times of crisis and decision making is a strong call for leaders in the present generation to pursue paths of nonviolence and humility in their quest for liberation and justice.

A Dream or a Nightmare? Legacy of the Beloved Community

The national holiday in America honoring King in January and the continual naming of streets, roads, and bridges after the esteemed leader have propelled King more into the mainstream of popular culture. It is now difficult to conceive that the man once viewed by the FBI as the most dangerous person in America currently enjoys a cordial and undisruptive presence in today's culture. And yet, thinking about King's legacy very seriously leads those of us who value his words and actions to a position of action and a prophetic call for change. Whether in the urban ghettos of America, the shanties of South Africa and Kenya, or the forgotten poor of Italy and

Croatia in Europe, the legacy of the slain Baptist minister from Georgia still provides inspiration and strategic insight for fighting against the dogs of oppression.

It must never be forgotten that King and the legacy of the Civil Rights Movement paved the way for Obama's win and historic inauguration on January 20, 2009. King's work transcended the boundaries of race, class, gender, and ethnic difference as he directed the consciousness of everyday people on the centrality of human dignity and personhood. King recognized very early on that human fulfillment comes through serving others, that all of our individual resources of thinking, being, loving, hoping, laughing, and living are perfected as we seek to uplift, heal, encourage, and bring justice and love to the lives of others. King gives insight to what it means to live faithfully and courageously in a disenchanted world of violence and human suffering.

Conclusion

Understanding the historical context of Obama's presidency and its indebtedness to the freedom fighters of yesterday and today better equips each of us to confront the persistent problems of race and racism in America today. The present situation of racial and ethnic conflict, now experienced on local and global levels, demands a critical reappraisal of the significance of King's witness. There have been few incidents in contemporary history where an oppressed group of people resisted the forces of injustice and dehumanization using nonviolent means and triumphed. History is replete with occurrences when interpersonal human persuasion is insufficient to advance the cause of freedom and justice. There are moments when, as we have seen in King's witness, faithful individuals and groups feel it is necessary to challenge social, political, and economic systems as well. We see examples of this when we think of the great atrocities experienced by the Jews in Hitler's Germany, Catholic-Protestant relations in Ireland, the Balkans, South Africans under apartheid, Rwanda, and American slavery and its effects. Through intentional systematic and structured forms of subjugation, individuals have been denied the opportunity to become all that they can be as made in the image of God. King was certainly aware of this when he began his involvement with the MIA.

Facing the challenges of difference and otherness today also requires a clear commitment to nonviolence and reconciliation. King's "letter from Birmingham Jail", perhaps on this occasion more than any other, revealed a leader who had come full circle and worked out within himself the social and theological foundations for his actions and the grounds for his pursuit of the beloved community. On Good Friday of April 1963, perhaps at the height of the Civil Rights Movement, King was faced with the daunting challenge of incarcerated child protesters and a depleted budget in his organization of the SCLC. He was faced with the problem of whether to leave Birmingham to do more fund-raising or to continue to break an injunction against protesting in the city. His arrest was all but guaranteed, with no certainty that he would be released. After stepping into the next room to pray, King returned with an affirmative commitment. He surmised that although he did not know the outcome, he could join the 160 protesters already arrested and continue the march.

Ironically, it was during his time in Birmingham Jail that King penned the "Letter from Birmingham Jail" on slips of tissue paper. In the letter, he eloquently articulated that the essence of Christian faith is radical and transformative love, fueled by the nonviolent life of Jesus Christ who was an extremist in his love for the other. He wrote that ultimately the universe is directed toward justice—that God's nature is love and justice. The quest for justice, human dignity, and reconciliation were at the core of the gospel message. That, in the final analysis, the Christian message is a message of hope, healing, liberty, and fellowship with God and the other. Here, his life serves as an exemplar into what it means to live faithfully, with compassion, love, justice, and dignity.

While Obama has said he is a Christian, he has said very little about the content of his faith and the ways in which Christianity informs his ideas about life, justice, or government. In his chapter on faith in *The Audacity of Hope*, he says very little about his own faith commitments. He does share his suspicion of uncritical religious belief and also acknowledges the power of religion in American politics. He was not raised in a religious household, but was taught to appreciate multiple religious and humanistic perspectives. At the end of the day, he wants to hold in tension his personal faith and what he describes as "democratic pluralism." Unlike King who forged his theological and philosophical ideas through years of formal preparation as a theologian and minister, Obama is a Harvard Law–trained professor who became an expert on both the constitution and community organizing. Although King and Obama appear to share many of the same commitments in general, the ways they arrive at those positions are dramatically distinct.

King's example of faithfulness also emerged from his open critique of the Vietnam War. After the dramatic successes and heartbreaks of campaigns in Selma, Alabama, Birmingham, Albany, Georgia, and Cicero in Chicago, the Martin Luther King, Jr., of 1967 was a leader who had come of age. On April 4, 1967, at Riverside Church in New York City, he gave a provocative message, entitled "A Time to Break the Silence," in which for the first time King made a direct link between the Civil Rights Movement and the Vietnam War. It was also the first time King had openly and directly challenged the war policy of the Johnson administration. The King of 1968 was acutely aware of the interlocutors of race, economics, and politics. He understood that war is intrinsically economic in motive and insidiously evil in moral claims. King recognized that war was a "never ending black hole" or vortex that sucks up valuable resources that could be used to end poverty, create jobs and economic development, improve education, and treat epidemic illnesses and more.

I find it quite ironic that according to most supporters of Obama, his position on Iraq was at the top of the list of priorities. Most found it quite compelling that as a junior senator, Obama openly opposed the war in Iraq. Obama viewed the war as unsubstantiated and strategically damaging. He disapproved of the war on what he essentially viewed as rational and pragmatic grounds. King, on the other hand, opposed the war in Vietnam because he felt it was morally bankrupt and was the product of an intrinsic social evil. The ultimate determinative factor for King was not necessarily to build a democratic society, but to advance the beloved community among the peoples of the world—a community of nonviolence, peaceable friendship, justice, and inclusivity.

An often-overlooked dimension in King's vision was that establishing the "beloved community" was not simply a distant, abstract conception of hope. The beloved community was also in a state of becoming as individuals and groups of different races, classes, religious orientation, gender, and ethnicity worked together to make justice a reality for all people. One of the most powerful examples of community that King gives from his own life was during the Selma voting rights campaign of 1965. After receiving the Nobel Prize in Oslo the previous year, King had returned with a renewed sense of vision and purpose. He approached the Selma campaign with a growing sense of urgency as he began to look toward issues of economic justice and criticism of the Vietnam War. Although his work in Selma proved to be one of his toughest challenges, it became a rallying cry for justice and reconciliation across the nation. For the first time in the Civil Rights Movement, whites and blacks, Jews, Christians, and Muslims, the poor and well-to-do, all descended to Selma in the affirmation of freedom and justice.

King's vision of nonviolence as a global ethic and justice as a guiding principle of the beloved community continue to have lasting value in our world today. His life and work offers hope and inspiration as we attend to the persistent problems of war and peace, poverty, housing reform, and even the cultural problems impacting youth and families. King gives every person a stirring call to speak truth to power in today's context. The ways in which he lived out the concept of agape love reflected in the life of Jesus Christ continue to forge pathways toward meaningful relationships and justice in the world.

King often stated that the aim of freedom is the affirmation and quest for human dignity. For King, God has created all humans in God's image and is therefore innately cloaked in human dignity and honor. The degradation, humiliation, and damage to the human person, whether material, psychological, political, or social, are an assault to human dignity. In his book *Where Do We Go from Here? Chaos or Community*, King anticipates the postmodern globalized world of today—a world much more economically ravishing and technologically treacherous. In this changing world, the lines between justice and injustice are not as clear as when the signs read "For whites only." Now we have entered into the age of mutual funds and stock options, of the manipulation of public opinion through massive media propaganda machines. Addressing these radical changes involves recovering history—good and bad—then appropriating that history for today's context.

It would certainly have to take seriously the frightening parallels between Vietnam and the War in Iraq. To his credit, Obama made similar connections to war and poverty throughout the campaign as King did more than forty years earlier in his critique of the Vietnam War. As Obama postulated, the War in Iraq is directly related to public education, homelessness, healthcare, and other immediate issues right at our doorsteps. The over four hundred billion dollars that has been spent thus far in the Iraq War could have been used to transform our urban centers, increase technology and resources in public education, raise teachers' salaries, establish smaller class sizes, and make our secondary junior colleges and technical schools tuition free for all who have the desire to learn.

The illusory activities of multinational corporations and private lobbying groups have infiltrated the very foundations of our democratic system. During the Bush administration, the revelations of corruption by leaders such as Tom Delay, the Republican lobbyist Jack Abramoff, and others prompted the demand for radical reform in campaign financing, transparent congressional hearings, and independent panels to prosecute with diligence and all assiduousness. Obama was able to win the election by attending to these concerns and calling upon the creative resources of community organizers, youths, and activists alike to literally do the absurd. Obama, by drawing the masses of small donors to support his campaign, was able to challenge the status quo and forge a new multicultural political coalition. When money can determine the shape and scope of public policy to serve the rich and powerful, then how can the masses of poor and powerless American citizens feel that they have fair and equal representation under the law? With the historical legacy of King as his backdrop, Obama's election gives us an opportunity to uncover the complex web of economic interest driving public policy, both foreign and domestic. One only needs to look as far as the most influential vice president in history, Dick Cheney. The same Dick Cheney, who was former CEO of Halliburton and currently owns millions in stock in the company, has benefited and continues to stand to benefit millions of dollars as the stock rises due to continued no-bid contracts in war-torn Iraq. In the following chapters, I continue to argue that the historical struggle for freedom and human dignity, as reflected in the Civil Rights Movement, helps us to more fully appreciate and understand what Obama's presidency means today and its implications for the future. I conclude with the instructive and riveting words of King when he writes:

the large house in which we live demands that we transform this world-wide neighborhood into a world-wide brotherhood. Together we must learn to live together as brothers or together we will be forced to perish as fools . . . We must work passionately and indefatigably to bridge the gulf between our scientific progress and our moral progress. One of the great problems of mankind is that we suffer from a poverty of spirit which stands in glaring contrast to our scientific and technological abundance. The richer we have become materially, the poorer we have become morally and spiritually.[19]

CHAPTER 2

Obama and Race in America

Between me and the other world there is ever an unasked question: unasked by some through feelings of delicacy; by others through the difficulty of rightly framing it. All, nevertheless, flutter around it. They approach me in a half-hesitant sort of way, eye me curiously or compassionately, and then, instead of saying directly, How does it feel to be a problem? They say, I know an excellent colored man in my town; or, I fought at Mechanicsville; or, Do not these Southern outrages make your blood boil? At these I smile, or am interested, reduce the boiling to a simmer, as the occasion may require. To the real question, How does it feel to be a problem? I answer seldom a word.[1]

Her message came to embrace black people generally. She would come home with books on the civil rights movement, the recordings of Mahalia Jackson, the speeches of Dr. King. When she told me stories of schoolchildren in the South who were forced to read books handed down from wealthier white schools but who went on to become doctors and lawyers and scientists, I felt chastened by my reluctance to wake up and study in the morning. If I told her about the goose-stepping demonstrations my Indonesian Boy Scout troop performed in front of the president, she might mention a different kind of march, a march of children no older than me, a march for freedom. Every black man was Thurgood Marshall or Sidney Poitier; every black woman was Fannie Lou Hamer or Lena Horne. To be black was to be the beneficiary of a great inheritance, a special destiny, glorious burdens that only we were strong enough to bear.[2]

Barack Obama, on his mother in *Dreams from My Father*

America stands in the whirlwind of a cultural revolution. Over the past few years, the nation has been experiencing a kind of numbness, despair, and lack of confidence in its political process and in whether politicians had remotely any connections to the concrete issues affecting the average person's life. In the age of what many scholars are describing as "postmodernity," people are now being driven less by rhetoric and ideology and more by concrete practices and changes that have to do with the betterment of human life. This is what makes Obama's candidacy and election so appealing. Obama did not stand alone, nor did his campaign take place in a social and historical vacuum. As the first black president of the United States, it is extremely important to recognize the ways in which Obama walks in the pathways of the black struggle to overcome slavery, Jim Crow segregation, and what Martin Luther King, Jr., called the "iron feet of oppression." Du Bois painted this picture well in his *The Souls of Black Folks* as he eloquently dissected the visceral pain of black life in America and the meaning of resilience and survival. He writes:

> After the Egyptian and Indian, the Greek and Roman, the Teuton and Mongolian, the Negro is a sort of seventh son, born with a veil, and gifted with second-sight in this American world—a world which yields him no true self-consciousness, but only lets him see himself through the revelation of the other world. It is a peculiar sensation, this double-consciousness, this sense of always looking at one's self through the eyes of others, of measuring one's soul by the tape of a world that looks on in amused contempt and pity. One ever feels his twoness—an American, a Negro; two souls, two thoughts, two unreconciled strivings; two warring ideals in one dark body, whose dogged strength alone keeps it from being torn asunder.[3]

Du Bois, like Obama, was a Harvard man. He was a sociologist by training and became the first African American to earn a PhD from Harvard University. Obama became the first African American to serve as editor of the prestigious *Harvard Law Review*. What these connections reveal is that for decades, courageous black folks, like Du Bois, have fought, bled, and died for the cause of freedom and justice, to make America what it can be and ought to be. Every significant political advancement in America, from the abolition of slavery to the adoptions of the thirteenth and fourteenth amendments to the Constitution, has resulted from the determined efforts of faithful individuals concerned about the uplift of downtrodden black peoples in America. It should be noted that black people in America are an extremely diverse community. Cubans, Puerto Ricans, Afro-Brazilians, Jamaicans, Somalians, Haitians, Nigerians, Ghanaians, and more reflect the rich and vibrant differences among black people in America. Since American slavery, there has been a continuous cross-cultural fertilization among black communities, which makes it difficult to make a distinction between those who can and cannot connect their ancestry to American slavery. Obama's father and father's father were not the descendents of enslaved Africans in America. He does, however, share the plight of Africans in the diaspora who have suffered the brunt of slavery and the dehumanizing sting of colonialism as well. For that reason, Obama rightly belongs to that troop of black bodies Franz Fanon called the "wretched of the earth," those whom Western society in the last five hundred years has looked upon with disdain and fear. Evan Thomas, in the *Time* magazine article "A Memo to Senator Obama," raised the question of whether America was ready for a black president.[4] Thomas surveyed the 2008 electoral map and conducted countless interviews to discover that Obama had to convince the majority white public that he could make them safer and better off, regardless of his skin color. Although Obama is grounded in the black experience, he was able nonetheless to build a multicultural coalition made up of blacks, whites, Latinos, Asians, and others to show that he had the vision and sensibilities to be their president.

America and Race in Context

John Hope Franklin observed in *The Color Line: Legacy for the Twenty-First Century* that "even as he [Du Bois] was predicting that the problem of the twentieth century would be the problem of the color line, new, effective if inane arguments advanced by journalists, politicians, even educators, insisted that the Negro was a beast, a threat to civilization, a drain on the economy, and even a scourge on the body politic."[5] Even after the abolition of slavery, racist attitudes about black inferiority continued to exist. The blacks in America and throughout the world, growing out of the Enlightenment, were viewed, according to Basil Davidson, as "beasts of burden" or relegated to a perpetual state of servitude, beholden to their white—specifically Eurocentric—masters.[6] Franklin, who was appointed chair of the Clinton administration's commission on race in the late nineties, argues that during this period and in the first half of the twentieth century new strands of racial segregation, intolerance, and discrimination emerged. When Du Bois died in 1963, a radical shift began to emerge, no doubt due to the fervent rise of the Civil Rights Movement.[7] Momentous historical events prompted a renewed commitment to racial progress. After World War II, African American service men and servicewomen who returned from foreign theatres demanded equal rights. Many asked why they were fighting for the freedom of others abroad but were denied that very same freedom at home. First, with the order to desegregate the military by Harry Truman on July 26, 1948, the Congress passed a series of civil rights legislation in 1957, 1964, and 1965, contributing to a new wave of economic and political leadership in the black community. Publications like *Ebony, Jet, Black Enterprise, Essence,* and *Dollars and Sense*, in addition to the historic black print media, all paved the way for a heightened awareness of racial identity and political solidarity. It was precisely the heightened sense of awareness and reflection on the black predicament during the mid-twentieth century that stimulated a new surge of political protest and activism by blacks leading up to and during the Civil Rights Movement.

Several texts in recent years have looked at race during the Civil Rights Movement and attempted to make sense of the current racial paradigm in America. Jim Sleeper's *Liberal Racism* (1997), Tamar Jacoby's *Someone Else's House* (1998), Dinesh D'Souza's *The End of Racism* (1995), Abigail Thernstrom's *America in Black and White: One Nation Indivisible* (1997), as well as Andrew Hackers's *Two Nations: Black and White, Separate, Hostile, Unequal* (1992), Cornel West's *Race Matters*, Randall Kennedy's *Sellout: The Politics of Racial Betrayal*, Derrick Bell's *Faces at the Bottom of the Well: The Permanence of Racism* (1993), and bell hooks' *Killing Rage: Ending Racism* (1996) are all important reflections on the current realities of race in America. I merely identify these texts to point the reader to the rich intellectual discussions that have taken place in recent years to underscore the nuances and challenges concerning race in America. Americans and the world must not be misled into thinking that somehow the Obama presidency diminishes or removes the sting of racism that continues to rage on in America. What these voices reveal is that the battle is far from over.

Many of these perspectives reflect a chorus emphasizing the growing racial divide in America. Like the Moynihan Report of 1965, the Kerner Commission Report of 1968, and Bill Clinton's Race Initiative of 1997—1998, all of these perspectives reinforce the persistent realities of racism and white racial privilege in today's world. The fact that Obama has become the first black president of the United States does not change this reality. What it does mean is that perhaps the social and political conditions emerging from the American culture of racism might receive some bit of attention.

Too Black or Not Black Enough?
Obama's Racial Identity and the Black Experience

Whether or not Obama grew up on the Southside of Chicago, like his wife, Michelle Obama, is of little consequence given the fact that the time and place of his political leadership has been directly shaped by these historical, political, and racial forces. But, who is Barack Obama and what are the origins of his understanding of hope? Why is this question even relevant given all the latest talk of moving toward a "postracial" society? I would argue that Obama's identity and the place he holds among the cadre of black political leadership in American history are indispensible to understanding the future of race in America. Throughout the presidential election, Obama became and has since remained a public symbol of the racial and political shifts taking place in America that are rooted in the Civil Rights movement. The following words illustrate the complexity of Obama's racial identity and the changing racial fluidity taking place across America and much of the developing world:

> As the child of a black man and a white woman, someone who was born in the racial melting pot of Hawaii, with a sister who's half Indonesian but who's usually mistaken for Mexican or Puerto Rican, and a brother-in-law and niece of Chinese descent, with some blood relatives who resemble Margaret Thatcher and others who could pass for Bernie Mac, so that family get-togethers over Christmas take on the appearance of a UN General Assembly meeting, I've never had the option of restricting my loyalties on the basis of race, or measuring my worth on the basis of tribe.[8]

Obama, with all of his multicultural roots, does not represent movement toward any notion of a so-called postracial society. In fact, to view Obama as an example of such an idea would be disastrous for real racial progress in the years to come. These theories are not new. They emerged from the "melting-pot" metaphors of the early-twentieth century as the nation struggled with what to do with the massive influx of European immigrants flooding into cities like Chicago, Philadelphia, and New York. Many of these ideas were based on social theories of assimilation, essentially conformity to Anglo-Saxon British religious and cultural values. These perspectives often flatly ignore the treasures of difference and the goodness of racial and ethnic particularities.

Race has fundamentally shaped the soul of America. For as long as America exists, race will be indelibly imprinted upon its psychic, individual and social practices, and political aspirations. Like a major childhood scare, the impact of race will always be a critical part of the shared narrative of Americans, its institutions, and all that it hopes to be. Situating Obama among those brave souls who have fought to overcome racism must be established for the future well-being of unborn black, Latino, Asian, African, white, and multicultural children. The power and force of racism lies in its ability to go unnamed. Its ferocious viciousness lingers in rose-colored glasses with the illusion of racial equality or a denial of racism altogether. Like in the case of an alcoholic who must acknowledge his or her addiction, the power to overcome such an illness lies in the refusal to forget its destructive tendencies. The same is true for Obama and the issue of race. While Obama may very well be the nation's first black president, he is still a black man in America. To deny such a truth would mean that the countless black souls who continue to suffer the ravages of racism and the systemic structures that stifle and undermine black family life could easily be dismissed as some form of pathological ineptitude.

The urgent debates in public discourse about the Obama presidency have reminded us once again that politics and race go hand in hand. It is with some reluctance that I, as an African American male, even broach this subject, in part because there is an invisible and unspoken norm with the African American experience to refrain from airing out "dirty laundry." It borders on near sin to speak honestly and openly about so-called black leaders. But those within and beyond the African American community are raising provocative questions about the handsome and charismatic gentleman from Illinois. One of those questions is concerned with whether Barack Obama is "black enough" or "too black." Many within the African American community are wondering about the entire fanfare of the Obama presidency, whether he truly identifies with the black experiences in America, entrenched in slavery and Hurricane Katrina, that give little cause for "optimism about a hopeful America." And rightly so. Obama's life and experiences do not resemble the historical and current realities of America's slave descendants. That does not at all diminish his import and connection to the black community and its causes. There are many middle class blacks who reflect Du Bois' talented tenth, those who may not have had a firsthand experience with poverty but care deeply about the cause of justice and social change. In the final analysis, the question of whether Obama is black enough or too black is a false distinction of little relevance to the nature of his commitments and what his achievement means for racial progress in America. What matters most are his commitments and where he stands in the quest for racial equality and freedom, which his lived story seems to vividly attest.

The first book Obama wrote was *Dreams from My Father: A Story of Race and Inheritance*. Here, Obama attempts to characterize his life story as a quest to understand and confront the complexity of his racial identity, to figure out who he is and his place in the world. "What strikes me most when I think about the story of my family is a running strain of innocence, an innocence that seems unimaginable, even by the measures of childhood."[9] The innocence to which Obama refers is the experience of a world naïve about racism, bigotry, and immense suffering. Obama grew up in Hawaii as the son of a single white woman from Kansas. His father was Kenyan. It wasn't until his father's death while Obama was studying in New York at Columbia University that he began to experience a real crisis of identity. He received a call from his Aunt Jane in Nairobi informing him that his father had been killed in a car accident. His father's death and the shock and mystery around it led Obama on a quest of self-discovery. This is illustrated in the following reflections:

> At the time of his death, my father remained a myth to me, both more and less than a man. He had left Hawaii back in 1963, when I was only two years old, so that as a child I knew him only through the stories that my mother and grandparents told. They all had their favorites, each one seamless, burnished smooth from repeated use. I can still picture Gramps leaning back in his old stuffed chair after dinner, sipping whiskey and cleaning his teeth with the cellophane from his cigarette pack, recounting the time that my father almost threw a man off the Pali Lookout because of a pipe . . . "See, your mom and dad decided to take this friend of his sightseeing around the island. So they drove up to the Lookout, and Barack was probably on the wrong side of the road the whole way over there . . ." "Your father was a terrible driver" [10]

Although Obama did not grow up with his father, it is obvious from his autobiography that his search to understand who his father was would have an enduring impact on his self-image, vision for his life, and profound sense of optimism around social and political change. Obama's father was a Kenyan of the Luo tribe. He was born in Alego near Lake Victoria. During the period around which Kenya was moving toward independence, Kenyan political leaders selected a few outstanding students to study in American universities as a step toward integrating into the global community and to train leaders for the new independent Kenya. Obama's father was among these students. He became the first African student at the University of Hawaii. It was at the University of Hawaii in a Russian language course where Obama's father and mother would meet. [11] Obama's father later won a scholarship to pursue a PhD at Harvard University. Because of a lack of funding, Obama's father did not take his new bride and young child with him. Indeed, like many young black males across America, this would be a decision that would haunt the young Obama for decades to come.

Kenya, as an African country and former British colony, has a particularly important history in studies around African liberation. Kenya was among the first African countries to establish its independence from Western colonialism in 1964 under the leadership of Jomo Kenyatta. [12] It has continually been one of the few African nations that have experienced relative democratic rule and stability over the years. [13] Because of its ties to Britain, it was also a country targeted for terrorist attacks, as evident in the 1998 bombing of the U.S. Embassy in Nairobi. Culturally, there is a strong sense of pride among Kenyans concerning its affirmation of independence, its enculturation of Western values, and its political progress. As Obama became more acquainted with his father's ancestral heritage, he also became heir to a powerful legacy of resistance and political leadership. I am not at all suggesting that Obama is a resister of any kind nor would I compare him to the likes of Kenyatta or other African liberationists like Nelson Mandela of South Africa or Kwame Nkrumah of Ghana. It is important to recognize that Obama was not simply a product of Western intellectualism, of Columbia and Harvard, or only a product of his white midwestern family roots. He is also both African and African American. His influences cover a broad range of racial, historical, and cultural influences—all of which should be recognized, celebrated, and thoroughly critiqued.

Obama was also influenced by his white maternal grandfather, affectionately called "gramps." But his grandfather, like many moderately progressive whites of his day, viewed racial difference as somewhat of an obstacle to race problems. According to Obama, his grandfather paid very little attention to race and seldom talked about it. In his household, the idea of race was rarely discussed and often flatly ignored. Unlike many, a number of African American households, the issue of race has been historically unavoidable for the larger black community as a matter of both survival and cultural understanding. Black boys in the South were taught that they ought to never forget who they are and what it means for the violent culture of lynching, segregation, and dehumanization, a legacy that still continues to the present day with police profiling, massive incarceration, and self-inflicted gang violence. The lynching of the fourteen-year-old Emmit Till in 1955 for allegedly whistling at a white girl is evidence of the stark brutality of racism. Till's body was thrown in the Tallahatchie River in Mississippi, which prompted a wave of protest and righteous indignation that marked the beginnings of the Civil Rights Movement. Obama was born several years later on August 4, 1961, in Honolulu, Hawaii. Although Obama did not have direct encounters with this form of racialized violence, his yearning for identity and connectedness to the African American experience provided an insight into these realities.

It wasn't until Obama aged that he began to grapple with a sense of racial consciousness and confusion. As he wrote, even at the tender ages of five and six, he was oblivious to racial difference. "That my father looked nothing like the people around me—that he was black as pitch, my mother white as milk—barely registered in my mind."[14] It wasn't until his teenage years that Obama began to take seriously this issue of race, who he was, and what it means politically and socially. What this part of Obama's narrative does suggest is that a major part of his formative experiences was shaped by a world that did not recognize, discuss, or engage issues of race in any meaningful way. Throughout much of his presidential campaign, Obama went to great lengths to try to keep race from becoming the sole issue of his campaign. With the exception of his Philadelphia speech on race, prompted to a large extent by the spectacular scandal around his relationship with the former pastor Jeremiah Wright, Obama has spoken very little explicitly about race during the campaign or as president. That does not mean that the subject of race was and is not important to Obama. On the contrary, his first book, *Dreams from My Father*, was in fact a critical reflection on the complexity of race as reflected in his own story. It is clear, however, that Obama wanted to delicately balance the need for a national dialogue on race and building a larger coalition within which race was merely one among many issues that would need to be addressed.

While some claim this was a calculated political move necessary to try to win over an American population that was racially insensitive and fearful of discussing the issue, his early childhood story also reveals this connection to his formative experiences. It seemed quite natural for Obama to avoid conversations about race during the campaign since it has influenced much of his own social and cultural formation. What Obama would learn about race, including his own father's identity, would come from sheer self-determination and admirable will. Unfortunately, some have clearly interpreted Obama's silence around explicit conversations regarding race as an opportunity to introduce (and advance) notions of movement toward a "postracial" society.

This kind of talk, similar to the "melting-pot" theories of the early twentieth century and language of conservative mantras emerging in the late 1990s like "color blind society," should be looked upon with both caution and consternation. As I indicated in the introduction, it is convenient, particularly, for a vast majority of white Americans to dismiss the issue of race altogether, as if whiteness is normative for all other peoples and cultures in America and abroad. It is dangerous, if not altogether nihilistic, to not recognize race. Affirming and recognizing racial difference is indispensible to the pursuit of justice, equality, and general social progress. During the presidential campaign, Obama was able to build a powerful multicultural coalition. Whites from Iowa as well as black South Carolinians were able to find common ground and solidarity related to platforms committed to health care, ending the war in Iraq, tax cuts for the middle class, and more. But the unique problems affecting black Americans, such as the HIV/AIDS crisis, incarceration of black males, gang violence, and dilapidated urban schools would continue to receive little to no real attention if absorbed into a mythical "postracial" society. Understanding racial difference is key to improving dramatic disparities that have both historical and cultural roots in America—a nation drenched in the blood of racial conflict, suffering, and struggle.

The broad spectrum of racial difference, blacks and whites of a vast range of ethnic backgrounds and persuasions, has always been part of the American racial and ethnic landscape. *Following the Color Line: An American Negro Citizenship in the Progressive Era* by Ray Stannard Baker was a major study originally published in 1908, and later used as a significant resource in the report by Gunnar Myrdal, *An American Dilemma* (1944).[15] Baker, a journalist at the beginning of America's postreconstruction climate, covered a number of race riots occurring in the deep south in the early 1900s due to high unemployment, a rise in lynchings, and general social neglect. This was particularly the case surrounding the events of the 1906 riots in Atlanta, Georgia. What Baker observed was the tremendous, perhaps even irrational, fear harbored by many whites in the South of black people. "Everywhere I went in Atlanta I heard of the fear of the white people, but not much was said of the terror which the Negroes also felt," he writes.[16] The reality of fear, Baker suggests, represents one of the most compelling impediments to racial progress in the country. Since the beginning of slavery in America, fear of black insurrection and overall suspicions about black people led to many of the dreadful violent practices during slavery and later in the covert activities of the Ku Klux Klan. To instill fear and intimidation in the hearts of black people was the ultimate aim.

The idea of a "color-blind society" or a "postracial" America has always been a wistful dream cooked up by primarily those who no longer wish to face the historical and systemic legacy of racism and white supremacy in America. It provides an opportunity for its proponents to ignore the racial disparities in education, the dramatic incarceration of thousands of black males by the U.S. penal system, gang violence, housing and employment discrimination, and the distinctive impact of HIV/AIDS on African American women. Although these are issues that affect all Americans, there is a sense in which these are particular areas of crisis and concern for the black community. In the book *Whitewashing Race: The Myth of a Color-Blind Society*, several scholars came together to argue that this pernicious myth must be confronted and situated in its proper place in order to establish the basis of a renewed progressive and social initiative to advance racial progress. They write:

> Today, as a new century begins, race is still a pervasive and troubling fault line running through American life. We are not divided because we fail to "get along" as Rodney King lamented after the Los Angeles riots a decade ago. Nor is it because diehard advocates of affirmative action insist on stirring

up racial discord. What divides Americans is profound disagreement over the legacy of the civil rights movement. At the core of our national debate are very different opinions about the meaning of race in contemporary America and the prospects for racial equality in the future.[17]

The legacy of Jim Crow racism and segregation in the South and cultural racism in the North, they argue, has been undermined and discredited by new understandings of race and racial inequality.[18] Early on, there were major differences on the objectives of the Civil Rights Movement. When King began his leadership of the MIA in 1955 mounting the pulpit of Holt Street Baptist Church, his primary aim was to breakdown the walls of segregation. He, along with his allies in the movement, was interested in affirming the inherent dignity and personhood of blacks in the South and across America by removing those dehumanizing symbols of segregation such as signs stating "for whites only" and segregated practices in restaurants, public facilities, and of course city buses. After the momentous rise of the freedom rides and desegregation movement among a wave of youth activism in the early 1960s, many turned their sights to the related issue of voting rights. The March on Washington of 1963 held as its primary objective the passage of the Voting Rights Bill then under consideration in congress. With the passage of the Civil Rights Act of 1964, a sense of fatigue set in among many leaders in the movement, and a painful breakdown occurred as King began awakening to a more global vision to struggle against poverty and war. Exactly a year before his assassination, King delivered a passionate and eloquent speech at Riverside Church in New York opposing the war in Vietnam. The speech was entitled "A Time to Break the Silence" as he chastised the Johnson administration to act with a sense of urgency to end the war. As Taylor Branch observes in his book *At Canaan's Edge: American in the King Years, 1965–1968*, black political and church leaders quickly parted company with the famed leader in his prophetic call for the nation to turn away from war and confront global poverty. The breakdown in leadership led to a fragmentation of vision concerning American race relations and the future of the Civil Rights Movement. It led to competing visions about the goals and objectives of the movement itself, producing divisions that continue to exist today.

Obama's Speech on Race and Pastor Jeremiah Wright

These historical divisions were exposed in bizarre fashion before the nation through the caricature of a well-respected African American minister and Obama's longtime pastor—Jeremiah Wright. Obama's speech in Philadelphia on race as a response was nothing short of brilliant and courageous. No other high-level political leader in the history of this country has confronted race with such precision, intelligence, and depth of wisdom as Obama. What is more compelling is that Obama's speech appeared at a time when America continues to be viewed as increasingly negative and domineering in much of the world. Here, Obama recognized that one cannot distinguish the history of racism (from slavery to the genocide of American Indians) and socially progressive policies that continue to stall at almost every level of government. From health care, education, unemployment to the war in Iraq and nuclear proliferation, the persistent issue of race remains one of the most divisive, yet promising, areas of public debate. Obama's speech will no doubt be compared to the historic speeches of old like Sojourner Truth's "Ain't I A Woman", John F. Kennedy's 1960 Democratic nomination acceptance speech, and Martin Luther King, Jr.'s "Letter from Birmingham Jail".

In Thomas Paine's December 23, 1776, speech, "The Crisis," he said, "These are the times that try men's souls." Indeed, Paine's words, which may have been shared over the tables of the drafting documents of the Declaration of Independence in Philadelphia over 200 years ago, found new meaning in Obama's speech. Clearly, America is at a crossroads. Will it go the way of reconciliation, healing, peace, and honorable leadership in the world? Or, will it go the way of the traditional pattern of cutthroat politics, racial animosity, growing divisions between rich and poor, intensification of anti-American sentiments in the world, and unending wars and militaristic conflict? Whatever may be said concerning the choices Americans faced in presidential election, a reality that cannot be avoided is that whatever has been happening is not working. In fact, it seems to be leading down a spiral of fragmentation, conflict, and suffering. With the downturn of the U.S. economy, not seen since the Great Depression, and the sixth anniversary of an open-ended war, America must make tough choices about what it wants its future to look like for its children and grandchildren.

The injection of Obama's beloved pastor, Jeremiah Wright, into the debate revealed the deep wedges along racial lines that still exist in America. It demonstrated the gross lack of understanding, disconnectedness, and outright fear and hostility among blacks and whites about this curious American experiment. As Obama highlighted in his speech, the words of Wright make little sense and would certainly seem anti-American and shocking were it not for the context of racial oppression and a mere generation-removed system of segregation, of which Wright is heir. As a black youth in the sixties, Wright was in lockstep with the black power movement. The longtime activist and executive director of the SCLC Ella

Baker borrowed eight hundred dollars from the SCLC to host the first conference to establish the SNCC on April 15–17, 1960.[19] The conference was held on the campus of Shaw University in Raleigh, North Carolina. Wyatt Tee Walker, Ralph Abernathy, Douglas Moore, Fred Shuttlesworth, and James Lawson, all leaders in SCLC, also attended the meeting to encourage and provide leadership for the new student organization. Unlike the hierarchical, religion-based SCLC, SNCC was a student-led organization primarily focused on organizing sit-ins and freedom rides across the south. SNCC workers became known as "shock troops of the Movement."[20] They came across as more radicalized and would venture into areas of the south that few others would go. SNCC began its voting rights project in August 1961 in McComb, Mississippi, under the leadership of Bob Moses and later initiated another voting rights project in Albany, Georgia, with Charles Sherrod. The SNCC arm of the movement caught momentum by the spring of 1963 as more students joined the movement, and the movement grew in confidence with several decisive victories for desegregation. With the Voting Rights Act passed in 1965, SNCC turned its attention, as with many other civil rights organizations, toward educating blacks in the nuances of local governmental politics. This was the beginning of the localized grassroots black political machine, which Obama fully employed during his campaign. While Obama reaped the harvest of this rich tradition, seeds were sown by the intentional efforts of SNCC workers. These workers recognized then that the key to racial process rested in the ability of blacks to become agents in the local political process. They recognized early on that all politics is local, even the national elections.

Without question, Wright was part of the SNCC tradition. He was a child of the Civil Rights Movement, a youth activist, and a student of Black Liberation Theology (a school of thought born in the era that emphasizes black freedom and liberation over and against religious doctrine or nationalism). The shock and horror perceived by many white Americans also points to the incredible lack of understanding among white and blacks about their particular communities of faith. As King said years ago, and what certainly remains true today, Sunday mornings at 11 a.m. are still the most segregated hour at anytime in the country. Wright was not speaking as a political leader of some covert conspiracy. He did not, nor has he ever, preached or advocated hating any racial group. What he has done, which is not uncommon in many black churches and has been so throughout the history of the black church, is elevate a message of the frustrated hopes and painful dreams of the black experience in America. Without taking seriously the events of Hurricane Katrina, slavery, Jim Crow, the gross disparities of race when it comes to health care, incarceration, housing, unemployment, and poverty,

Wright's sermon would certainly not make sense; neither would Obama's speech on race.

In the black church, the preacher has always been much more than a professionally appointed ministerial leader who advances and preserves the doctrines of the church. The black preacher has been the one who has voiced the pain and suffering of black folks in the pews. The black preacher has been one who has been compelled to speak to all areas of black life, including the social, political, and economic dimensions of their reality. It is not surprising that Obama would have connected with Wright as a father figure. In *Dreams from My Father*, Obama talks about his longing for that fatherly relationship arising from the abandonment of his biological father. As a student of African Studies at the University of Chicago Divinity School, Wright studied the complexity of the African diaspora and would be one of the few pastors who would really understand Obama's struggle with racial identity and the broader context of the black experience. Wright, like many black pastors, is also very accustomed to stepping in as a surrogate father figure for many young black boys and men. This is supported by the fact that nearly two-thirds of all black households are single parent led by women.

Obama's speech on race, though reacting against the onslaught of negative ads about his longtime pastor, did elevate Obama's integrity as an African American leader deeply concerned about race in America and awareness of the complexities America's history and present racial context. In his speech, he said:

> This was one of the tasks we set forth at the beginning of this campaign—to continue the long march of those who came before us, a march for a more just, more equal, more free, more caring and more prosperous America. I chose to run for the presidency at this moment in history because I believe deeply that we cannot solve the challenges of our time unless we solve them together—unless we perfect our union by understanding that we may have different stories, but we hold common hopes; that we may not look the same and we may not have come from the same place, but we all want to move in the same direction—towards a better future for of children and our grandchildren . . .
>
> I am the son of a black man from Kenya and a white woman from Kansas. I was raised with the help of a white grandfather who survived a Depression to serve in Patton's Army during World War II and a white grandmother who worked on a bomber assembly line at Fort Leavenworth while he was overseas. I've gone to some of the best schools in America and lived in one of the world's poorest nations. I am married to a black American who carries within her the blood of slaves and slaveowners—an inheritance we pass on to our two precious daughters. I have brothers, sisters, nieces,

nephews, uncles and cousins, of every race and every hue, scattered across three continents, and for as long as I live, I will never forget that in no other country on Earth is my story even possible.

It's a story that hasn't made me the most conventional candidate. But it is a story that has seared into my genetic makeup the idea that this nation is more than the sum of its parts—that out of many, we are truly one."[21]

In this brief speech, Obama delivered one of the most thoughtful reflections on race in America by a national political leader since Martin Luther King, Jr.'s "I Have A Dream" speech in 1963. This may come as a surprise to some. To others, this was made dramatically apparent by the attention it received in all sectors of American society, from religious communities to schools and political spaces. It was indeed refreshing to have once again the language of race injected into mainstream public debate. Obama's speech affirmed what Jonathan Sacks called the "dignity of difference." His achieved his aim to emphasize the inherent humanity of both blacks and whites in America, of which his own biographical experience reflects. He wisely stayed away from talk of social structures, system racism and the painful legacy of slavery, Jim Crow segregation, and economic racial disparities across the country. In spite of its limitations, Obama was able to adequately address the rage of Pastor Jeremiah Wright, while offering a renewed vision for a national dialogue on race in America. His speech ultimately called for a new public dialogue on race in America. Regrettably, few took up his call, and his speech on race was short lived.

The brief 10 to 20-second clips of Wright circulating on the Internet, YouTube, CNN, FoxNews, and other stations did not reflect the fact that Wright is a U.S. Marine veteran, studied at some of the best schools in America, and has never been associated with any anti-American activities or antiracist/anti-Semitic language or practices in his over-thirty-year tenure at Trinity United Church of Christ in Chicago. The clips said little about the hundreds of ministries Wright helped to develop as pastor, ranging from drug-treatment programs, marriage counseling, homelessness and joblessness programs to prison ministries, youth ministries for inner city gang members, and programs for the elderly. Located in one of the roughest areas in Southside Chicago, Wright has been committed to the work of social justice and bettering the community for more than thirty years. The barrage of media attention on Wright, the retired pastor, demonstrates more than anything the cheapening of real journalism and the out-of-control sensationalism of the infotainment industry today that will do almost anything to spur conflict and increase fear and anxiety to fuel their ratings. On the one hand, the Reverend Wright's sermon served as a distraction for the Obama campaign that desperately needed to focus its attention on the working people of Philadelphia and more broadly Pennsylvania. On the other hand, the ways in which Obama used the controversy to introduce a historic and indispensible dialogue on race into the discussion could prove to be a defining moment for the nation. Obama's speech in Philadelphia moved him beyond a simple politician. His "improbable quest" took on a new, more pronounced level of intensity, depth, and sincerity as he confronted an issue with ancient roots and incomparable promise.

In those brief words, Obama revealed his honor and integrity as a man of faith and one who doesn't sell out those closest to him for political expediency. He also showed his commitment to restoring the nation to a path of greatness and hopefulness, not just for a few elites but for all. In Philadelphia, amid the shadows of the nation's founding fathers, and just steps away from the bell that stills rings of liberty, Barack Obama became a leader.

Conclusion

I have tried to show, in this chapter, that first of all the issue of race and racism in America is as alive and well today as it was during the turn of the twentieth century. If America forgets its racial past, it is doomed to repeat it. Now, however, more is at stake. Because of the role America plays in international affairs, the ways in which it views race and relates to other nations of the world has far-reaching global implications. The Obama presidency, in as much as it is about the triumph of optimism and hope over skepticism and fear, is about the nation attempting to come to terms with its racist past. When Obama was sworn in on January 20, 2009, in Washington, D.C., the nation and the world saw not only a young, idealistic, gifted visionary. They also saw a black man being elevated to a seat of power, formerly held by forty-three consecutive white males. They observed a black man leading what might truly become a multicultural nation that respects and honors all people. Throughout many controversial moments of the presidential election, including the Jeremiah Wright media blitz and Obama's eloquent race speech, we bore witness to the dramatic unfolding of racial politics, power, and the meaning of the American dream. As I take up in the next chapter, understanding these connections, particularly Obama's identity, may tell us volumes about who we are as individuals and collectively as a people.

CHAPTER 3

A Black Man in White America

A powerful preoccupying factor in the history of this country since its founding in seventeenth century has been the matter of color. Color and race have never been far below the level of awareness, even anxiety, on the part of white Americans. The matter of color justified the establishment of African slavery; and then white Americans argued that slavery was not only the natural lot of blacks but the most beneficial state of existence for persons from the "Dark Continent." Indeed, freedom for blacks was not only undesirable but inconceivable. Consequently, every effort should be made to prevent their manumission and even to return to bondage those who were free.[1]

On the day of Obama's inauguration on the cool, crisp, winter morning of January 20, 2009, the nation and world saw something not seen perhaps in the last few centuries of human history. The world witnessed a black man taking the reins of the lone superpower and greatest militaristic empire of our time. With every word echoed in his oath, flashes of the slave trade, the bitter neglect of reconstruction, the lynching, the quest for desegregation, and the Civil Rights Movement all flickered with maddening clarity. Who Obama is as president, because of the historical legacy of racism and struggle, is perhaps as important as what he stands for.

From here, it is essential to give some treatment to Obama's place as an African American male serving in the highest office in the land within the broader contours of American society. What does it mean to be a black male in America today? Raising this question, of itself, is a subversive undertaking because in doing so one is stating a political reality steeped in neglect and marginalization. It also makes it difficult to avoid the common gender wars of who is suffering most. One must take seriously the multiplicities of oppression, particularly the sting of patriarchy, homophobia, classism, sexism, and ableism. In raising such a question, I do not wish to reduce or somehow lessen the significance of black women and their unique struggles. In fact, black women have been and continue to be the backbone of the black experience in America. Women are now leading nearly 70 percent of black households. They have been and continue to be the bearers of black tradition and culture, protectors, providers, lovers, and saints. Black males owe their very survival in this nation to black women. But given the degree to which Obama participates in, and some might say even benefited from, the patriarchal dimensions of American society, what insights might we gather about the persistence of racism today? Racism, in fact, gives dramatic insight to how other forms of oppression function, and lives within social structures and institutions. In this chapter, building on the broader context of racism and America, I take a closer look at the peculiar aspects of race and racism, including its institutional and structural configurations with Obama in view.

John Hope Franklin masterfully points out that in America race has fundamentally shaped the social, cultural, religious, and ideological psyche of its members. The very nature and consciousness of America are unintelligible without the issue of race. Obama's run for president gives us an occasion once again to revisit the history of such a devastating racist past and consider its present meaning. There is an ancient African proverb, echoed in the words of the twentieth-century Harvard philosopher George Santayana, that says if people do not know their history, they are destined to repeat it. Like other black folks, I am deeply optimistic about the prospects and possibilities of an Obama presidency. As a theologian, I am also aware of the pitfalls of human life, that human nature is a dismal reality that makes sin and evil inevitable. In spite of how brilliant Obama may be, all Americans (especially the vast majority of black people who celebrate Obama's presidency) would do well to keep in view the reality of American racism, its history and painful legacy. By doing so, we are much better positioned to critique, analyze, and challenge any political structure or administration that neglects the plight of black suffering in America. We must never forget that Obama is part of a larger systemic political apparatus that has been hell-bent on keeping those at the bottom on the bottom. Obama is a courageous leader who will no doubt do his part. However, it would be a mistake to view Obama as some sort of messianic figure who can "do no wrong" or the one who alone holds the key to the redemption and prosperity of all of black America. Considering the deep roots of race and racism in America helps to more forcefully attend to this issue at the present moment.

The New Racism and American Society

Racism in America now comes in the form of exclusion, dismissal, and outright rejection—of ideas, needs, perspectives, stories, and resources. Black folks may have made it to the table but have officially been shut out of the conversation. Although the signs stating "for whites only" have been dismantled, the normative structures of white privilege are fully erect. The presuppositions upon which racism was built, essentially a divinization of whiteness arising from enlightenment claims about human nature, are still in full force in American society. Although the visible signs of Jim Crow racism were removed through the courageous witness of black folks more than forty years ago, the invisible (and often subconscious) ideologies of white supremacy continue to be a driving force behind the systemic issues impacting black life today.

As a black man in white America, Obama himself acknowledges the ways in which his experiences are uniquely different from the average black male who could trace his roots to American chattel slavery. In his book *The Audacity of Hope*, Obama clearly points out that he rejects notions of a "postracial" society that denies or reduces the particular racial identity of its peoples. Some have used Obama's speeches to further their own political agendas and to minimize the lingering significance of race in American society. The speech he delivered at the 2004 Democratic Convention, where he decried that there is only the "United States of America" at the end of the day, is a good example. To this end, Obama offers a word of caution. He wrote, "To say that we are one people is not to suggest that race no longer matters—that the fight for equality has been won, or that the problems that minorities face in this country today are largely self-inflicted."[2] It is refreshing to know that Obama is indeed conscious of the particular issues affecting certain communities in America. He further observed that "to suggest that our racial attitudes play no part in these disparities is to turn a blind eye to both our history and our experience—and to relieve ourselves of the responsibility to make things right."[3] As someone who was able to assume presumably the most powerful position in the world, the insights and perspectives Obama will bring to the presidency will be nothing short of revolutionary.

Throughout the history of America, the presidency has been engrossed in white supremacist ideals, where its leaders were shaped and formed largely in a world that positioned whites as near divinity and superior to another group of human beings. For instance, Ronald Reagan's assault on social programs and his legacy of casting black women as "welfare queens" is still being felt today. This predicament dehumanized both blacks and whites. It gave whites the false impression that they were and are more advanced and normative for other peoples and cultures across the world, while filling blacks with the venom of psychological inferiority, low self-worth, and incredible physical hardship and suffering. Although Obama's experience has been unique, he nevertheless recognizes the deep roots of racism permeating the veins of the American body politic. In his reflections of race, he writes:

> Moreover, while my own upbringing hardly typifies the African American experience—and although, largely through luck most of the bumps and bruises that the average black man must endure—I can recite the usual litany of petty slights that during my forty-five years have been directed my way: security guards tailing me as I shop in department stores, white couples who toss me their car keys as I stand outside a restaurant waiting for the valet, police cars pulling me over for no apparent reason. I know what it's like to have people tell me I can't do something because of my color, and I know the bitter swill of swallowed-back anger. I know as well that Michelle and I must be continually vigilant against some of the debilitating story lines that our daughters may absorb—from TV and music and friends and the streets—about who the world thinks they are, and what the world imagines they should be.[4]

With all of his optimism, it is impossible even for Obama to escape the reality that race is still the most pervasive and persistent problem facing the American consciousness. Because of the role America plays in the world, through militarism, international markets, and a host of other global influences, American racism has spilled over to its racial policies and treatment of other non-Western nations as well. The words of Du Bois more than a hundred years ago still ring true today. "The problem of the twentieth century is the problem of the color-line—the relation of the darker to the lighter races of men in Asia and Africa, in America and the islands of the sea."[5] So, on the one hand, while race may be an issue directly connected to America's past and its citizens, on the other hand, it is also true that America does not live in a world of isolation. Its views, ideas, and policies, which have indeed been informed by racism and white supremacist ideals, have now dramatically impacted the world abroad as developing nations of Asia, Africa, and the Middle East continue to feel the brunt of inequitable economic and political practices. The roots of these practices, I believe, may be found in the peculiar racial dynamics in America and Europe as well.

Cornel West has been one of the most outspoken public intellectuals exploring the reality of race in America. His acclaimed book *Race Matters* provides creative insights into the nuances of American racism. Given the fact that Obama as the first black president will clearly influence how the issue of race is discussed in the public square, a conversation between Obama and the analytical resources on race offered by West is indeed called for and essential to how this discussion is situated for the years to come. According to West, the proper place to begin discussing race in America is not with the problems of black people but with the flaws of American society. How race is discussed, viewing blacks often as the "other," with whiteness as normative, places the responsibility of challenging the moral and cultural dimensions of race on blacks. A sort of policing of what it means to be "American" occurs in a way that attempts to force peoples who are not of European descent to simply assimilate. This destructive pattern of racial discourse has led to a refrain in the public square that someone's race is a "black" problem, not necessarily an American dilemma. At a time when the issue of race has once again taken center stage by virtue of the historic campaign and election of Obama, new opportunities have emerged to establish a new framework, one that calls for "a frank acknowledgment of the basic humanness and Americanness of each of us."[6] West puts it this way:

> We must acknowledge that as a people—*E Pluribus Unum*—we are on a slippery slop toward economic strife, social turmoil, and cultural chaos. If we go down, we go down together. The Los Angeles upheaval forces us to see not only that we are not connected in the ways we would like to be but also, in a more profound sense, that this failure to connect binds us even more tightly together. The paradox of race in America is that our common destiny is more pronounced and imperiled precisely when our divisions are deeper. The Civil War and its legacy speak loudly here. And our divisions are growing deeper. Today, eighty-six percent of white suburban Americans live in neighborhoods that are less than 1 percent black, meaning that the prospects for the country depend largely on how its cities fare in the hands of a suburban electorate. There is no escape from our interracial interdependence, yet enforced racial hierarchy dooms us as a nation to collective paranoia and hysteria—the unmaking of any democratic order.[7]

In these words, West speaks as both prophet and sage in recognizing that the destiny of whites and blacks in America are intertwined. Blacks have historically offered an alternative vision for America and a radical critique of its democratic ideals. From Henry Highland Garnett, Sojourner Truth, and Frederick Douglass to Martin Luther King, Jr., Jesse Jackson, Al Sharpton, and Marian Wright Edelman, the aim has been to call America to live into its own hopes. West was speaking out of the explosive context of the Los Angeles riots of 1992 sparked by the verdict acquitting white police officers in the beating of Rodney King. For many blacks, the Rodney

King case unveiled the deep, corrosive racial divisions existing in America. It brought to the surface the pain of black suffering experienced in poor housing, dilapidated educational system, and higher rates of incarceration, police brutality, and lack of health care. It was also a powerful indication that in as much as whites and blacks have different (often competing) views of what America is, their lives are inextricably bound together.

The great American literary genius Ralph Ellison captured the essence of this interconnectedness when he wrote,

> Since the beginning of the nation, white Americans have suffered from a deep uncertainty as to who they really are. One of the ways that has been used to simplify the answer has been to seize upon the presence of black Americans and use them as a marker, a symbol of limits, a metaphor for the 'outsider.' Many whites could look at the social position of blacks and feel that color formed an easy and reliable gauge for determining to what extent one was or was not American.[8]

Martin Luther King, Jr., intimated more than a generation ago:

> We are caught in an inescapable network of mutuality, tied in a single garment of destiny. Whatever affects one directly affects all indirectly. I can never be what I ought to be until you are what you ought to be. The rich man can never be what he ought to be until the poor man is what he ought to be.[9]

It remains to be seen as to how Obama will respond to the particularities of race in America—whether he will directly challenge the white supremacist ideologies of his colleagues in Washington, D.C., and American white elites or avoid questions of race altogether. Either way, the problem of race is with us and must be dealt with. Even Obama acknowledged that in many of our urban cities, quiet storms and wars are raging and, if left unattended, will expand to the neatly manicured gated communities of the suburbs and mainstream American life. But, what can Obama's story, his campaign, and election as president tell us about the present conditions of race in America, its implications for all Americans and an increasingly globally connected and culturally diverse world?

From Birmingham to Jena: Systemic Racism and Black Males

For many, the American dream has truly become a nightmare. The vast amount of statistical data, research, and information today makes it virtually impossible to come to a consensus on the problems facing black life in

America, much less to explain why so many African American males are being incarcerated at alarming rates. Nonetheless, the U.S. legal system, especially related to prisons, is one very important example of systemic racism today. In merely three decades, the prison population in America has grown from 330,000 in 1972 to 2.1 million in 2001, and the rate of imprisonment in the United States is almost ten times greater than most of the industrialized nations of the world.[10] Addressing this issue has been stifled by the changing cultural dynamics in America, in addition to the rapidly expanding gap between rich and poor. As the Latin American activist, philosopher, and theologian Leonardo Boff has observed, human civilization is now experiencing a kind of cultural and historical shift, akin to the Bronze and Iron Ages. Except, now technology has become the fulcrum on which new ways of relating, knowing, and being in the world is being realized. According to Boff, we are currently experiencing a new kind of technical development, which brings with it new kinds of social relations. The basis of social relations, he argues, is no longer labor, but communication and informatics.[11] What this perhaps infers about the research enterprise is that it is becoming much more individualistic, fragmented, and less dialogical, and occurring through electronic pulsations and virtual images and monitors. Racism now arrives in the form of perceived intolerance, neglect, and individual choice. Most would attribute the problems facing young black males primarily to individual moral behavior without closely analyzing the structural realities related to poverty, geographic location, and public indifference. There is a kind of cultural attitude that reflects the illusion that somehow technological progress translates into moral progress. As Gianni Vattimo highlighted, notions of progress, particularly when it comes to matters of justice, equality, or human freedom, now come under the guise of technological progress.

Institutional Racism in New Clothes

But what do the changing cultural realities related to research and technology more broadly have to do with the present quest for social justice, which some may now feel was one of the factors that led to the Jena Six situation? The recent, and still persistent, events concerning six African American high-school students in the small rural town of Jena, Louisiana, are a dramatic case study for exploring the historical, social, and economic trajectories of race and legalism in the American experience. Jena Six also creates new opportunities for exploring the quest for social justice in the age of Obama and the challenges of pluralism in building a sense of collective consciousness.

Is there a connection between the Civil Rights Movement, particularly one of its most significant theaters in Birmingham where King penned possibly one of the most important writings of the twentieth century, and the Jena Six story? What are Obama's views on issues like this, and how will he respond? Now, nearly forty years later after the civil rights era (in fact, April 2008 marked the fortieth anniversary of Martin Luther King, Jr.'s assassination on the balcony of the Lorraine Hotel in Memphis, Tennessee), how do we understand the legacy of King in light of continual, more nuanced social inequities? Indeed, there are clear and blatant differences between Birmingham and Jena. Birmingham, coming as a backdrop of the March on Washington in 1963, was an intentional and strategic direct action campaign aimed at desegregation of store and public facilities and establishment of conditions for equal employment practices. In his "Letter from Birmingham Jail," written as notes on strips of tissue paper, King was attempting to publically respond to eight liberal white clergymen who bashed the protest as "untimely and unwise."[12]

In the letter, King made a fundamental distinction between human law and eternal law. Drawing on the theological and philosophical insights of Augustine and Thomas Aquinas, King argued that human law is simply an approximation or an attempt to achieve the greater, intrinsic law of the universe. Segregation, though legal, he wrote, was irreconcilably inconsistent with God's eternal law. He grounded this distinction in the notion that the proper goal of the law or law at its best purports to preserve, sustain, and enrich human life and social relations. Because the system of segregation, by its very existence, separated human beings, social relations, and institutions, it undermined the very core of what it means to be human and to live together in what he called the "beloved community." Herein lies one of the fundamental differences between King and Obama. Indeed, King as a black Baptist preacher and theologian envisioned the beloved community in a way that challenged systemic racism and its impact on interpersonal relationships. Obama, on the other hand, is a pragmatist with strong commitments to the underclass and marginalized communities. He has said that his chief aim is to seek to perfect America's constitutional ideals, whereas for King, establishing the beloved community was the motivating source of all his work in the movement. The Obama administration can learn a great deal from King's vision in responding to social structural issues like the U.S. penal system. As the philosopher and social critique Michel Foucault recognized more than a generation ago, prisons simply serve as a canary in the cave, a dramatic symptom of what is so desperately wrong with contemporary American life, Western life in general. The recent events surrounding the story of six young black high-school students in

Jena offers a glimpse into today's collision of systemic racism and its lingering effects.

Of course, the events of Jena Six were not, like Birmingham, a demonstration of any kind. It was not an intentional protest or a kind of systematic and strategic effort like that of Rosa Parks. In fact, there is evidence to suggest that the circumstances stemming from a "whites only" tree on school grounds, which sparked outrage and national protest, were nothing more than a school-yard brawl. On the other hand, these events of Jena Six left a deep expression of one of the most lingering tragedies haunting the soul of America—that which Derrick Bell has called the permanence of "racism." According to reports, in September 2006, a black student asked a school administrator if he could sit under the "white tree". After he was told he could sit anywhere, he sat under the tree, and the next day three nooses (reflecting school colors) were hung from the tree. Now this event makes no sense apart from the troubling and violent history of lynching, segregation, and humiliation of blacks in across the Deep South. When no action was taken by school administrators, black students at the school protested, and it was essentially written off as a distasteful prank. The situation escalated when a black student was beaten up on December 1 (Friday) night, by a group of white students for attending a "white party." The next day, at the "Gotta Go" convenience store, the black student who was beaten up confronted one of the white students who participated in the fight the night before. As the story goes, the white student retrieved a shotgun from his vehicle. The gun was taken by the black students, and the white student was severely beaten. On December 4, white students along with Justin Barker, hung nooses and hurled racial insults at the school under the "white tree." Later that day, a fight ensued and Barker was severely beaten by students at school. Over the next couple of days, December 5–6, the students, Robert Bailey, Theo Shaw, Carwin Jones, Bryant Purvis, and Mychal Bell, were charged. Bell was the only student unable to post bail and remained in jail. None of the other students were charged in the incident.

The story is a searing indication of the systematic exploitation of primarily poor young black males at the hands of the penal system. Black communities communities across the nation, both urban and rural, are watching their most gifted sons plucked away at levels not seen since the theft of black men and boys during the transatlantic slave trade in villages across Ghana, Sierra Leone, Cote D-Voire, and Angola. Indeed, Obama must directly address these issues as president.

What Birmingham and Jena share in common are essentially three things. First, both events reflect the pervasive interconnections of race, law and incarceration, and power in American society. King recognized that to dismantle the power of incarceration as an instrument of social control was to unveil its abuses and misuses, and that when the innocent are jailed for righteous reasons, this punishment strips away the moral authority and hegemony of the system itself, causing others to call into question its very legitimacy in that particular context. Second, these instances demonstrate the ways in which black experiences with incarceration also signal other deep systemic problems, such as poverty, political disenfranchisement, violence, housing, and education, that have their origins in the history of the black freedom struggle in America. There is a direct connection and line of succession, from Birmingham to Jena, linked to slavery that continues to suppress blackness or to "keep blacks in their place." The relationship between Birmingham and Jena also gives us insight into the broader, more fundamental dilemmas affecting the cultural and political landscape of America—namely, that prisons, surveillance, state coercive power, and control of the knowledge have become the primary tools of social control.

Prisons as an Indicator of Structural Racism Today

Foucault, who argued that racism was essentially a product of Western culture and linguistic structures and attempts to establish systems of "normality," saw the modern penitentiary as an expression of Western culture in general, and American culture in particular. Foucault helps us to think critically how modern linguistic structures, perpetuated by so-called Christians and non-Christians alike, enable the conditions for ghettos and massive prison structures to exist. The modern prison, of which black males in America have become the primary benefactors, was for Foucault the result of a binary linguistic structure that creates systems of normality and abnormality (i.e., white/black, good/bad, high/low, etc.). These modes of describing the world produce structures of oppression in the same manner the "leper" in ancient cultures was considered the "outcast" and the "abnormal" other. Using Foucault's observations, one can see how black males in popular culture historically have been deemed the "leper" or the "abnormal" other, making their disproportionate representation in prison both acceptable and possibly even justifiable. Foucault's description of modern prisons as symbolizing the destructive tendencies of modernity helps us to think anew about the issue of prisons in a postmodern context. In terms of structure, prisons are built with the purpose of maximum surveillance with minimum guard personnel for efficiency. Foucault alone leaves us with little hope of overcoming the problem. For Foucault, the world ends in hopelessness. Obama started his campaign on the platform of hope and change. It would seem that Obama and his campaign had an acute awareness of the broader cultural problem of nihilism. More specifically, the Obama camp responded to the ways in which the Bush administration dramatized the deepest of human fears. The modern-day concentration camp at Guantanamo in Cuba was a powerful example of hopelessness and desperation translated into a concrete institution of social control. The concentration camp at Guantanamo was established by the Bush administration to house suspected terrorists without any access to trial and jury, breaking all constitutional and even military justice laws.[13] Guantanamo, more than anything, signaled the way power seeks to control and isolate and how prisons are often used as the primary instrument of social and political subjugation.

Like much of our society, prisons have to do with power, social control, isolation, individuality, and efficiency. Prisons, according to Foucault, are dramatically similar to other modern institutions such as shopping malls, schools, psychiatric institutions, nursing homes, the military, and the government. In prisons, truth and justice are defined by the systems of power that control the institution. The power of the institution arises from its ability to isolate its members from each other, always seen but never able to see. The primary tool of prisons, like much of the wider society, is surveillance. What makes surveillance so dangerous is that black men are often targeted and criminalized from the first contact with law enforcement officials simply because of surveillance and skin color. As Earl Ofari Hutchinson insists in *The Assassination of the Black Male Image,* the effects of mainstream media's obsession with criminalizing young black males merely intensified surveillance, contributing to more negative contacts with the police and abuses by the criminal justice system.[14] With the now nearly two million incarcerated bodies in America's prison industrial complex, one has to seriously reflect on the forces that has shaped the largest prison system in the world.

Poor Blacks, Joblessness, and Incarceration: Is the U.S. Penal System a Legitimate Legal System for the Poor?

The real issue that most Americans are reluctant to face, and that Obama must confront as president, is the inescapable connection between race, poverty, and the U.S. penal system. High rates of black male imprisonment are directly related to the scourging economic disparities between black and white in America. With the combination of poverty and racism at the center of the crisis, our nation is faced with the difficult question about the very legitimacy of the system. According to William Julius Wilson, the Harvard sociologist who has conducted extensive studies related to urban poverty and the impact of joblessness in shaping behaviors and cultural life, black male engagement with the prison system can in no way be divorced from the social and economic conditions of their context. From the moment of birth, if you are poor and black, you are more likely to end up in prison than college. Poor black males are more likely to be targeted, policed, harassed, and left with fewer life options for avoiding a confrontation with the massive system of incarceration.

Certainly, the efficacy of the system hinges on the fulcrum of fairness for both victim and the accused. Now, the unfortunate reality is that fairness more than ever before looks white and wealthy. Addressing the issue of poverty, which creates the conditions that exacerbates criminality and disparity, is essential for meaningful reform to take place. Attaching poverty and the policies that allow racism to persist with the bang of every gavel is the key to moving toward a more just and equitable system for all.

Bruce Wright: former New York Supreme Court Judge and author of *Black Robes, White Justice: Why Our Legal System Doesn't Work for Blacks*, affirms that racism is an inescapable reality. Wright maintains there is a pervasive presence of racism on the benches and in the courtrooms across the nation. Much of this, says Wright, hinges on the notion that "the fear of black men rests upon the white posit that most, if not all, black males are criminals and dangerous." As Hutchinson points out, the constant portrayal of black males in the media as violent, shiftless, sexually deviant, and undisciplined is not excluded from the ways in which white and black judges alike engage in the interpretation of laws, prosecution, and treatment of blacks. Why is it, says Wright, that white judges and law makers are resistant to address the question of such high rates of black defendants in court cases? He writes:

> Do white judges ever wonder about why there are so few black lawyers appearing before them? Do they ever inquire about the history of bar associations that used to exclude Jews and blacks? Do they ever ponder aloud or in silence the reasons that there are so few black judges? Whenever I have raised the subject of bar association discrimination against blacks, my white colleagues profess never to have noticed any such thing.[15]

The deep roots of racism have not disappeared from American consciousness. Even in the midst of an Obama administration, racism rages on. It is not as if the assassination of Martin Luther King, Jr., on a crisp April morning in 1968 outside the Lorraine Hotel, created the conditions for a miraculous awakening and transformation of racism and bigotry. On the contrary, through family systems laced within the fabric of institutions and structures, racism and injustice have found more comforting refuge under the allusion of racial progress and technology. Racial attitudes and practices are often passed from generation to generation unless intentional and conscious intervention and awareness take place. But even this alone is not sufficient to break the cycle of racism and discrimination. Nearly exclusive white neighborhoods, schools, businesses, clubs, and social organizations create the conditions for negative racial attitudes to persist, and sometimes worsen. So there is a need to take personal responsibility in families both to curve racist attitudes and behaviors as well as transform systems, such as the courts. As Wright points out, and also reported by the American Bar Association, the lack of black judges, lawyers, court clerks, legal assistants, wardens, police, prison guards, local/state/federal policy makers each contributes to the conditions that intensify painful mistreatment of black males in the judicial system.

Wright is right to point out the persistent reality of race as it informs the legal process. He, however, does not emphasize the broader role that poverty plays in the legal process. There is a direct correlation between poor defendants and prosecutorial activities. William Julius Wilson, the Harvard sociologist, has gone to great lengths to point out the ways in which poverty not only shapes the culture, moral choices, and prospects of blacks, but also indicates that by the very reality of being both black and poor, persons are faced with an inevitable possibility of being sucked into the spiraling grip of the penal system, from youth on into adulthood. His classic works, *Power, Racism and Privilege, The Declining Significance of Race, The Truly Disadvantaged,* and *When Work Disappears: The World of the New Urban Poor,* all attest to the need for urgent dialogue and prophetic action aimed at redeeming and transforming a currently fractured and dangerously imbalanced judiciary. If we agree with Immanuel Kant that human beings are both moral and social agents, then we cannot reasonably assess the high rates of black male incarceration without considering moral choice related to established laws and rules of behavior, or what happens at the first level of contact between black youth and police, and the social situations that influence moral choice.

There are some things that can be done. It will take direct comprehensive action from the Obama administration and local leaders to confront these challenges. There needs to be a robust debate in local and national spaces about the nature of judicial prudence concerning the poor, not simply as an individual reality, but as a social condition that has political, economic, and cultural consequences. Also, there is a need to establish advisory councils that might provide oversight of court decisions by local communities in ways that reflect the diversity of that particular community.

Here, it means revising this notion of a "jury of our peers"—where "peers" has a more particularized and local configuration. Activists and political leaders must also advocate for local and national initiatives designed to increase representation of judges, lawyers, and police. Additionally, policies and codes that provide regular oversight of judicial conduct related to the treatment of racial and ethnic communities must be written into the legal system. More broadly speaking, marginalized communities must become more engaged in the political process, especially in local elections. It is often the case that poor communities, particularly the black communities (and studies have borne this out), often neglect local elections that often determine key positions like judges, sheriffs and police chiefs, local and state legislators that really have a tremendous impact on determining critical decisions about our day-to-day lives.

Conclusion

At the end of the day, America's prisons, inasmuch as they disproportionately impact African American males in America, are not just about this segment of American society. The same ideas and racist tendencies informing America's prisons also influence foreign policy in the global community, militarism, and even domestic policies related to children and the elderly. Racism also spills over to the relative abandonment of constructive policies and initiatives toward African countries, the Caribbean, and parts of Latin America. Racism in America is profoundly interrelated to racism in the global community, which can be most visibly seen throughout the African diaspora. As we will address in the next chapter, looking at the broader implications of racism in America for the global community deserves serious attention. As the first black president, what impact will Obama's administration have on the rest of the world, especially the African diaspora? Furthermore, is it possible to once again forge a collective African consciousness in thinking about the new, more fluid dimensions of black identity in today's world?

CHAPTER 4

Obama, African Diaspora, and the New Meaning of Blackness

Little of beauty has America given the world save the rude grandeur God himself stamped on her bosom; the human spirit in this new world has expressed itself in vigor and ingenuity rather than in beauty. And so by fateful chance the Negro folk-song—the rhythmic cry of the slave—stands to-day not simply as the sole American music, but as the most beautiful expression of human experience born this side the seas. It has been neglected, it has been, and is half despised, and above all it has been persistently mistaken and misunderstood; but notwithstanding, it still remains as the singular spiritual heritage of the nation and the greatest gift of the Negro people.[1]

Africans are going to have to be responsible for their own salvation. We have to be partners with them in that process. The African American community here has to be attentive to their issues. On the flip side, African leaders have to create a rule of law that is not corrupt, that is transparent.[2]

In February 1959, Martin Luther King, Jr., visited India on a trip arranged by the Gandhi National Memorial Fund along with Lawrence D. Reddick, his biographer, to study Gandhi's nonviolent philosophy. As David J. Garrow records, there were three things King shared with his Dexter Avenue congregation about his trip upon his return.[3] King first admired Gandhi's incredible capacity for self-criticism, and second, his ability to reject capitalism by relinquishing all material possessions. King also told his congregation how much he admired Gandhi's self-discipline. What is undeniable is the fact that King's travels introduced him to the larger, global scope of his campaign for justice in the South. King understood that although the primary theaters of his leadership in the movement was the American South, he was really engaged in a global (albeit cosmic) struggle for truth, justice, and human freedom in the world. In King's mind, the struggle was much greater than he and his immediate colleagues in the MIA and the SCLC.

The same sense of global awareness seemed to have bitten Obama, not only in growing up in Hawaii and Indonesia, but in his trip to several African countries, like South Africa and his fatherland of Kenya as a newly minted U.S. senator in 2006. For the third time in his life, in August 2006, Obama once again traveled to Kogelo, Kenya, a small grassless village in the western region of the country. It was the land of Obama's father, who had grown up as son of a Muslim goat herder.[4] His grandmother still lives in the village. In Kenya, Obama was greeted by massive crowds, all claiming him as one of their own. While in the village, thousands of people came out, clogging the thatched houses and dirty streets; surrounded by black faces, the crowd shouted "*Obama biro, yawne yo,*" meaning "Obama's coming, clear the way."[5] The tremendous affection shown to Obama by the Kenyan people expressed the amazing adoration many developing countries across Africa, Asia, and Latin America feel about the young leader. It also presents us with an opportunity to explore Obama and, in a real sense, America's connections to the African diaspora and the world community.

As we now know, Obama's inauguration as the first black president of America is not just about America. It represents something very compelling happening in the world. Since the Civil Rights Movement, the forces of integration have dramatically changed the landscape of race in America. Obama's campaign, if fully appreciated, must be situated within a historical saga of racism, segregation, colonialism, and the emergence of a technocratic culture where global forces are creating conditions in which people learn to coexist with their differences.

Race, the Legacy of Colonialism, and the Global World

The history of racism in America is not just about America. If America (its policies, economic and cultural influences, military presence, etc.) were isolated to its own geographic boundaries, the history of racism in this nation would still be intricately connected to the ways in which race and ethnicity are viewed throughout the world. Obama, who considers himself a "citizen of the world," will have to contend with the meaning of his presidency for nations throughout the world who have long recognized the white supremacist ideologies of the West in general, America in particular. As president, Obama must not only reckon with the matrix of American power in the world, he must also take seriously the painful shadows of colonialism and neocolonial economic systems of globalization. Old forms of colonialism sought to control geographic territories, bodies for physical labor, and natural resources. Neocolonialism now seeks to control the economic and political structures of developing nations to advance the interest of the few developed nations. Global organizations such as the International Monetary Fund, World Bank, United Nations, and the Group of Eight (or the G8) have been at the forefront of directing the policies and programs that order the lives of millions across the developing world.

The history of colonialism in many developing nations across Africa, Asia, and Latin America is still fresh on the minds of countless individuals who in recent years have come to hate America with a kind of diseased fury. Current attitudes about America did not begin with George W. Bush or the aftereffects of 9/11 alone. Since the dawn of the nation, they have been rooted in memory of slavery, genocide of the native Indian population, America's involvement in colonialism, and countless other global travesties. While Americans may have short memories, the world community does not. The interconnectedness of cultures across the globe now makes the radical changes taking place around issues of identity and race much more apparent.

As we think about how the Obama administration, and America in general, ought to relate to the broader African world, Aimé Cesaire is a very engaging and helpful conversation partner because of his insights into Western imperialism and the liberationist struggle against colonialism. Cesaire's ability to flow freely between the Western world and African consciousness under colonialism is rare and necessary. It is quite disturbing how little U.S. policy makers know about the developing African world. The poor people of the world have paid the price for such ignorance and denial. There is hope, however, that Obama will bring fresh perspectives and vision to U.S. relations toward Africa and other countries like Brazil, the Republic of Haiti, and the Caribbean. Obama's meeting with Brazilian president Luiz Inacio Lula da Silva on March 14, 2009, is an example of the kind of serious engagement (among equals) that must take place to advance U.S. foreign and domestic policy. Of course, this is not new. The United States has historically supported foreign governments in developing nations that adhered to its political interests. In either case, there is a need to deepen American understandings of the developing world, especially across the African diaspora. Dialogue between the Western world and developing nations has often taken place around the historical legacy of colonialism, which needs to be contextualized for today's world. In Cesaire's *Discourse on Colonialism*, a book first published in 1950 as sort of a "third-world manifesto," the call was issued for oppressed peoples to decolonize both their bodies and their minds. For most of the developing nations, the experience with colonialism has been one of the definitive experiences that has shaped racial attitudes and suspicions toward Europe and its golden child, America. Cesaire observed:

> A civilization that proves incapable of solving the problems it creates is a decadent civilization.
>
> A civilization that chooses to close its eyes to its most crucial problems is a stricken civilization.
>
> A civilization that uses its principles for trickery and deceit is a dying civilization.[6]

According to Cesaire, the problem with Western civilization and modernity, of which American democracy is the rightful heir, is its deceit and lies. Its failure to live up to its own values and commitments, its inability to speak openly and honestly about its intents, and, most of all, its unabashed determination to manipulate its own principles (of freedom, democracy, justice, etc.) to dehumanize others around the world may very well be its greatest threat to survival. What Cesaire so eloquently intimates is that developing nations have awakened from their slumber and are no longer blindly accepting the language and ideologies of "freedom" or "democracy." They are calling into question the presuppositions and the very foundations upon which Western society has constructed its identity and place in the world. They no longer simply believe the hype around Western values and ideas. The colonialists, he says, "may kill in Indochina, torture in Madagascar, imprison in Black Africa, crack down in the West Indies. Henceforth the colonized know that they have an advantage over them. They know that their temporary "masters" are lying."[7] Therefore, he argued, "they are weak." What Obama and his administration have before them is a much more skeptical, resentful, suspicious, and hostile world that is no longer convinced that America is what it says it is. The colonialism that Obama and his administration must face is an ideological colonialism that says America's religious, cultural, and political values are somehow innately superior to all others in the world. Of course, any administration in office would have to take up these concerns. However, because of Obama's sensibilities to multicultural issues as expressed in his writings, travels, and experiences as a community organizer, there is a sense that he is more attentive to these matters. Whether he is or not, people in developing nations (and Americans who are in solidarity with them) must take seriously the provocative insights of Cesaire here in particular. Somehow, Americans have convinced themselves that other nations, especially those of the developing world, have nothing meaningful or significant to contribute to their flourishing other than labor and natural resources. Although the language of colonization is rarely used these days, the reality of military occupation, for the United States, in Iraq, Afghanistan, Germany, South Korea, Japan, and other parts of the world represents the same colonialist practices as before. Cesaire surmised that colonialism, as was the case in Europe, breeds exploitation and leads to the kind of evil leadership aspirations as was the case in Germany under Hitler. He intimated that

> no one colonizes innocently, that no one colonizes with impunity either; that a nation which colonizes, that a civilization which justifies colonialization— and therefore force—is already a sick civilization, a civilization which is morally diseased, which irresistibly, progressing from one consequence to another, one denial to another, calls for its Hitler, I mean its punishment.[8]

Hitler was the underside of European Enlightenment claims about human rationality and morality. And while the Obama administration may seem far removed from the historical context of Cesaire, the lingering effects of the colonial age and the ushering in of a neocolonial militaristic imperialism is immediately at hand. In Iraq, the United States now occupies a state once viewed by the international community as fully independent and sovereign. U.S. oil and gas industrial services companies like Halliburton are deeply engaged in the economic depletion of Iraq's oil and natural resources. So, although colonialism as once experienced may be a thing of the past, economic and militaristic colonialism continue to wreak havoc across the globe, the consequences of which are indeed felt most, perhaps, on the African continent and throughout its diaspora.

Here, it is important to explore the relevance of human suffering on the continent of Africa. Specifically, I am concerned with the ways in which the West has failed to adequately attend to the legitimacy of African indigenous life, in large part due to the privileging of modern Hegelian theological presuppositions toward non-European peoples. Georg Friedrich Hegel, in his *Philosophy of History*, which was a pivotal text that laid the groundwork for Western cultural interpretations of Africa, Asia, and Latin America in the early nineteenth century, essentially cast German culture as the culmination of human civilization, while describing much of the non-Western world as subhuman and innately inferior. It was here that Hegel infamously called Africa the "dark continent" with its uncivilized inhabitants. Hegel's assessments paved the way for many of the racist and white supremacist attitudes and policies that would follow, often under the guise of fostering "rationalism," personal autonomy," and "human freedom." More could be said about Hegel's influence, but focusing on his (and other nineteenth-century Western thinkers) condemnation of African deities is worth noting. This was done by subjugating the African's God to the realm of mysticism and animism, it further negated the dignity and inherent virtues of Africa in general, its culture, spiritual practices, and ways of being in the world. Talk of nihilism that has now infiltrated the fortress of the Western metaphysical tradition creates the opportunity to reassess the social ontology of African religious systems. By doing so, it will also give rise to a more urgent appreciation of the need to respond to pain and sorrow endured on Africa's soils, wrought by HIV/AIDS, genocide, poverty, civil strife, and economic exploitation. When the history books are written centuries from now, what will be said about the current generation and its obligatory response to suffering African children in the Congo, Zimbabwe, Tanzania, Namibia, South Africa, and the better part of sub-Saharan Africa? Obama's position on these issues has been one of empowerment. Inasmuch as he has expressed a commitment to helping solve many of the problems facing developing nations, Obama has also emphasized that developing countries too must become direct agents in their own social transformation. As Ben Wallace-Wells writes on Obama's trip to Kenya, in his response to massive crowds in his father's village of Kogelo, "He [Obama] wants to help Kenyans, but he also wants them to help themselves."[9] At first glance, Obama's response of self-empowerment is quite a typical response of most politicians when traveling to the developing world. But, as the first black president of America, even then as the only black U.S. senator, Obama surmised that his role was not just about the American context but also about the global world. In Kibera, Kenya, as with most parts of the African continent, the fact that Obama is black is all that mattered. His ancestral connection as an African descendant, specifically Kenyan, was of the utmost importance. It meant, in some intrinsic and profound sort of way, that Obama was linked to their experience by blood and by duty. In their eyes, Obama has the solemn responsibility to share in their plight and their liberation. In one instance, Obama picked up the megaphone and said to the people of Kibera during his visit, "Everyone here is my brother! Everyone here is my sister! I love you Kibera." It was as though the energy and passion of the crowds had brought Obama into a grand collective consciousness of struggle, hope, and redemption bearing in the hearts of African peoples.

Deconstructing the Roots of Western Hegemony

In identifying, even remotely, with African peoples, Obama is in many ways challenging the very historical presuppositions and ideologies that have governed the policies of Western nations toward the African diaspora since the Berlin Conference of 1885 and since Western expansionism in the seventeenth century. Specifically, the privileging of Western language and culture over the peoples and lands of Asia, Africa, and Latin America might even be seen in the early organization of the World Council of Churches. Established in the ruins of a post–World War II world, the three official languages of the first meeting of World Council of Churches were English, French, and German, the dominant languages of Europe during the time. What has become increasingly apparent is the dramatic shift of the Christian epicenter to those regions of the world formerly viewed as uncivilized and primitive. Peoples and cultures all across the world are now calling into question modern notions of progress, scientific exploration, and Western notions of personal autonomy and rationalization. Although many scholars in the West have cast these moves as an "end of history," when really they signify the decline of Western hegemony in the world, they come as a beginning (again) of the prominence and legitimacy of Asian, African, and Latin American cultures as irreducible voices in directing human affairs.

Specifically, the rising prominence of the Christian church on the African soil has created the opportunity for renewed conversation about the significance of African religions and practices in challenging the nihilistic pitfalls of modernity. Hegelian and Cartesian ideas about "personal autonomy" and "rationalism" must now come face-to-face with the social autonomies of African indigenous religious systems that place community at the center of what it means to be human.

Two figures helpful in unpacking the ways in which the treatment of Western nations toward African peoples is fundamentally a theological and philosophical problem are Cornel West and John Mbiti. Cornel West, an outspoken critic of the Western philosophical tradition, approaches the question through a "genealogy of race" where he views the "binary linguistic system" that has characterized philosophical discourse since the Enlightenment and onward as fundamentally a Western phenomenon and insidiously dangerous and damaging for the "other;" primarily because it creates an "either/or" way of thinking that privileges one thing over the other. In order to define what something "is," it must be pitted against what something "is not." One of the points of connection between West and Mbiti as it relates to Obama is seen in the radical Afrocentric Christianity of Rev. Wright and the Trinity United Church of Christ in Chicago. In this congregation and through its leader, Afrocentric Christianity challenges the kinds of distinctions (i.e., mind/body, etc.) often assumed within a binary system. Wright and his followers at Trinity appropriated the view that Afrocentrism and Christianity are compatible, especially for African Americans, insofar as both celebrate black humanity while challenging systemic evils in the world. Afrocentrism elevates black genius and the unique contributions of Africa to world. Because various religious traditions, including Christianity, Islam, Hinduism, Buddhism, and Judaism, all have long histories on the continent, Afrocentrism also celebrates the various ways in which black people have expressed their religious selves. Hence, Afrocentrism and Christianity are natural siblings for black people who wish to live out their faith amid the demons of dehumanization in a racially hostile world.

As both a spiritual and socially engaged institution, Trinity has employed Afrocentrism as a way of interpreting the meaning of Christianity for their context on the Southside of Chicago. This also included an agenda of economic and political empowerment. In addition to a cultural arts center, Trinity has encouraged economic development through education, home ownership, small business development, and many other programs. The kinds of concerns Trinity has taken up in its local community often, unfortunately, get left out of larger debates around globalization, which often directly impact local communities such as the residents of 95th Street in the South side Chicago. These communities are often affected by the massive transitions in job creation, access to capital, public transportation, and the like. It is quite odd that much of the talk about the ills of globalization in the West has yet to seriously take into account the voices of those who are at the bitter receiving end of economic exploitation and abandonment. Why is it that many Western scholars refuse or seem incapable of integrating the theological and philosophical perspectives of Africans themselves in addressing the question of globalization or other forms of neocolonialism?

President Obama, if he is true to himself, will bring a very refreshing global perspective to the ways in which blackness, and in many ways America more broadly, is now being shaped by a larger global context. Engaging the interconnectedness of cultures, languages, societies, and economies across the globe can no longer be denied. Obama's life speaks to this reality. In his second memoir, *The Audacity of Hope*, he speaks very positively and eloquently about his experience with the "world beyond our borders." He writes:

> In the field of international affairs, it's dangerous to extrapolate from the experiences of a single country. In its history, geography, culture, and conflicts, each nation is unique. And yet in many ways Indonesia serves as a useful metaphor for the world beyond our borders—a world in which globalization and sectarianism, poverty and plenty, modernity and antiquity constantly collide.[10]

Obama reflects on the growing temptation of world powers, such as the United States under the Bush administration, to retreat and withdraw into isolation as a way of punishing or making foreign governments conform to U.S. foreign policy agendas. While Obama primarily speaks out of his experience with Indonesia, the land of his childhood, he is right to point out that Indonesia shares a great deal in common with other developing nations across the African diaspora, including his father's land of Kenya.

It is Obama's assertion that the best course of action for the United States is not to superimpose its "way of life" beyond its borders or to somehow create global policy as it engages in the business of nation building abroad. On the contrary, America must attempt to perfect its own vision of democracy and freedom, and as a consequence serve as a model to the broader world in a way that invites both adoration and respect. He observes:

> Moreover, while America's revolutionary origins and republican form of government might make it sympathetic toward those seeking freedom elsewhere, America's early leaders cautioned against idealistic attempts to export our way of life; according to John Quincy Adams, America should not go "abroad in search of monsters to destroy" nor "become the dictatress of the world." Providence had charged America with the task of making a new world, not reforming the old; protected by an ocean and with the bounty of a continent, America could serve the cause of freedom by concentrating on its own development, becoming a beacon of hope for other nations and people around the globe.[11]

The impulse toward imperialism and "manifest destiny," according to Obama, has continued to be one of the greatest barriers to the flourishing of American ideals in the world. As Obama rightly indicates, the thrust for imperial domination has often been accompanied by violence and destruction. It meant trampling on the very ideals it has held dear. From the extermination of the native Indian to slavery and internment of Japanese Americans during World War II, American imperial aspirations have often arrived at the doorsteps of other peoples and cultures as death and suffering. Obama further adds:

> To begin with, we should understand that any return to isolationism—or a foreign policy approach that denies the occasional need to deploy U.S. troops—will not work. The impulse to withdraw from the world remains a strong undercurrent in both parties, particularly when U.S. casualties are at stake. After the bodies of U.S. soldiers were dragged through the streets of Mogadishu in 1993, for example, Republicans accused President Clinton of squandering U.S. forces on ill-conceived missions; it was partly because of the experience in Somalia that [the then] candidate George W. Bush vowed in the 2000 election never again to expend American military resources on "nation building."[12]

The world of competition and conflict between the great superpowers of the world has dissolved. The greatest threats of today, says Obama, are among those nations on the margins, those essentially locked out of the prosperity promised from participation in the global economy. They are primarily poor nations, with fragile governments and little means of sustenance. They are also nations that have been historically, and continue to be, exploited by former Western colonial forces in the world. Depleted of their natural resources, and exploited for their labor, many developing nations are fed up and hopeless about the chance to relate to Western nations as equals, and see revolutionary change as the only way forward. In many ways, Obama is raising the same kind of awareness spoken by Frantz Fanon decades ago when he proclaimed in *A Dying Colonialism,* "This is the age of revolution; the 'age of indifference' is gone forever."[13] Fanon's prophetic assessment of the global world concerning its marginalized peoples still speaks today, even as Obama gets comfortable in his new digs as president:

> Today the great systems have died or are living in a state of crisis. And it is no longer the age of little vanguards. The whole of humanity has erupted violently, tumultuously onto the stage of history, taking its own destiny in its hands. Capitalism is under siege, surrounded by a global tide of revolution. And this revolution, still without a center, without a precise form, has its own laws, its own life and a depth of unity—accorded it by the same masses who create it, who live it, who inspire each other from across boundaries, give each other spirit and encouragement, and learn from their collective experiences.[14]

Although Fanon was speaking primarily out of the revolutionary spirit of the mid-twentieth century as Algeria was experiencing its own independence movement, the fact is that for most developing nations, not much has changed since those times. The greater part of the developing world still lives on less than a dollar a day. Much like the dynamics of colonialism, at the heart of this new or neocolonialism at work today is racism. It is the persistent reality of how developing nations are viewed by the vast majority of the wealthiest Western nations. Racism now appears as radical indifference to the suffering and starving bellies of children under the rubric of a free market economy. The notion was that somehow an uninhibited free market economy, in spite of the hardship it may cause for those unable to participate in such a system, will work out best for everyone body in the long run. But, as the Wall Street economic crisis hit the Obama-McCain campaign trail in late September 2008 and continued to spiral out of control late into December and January 2009, not only has colonialism become a dying narrative, so has free market capitalism. As Howard Winant observes in *The New Politics of Race: Globalism, Difference, Justice*, the language of racism and its connections to international policy are now being shaped by a "New Right," hegemonic agenda that wishes to dismiss racism as "invisible and marginalized" or as an "artifact of the past."[15] Using front organizations like Ward Connerly's American Civil Rights Institute, right-wing conservative groups have lead a provocative and intentional effort to distort the very legacy of the Civil Rights Movement and divert attention from the reality of racism today and how it functions both at home and abroad. Racism has been cloaked under the illusion of a false progressivism. Or, as the famous Italian philosopher Gianni Vattimo says, the illusion of progress, especially when it comes to systemic racial realties, comes under the guise of "technological advances."

Racism not only continues to persist, it continues to rage onward cloaked within a largely neoconservative agenda that has white American global domination as its primary goal. Some conservative streams of white American Protestant Christianity often disguise racist attitudes through organizations such as the Southern Baptist Convention, Focus on the Family, Jerry Falwell's Liberty University, and the Moral Majority. These organizations, which claimed to promote evangelical Christian-oriented policies, also advanced agendas that promote militarism and laissez-faire economic policies, especially concerning the poor. Racism, often cloaked in the white conservative right-wing agenda, is not isolated to domestic policies; it is now at the direct front and center of the shaping of international policy. The paternalistic policy of the Bush administration of not talking to foreign leaders, particularly "enemies," who do not conform to U.S. policy, has proven to be both ineffective, supremacist, and simply arrogant.

As Winant argues, racism as a modern construct is infused with the underlying claims of the Enlightenment and its high ideals. On the one hand, modernity gave way to the miraculous technological advances in medicine, the sciences, and the language of human dignity, personal autonomy, and human freedom. On the other hand, it is impossible to talk about modernity without invoking the horrors of nuclear war and proliferation, slavery, genocide, colonialism, and the Holocaust, all of which have racial overtones. Cornel West offers a very compelling explanation about the connections between modernity and racism in terms of their global significance when he emphasizes the ways in which modernity purported a linguistic system that created a hierarchical vision of the world, placing white Europeans at the very top of the created order. By affirming the

Cartesian notion that rationalism presupposes what it means to be human, modern philosophers, such as Hegel, Kant, Descartes, Bacon, Rousseau, and others, cast a shadow upon other peoples and cultures in the world as "native," "savage," "indigenous," less civilized, or simply subhuman. The either/or binary linguistic system produced a system where "whiteness" became synonymous with goodness and divinity, while "blackness" as the negation of whiteness became increasingly viewed as "evil," dangerous, and the absence of life, that is, the great void. White supremacist ideals still inform policies, primarily operating in global financial organizations such as the World Bank, International Monetary Fund, and the G8 covenant. What we now see with an Obama presidency and what it might mean for the global community is a convergence of a narrative that has mainly viewed America as fundamentally white and Christian, and the emergence of a narrative that goes beyond a white supremacist orientation that is much more multicultural, inclusive, and global in consciousness. Winant does a good job of mapping this transition when he observes:

> Massive migration, both internal and international, has reshaped the U.S. population, both numerically and geographically. A multipolar racial pattern has largely supplanted the old racial system, which was usually (and somewhat erroneously) viewed as a bipolar white-black hierarchy. In the contemporary United States, new varieties of inter-minority competition, as well as new awareness of the international "embeddedness" of racial identity, have greater prominence. Racial stratification varies substantially by class, region, and indeed among groups, although comprehensive racial inequality certainly endures. Racial reform policies are under attack in many spheres of social policy and law, where the claim is forcefully made that the demands of the civil rights movement have largely been met, and that the United States has entered a "postracial" stage of its history.[16]

The racial vision of King, as Winant points out, was radically different from what we are now seeing under the language of a "postracial" society. Because, for King, racial justice was central to any move toward the "beloved community." "To be 'free at last' meant something deeper than symbolic reforms and palliation of the worst excesses of white supremacy. It meant substantive social reorganization that would be manifested in egalitarian economic and democratizing political consequences. It meant something like social democracy, human rights, social citizenship for blacks and other 'minorities.'"[17] The problem that Obama must take up in his administration is to acknowledge the ways in which race and racism function in the shaping of international policy, and have the courage to listen to the voices on the margins in setting his agenda.

King's revolutionary global vision of the beloved community was also an ethic of community that forced the world to deal fairly with the most vulnerable peoples of the world. It was a global ethic that affirmed racial difference while challenging institutions and policies that treat people unfairly based on racial, ethnic, cultural, or social identity. Winant defines racism in today's fluid, complex world as that which "creates or reproduces hierarchical social structures based on essentialized racial categories."[18] I do think that Winant's understanding of racism in the current global world is quite limiting in the sense that racism is much more than constructing social systems or producing policies that relate to folks on the basis of hierarchical systems and social structures. Racism is also a cultural attitude of superiority that has to do with not only structures but indifference toward the poor and marginalized peoples of the world. It also has to do with the paternalistic manner of Western nations' relating to, more often than not, developing nations. In recent years, the New York Police Department (NYPD) and the Immigration and Naturalization Service (INS) have ratcheted up their racialized policing of cultural spaces, such as a New York Indian restaurant. In that experience the convergence of racism, as a historical and domestic problem in the United States and how it now functions in the broader world, may be seen in the following areas:

Racial profiling. They do not operate this way in French restaurants in New York.

Immigration restriction. Immigrants are the chief target. This is an old story and dilemma, because immigrants provide cheap labor.

Surveillance. The action in the restaurant was carried out by a combination of mainstream and secret police; the latter are building dossiers not only on immigrants but on everyone. Does the name Stasi ring a bell? This stuff is also unconstitutional, if anybody cares.

Harassment of low-wage labor. Racism generally fortifies and deepens exploitation, which means it is different at different class levels. The NYPD and INS do not carry out raids of this type at Morgan Stanley or Microsoft, which have plenty of South Asian staff too.[19]

Racial profiling, in particular, which has always been a problem for black folks in America since the days of slavery, is now practiced among Latino, Muslim, and Indian communities. Racial profiling as a practice of unduly identifying and engaging in surveillance of black- and brown-skinned peoples, unprovoked, remains a perennial problem at home and abroad. Racial profiling also becomes a metaphor for understanding the kind of exclusion felt by many African nations across the diaspora as they desperately try to participate in the global economic and political systems. Many of the developing nations that hold the majority of seats in the UN vehemently opposed the war in Iraq as the United States sought UN approval for the war. Bush's doctrine of "preemptive" war emerged as a result of the primarily black and brown nations rejecting the Bush-led American argument for war.

Though Obama doesn't give much attention to the African diaspora in his writings, he does recognize the need to engage the multidimensional issues that plague the African continent and many developing nations outside. Obama knows all too well that the problems facing these nations are also America's problems. The world is far too interrelated and interdependent to avoid our profound sense of connectedness. Obama insists:

> Of course, whether in Africa or elsewhere, we can't expect to tackle such dire problems alone. For that reason, we should be spending more time and money trying to strengthen the capacity of international institutions so that they can do some of this work for us. Instead, we've been doing the opposite. For years, conservatives in the United States have been making political hay over problems at the UN: the hypocrisy of resolutions singling out Israel for condemnation, the Kafkaesque election of nations like Zimbabwe and Libya to the UN Commission on Human Rights, and most recently the kickbacks that plagued the oil-for-food program.[20]

Conclusion

The tremendous degree of suffering throughout the African diaspora, including Obama's paternal land of Kenya, has reached epic proportions. There will be an air of expectation in the Obama administration that he will do what presidents of the past have failed to do. And that is to engage African-descendent peoples as equals. The task is to somehow make right the wrongs of a racist and colonialist past. The task is to engage in a comprehensive policy agenda that leads the wealthiest nations in an effort to address the ecological crisis on the African continent, the Caribbean, and the Republic Haiti. It is not quite clear that Obama has nostalgic connections to the African diaspora or that he is Afrocentric in any way. On the contrary, it is very clear that Obama views himself as an African American who is creatively connected to the global world. The following two quotes speak to his attitude toward his own identity and the African diaspora in general.

> Black Americans have always had an ambiguous relationship with Africa. Nowadays, we wear kente cloth, celebrate Kwanza and put up posters of Nelson Mandela on our walls. And when we travel to Africa and discover it's not all sweetness and light, we can end up deeply disappointed.[21]

The starting premise for me that my mother instilled in me, and my father inadvertently instilled, was that everybody was the same.

I've always been clear that I'm rooted in the African-American community but not limited to it.[22]

From these words, one can see that Obama's connection to the African diaspora is complex to say the least. Although he has found renewed relationships with his father's tribal community, in the wake of his presidency, there will be a passionate outcry across the African continent for Obama to speak directly to their social and political concerns. For instance, the problem of HIV/AIDS on the African continent is perhaps more serious than ever before. According to the World Health Organization, over 34 million people have contracted the HIV/AIDS virus. Other statistics concerning the AIDS crisis point to its severity and global consequences:

24.5 million of them in sub-Saharan Africa.

Nearly 19 million have died from AIDS, 3.8 million of them children under the age 15.

5.4 million new AIDS cases in 1999, 4 million of them in Africa.

2.8 million died of AIDS in 1999, 2.4 million of them in Africa.

13.2 million children orphaned by AIDS, 12.1 million of them in sub-Saharan Africa.

Reduced life expectancy in sub-Saharan Africa from 59yrs to 45yrs between 2005 and 2010, and in Zimbabwe from 61yrs to 33yrs.

More than 500,000 babies infected in 1999 by their mothers most of them in sub-Saharan Africa.[23]

President Obama will have to respond to these issues as a political commitment. The systemic issues exacerbating the AIDS crisis caused by mounting national debt, economic instability due to globalization, and corporate exploitation will all require global policy responses. Obama must be at the center, leading the way for a better, more flourishing Africa, and throughout the African diaspora as well.

CHAPTER 5

Race, Identity, and the Roots
of Black Nationalism

In the African American community in particular, I think sometimes we have a tendency for our leadership to be very protective of their turf and not invite young people in until it's way too late. The earlier we're grooming young people and giving them leadership opportunities, and pushing them up front, the better.[1]

We have a certain script in our politics, and one of the scripts for black politicians is that for them to be authentically black they have to somehow offend white people. And then if he puts a multiracial coalition together, he must somehow be compromising the efforts of the African American community. To use a street term, we flipped the script.[2]

For better or worse, Obama's presidency has forever transformed the paradigm of black political leadership, collective identity, and constructions of black nationalism in America. In this chapter, I would like to argue that, although Obama will make a difference in how the black community thinks about itself, there is a need to recover the historical legacy of voices in the tradition of black nationalism and broaden the cultural movement of Afrocentrism as a perspective from which to view the world, and black cultural and political identity. The black community is fragmented. We have now entered a new phase where differences are celebrated and elevated. There seems to be a growing appreciation for the complexity of the issues and challenges confronting America in general, black folks in particular. Also emerging is a deepening respect for competing viewpoints. Michael C. Dawson, in *Black Visions: The Roots of Contemporary African American Political Ideologies*, demonstrates the ways in which black nationalism has shaped black politics.[3] As discussed in this chapter, Dawson recognizes the various sources and converging viewpoints that, though different, have contributed to the realizing of black liberation. Historically, black nationalism and efforts toward building a collective consciousness to bring about change centered on a single, grand, all-encompassing narrative that would hopefully lead to liberation. In former generations, individuals longed for a way of situating their personal lives into some greater collective reality. This desire for sharing in some broader sense of liberation is what informed political struggles dating back to the abolitionist movement, reconstruction, and the Civil Rights Movement.

Several essential texts have reflected the general meaning of black nationalism, which provides a context for our discussion. Sterling Stuckey's classic book, *The Ideological Origins of Black Nationalism*, outlines a few key writings that have come to shape the movement and its message. Though not exclusive, those texts include: *The Ethiopian Manifesto* by Robert Alexander Young, *Walker's Appeal* by David Walker, Augustine's *Ten Letters*, Sidney's *Four Letters, Henry Highland Garnet's Speech*, and the *Political Destiny of the Colored Race* by Martin R. Delany. All of these texts are grounded in positive attitudes concerning Africa as the black ancestral homeland and Pan-African unity and acculturation.[4] The origins of black nationalism were geared toward igniting the fire of black political consciousness, mobilizing people against institutional slavery and colonialism, and establishing a healthy sense of black identity in all areas of life, from stabilizing the family to politics.

As the noted scholar and cultural critic Robin D. G. Kelley observed, "Politics is not separate from lived experience or the imaginary world of what is possible; to the contrary, politics is about these things."[5] For Kelley, politics is exactly about the day-to-day struggles with identity, about who we are, and about our place in the larger world. Stephen Ray, a prominent theologian and activist in Chicago, suggested that the problem with shaping a collective identity or even thinking about black nationalism today is that before black folks even leave their homes in the morning, they are fragmented, with splintered identities, struggling to figure out who they are amid some many competing visions and understandings of the self. According to Ray, in the black experience, you have a fragmented self encountering a fragmented world, which merely intensifies the reality of brokenness and conflict in the world. What this amounts to is a more challenging dilemma in trying to recover a sense of black unity and collective consciousness in our time. I am not advocating for the more violent strands of black nationalism, which were really marginal within the larger scope of its historical development. Rather, I believe that those elements of black nationalism that have urged black unity, collective consciousness, empowerment, and social change are essential to sustaining and developing flourishing black communities in today's context. It would be a grave mistake to think that Barack Obama (and his administration) can bring about change alone. It will require the slow, persistent, unified efforts of black folks around the nation working in partnership with other groups to realize the change that black folks so desperately long for and deserve.

Before exploring the connections between Obama, Afrocentrism, and black nationalism, I need to put in a brief word about why these connections are important and where they intersect. These connections are important because Obama has now become the "face" of the empire. America, as the lone world superpower, is now represented in the bronze faced, baritone voice of Obama. Symbolically, it carries tremendous significance for shaping black cultural imagination which influences creative political action. As a member of Trinity and a mentee of Wright, Obama was directly exposed to both Afrocentrism and black nationalism. While to the ears of many white Americans, these two themes sound radical and invoke images of extremism, they have been widely regarded, culturally, by millions of blacks across the world as positive and uplifting.

Trinity's 10-point Vision and mission statement, and its "Black Value System" statement (which all members are called to affirm) reflects strong Afrocentric themes. For instance, in the 10-point Vision, congregates pledge commitment not just to God, salvation, and the church, but also to Africa, education about the African diaspora, and black liberation.[6] The mission statement makes a similar commitment to certain Afrocentric ideals when it says that Trinity is a congregation that is "not ashamed of the gospel of Jesus Christ and that does not apologize for its African roots!"[7] Additionally, the "Black Value System" statement crafted in 1981 by the Byrd Recognition Committee led by Vallmer Jordan (a member of the congregation) speaks to the church's attempt to reconcile the Christian message and blackness in America. They reveal the extent to which the church has taken seriously the core messages of Afrocentrism and black nationalism, although there is a distinction between the kind of black nationalism and Afrocentrism espoused by Asante and Garvey or Malcolm X.

Wright and Trinity represent a particular expression of black nationalism and Afrocentrism very much grounded in Orthodox Protestant Christianity. Trinity incorporated Afrocentrism as a resource for building cultural pride and political empowerment. They used Afrocentrism to respond to the question of what it means to be both "black" and "Christian." In a world where black identity was denied and degraded (as seen in the minstrel shows of the late nineteenth century, black lynching, and even police profiling of today, for instance), Trinity has understood the need to give black folks the language to understand both their deepest spiritual longings and their need to make sense of who they are as black people. As a member of the congregation for over a decade, Obama, his wife, Michelle, and children, Sasha and Malia, were actively involved at every level, as were thousands of other people across the Chicago metropolitan area, even as far as Indiana, Michigan, and Wisconsin. The racism of the mainstream media distorted both the interpretation and practice of the Afrocentrism at Trinity, which promotes self-love, empowerment, and social justice—not hate. At Trinity, Obama seemed to have been able to hold together his faith, desire for social change, and commitment to multiculturalism, which of course would be fully tested throughout the presidential campaign.

Obama, Politics, and the Roots of Black Identity

Obama has been able to successfully navigate the turbulent waters of walking in the legacy of the black freedom struggle and also representing a new day of multicultural coalition building in American politics. Some have optimistically predicted that perhaps Obama would offer a corrective to the problematic history of exclusion and neglect from the Democratic Party over the years. Paul Street, in *Barack Obama and the Future of American Politics*, argues that this attitude may have merit given the fact that Obama has made many positive references to former black leaders like W. E. B. Du Bois, Malcolm X, Frederick Douglass, and Martin Luther King, Jr. Obama is also a former community organizer who devoted much of his young adult life to helping poor black people on the South Side of Chicago.[8]

With Obama in view, invoking the experiences and perspectives of figures like W. E. B. Du Bois, Marcus Garvey, Malcolm X, and others, Molefe Asante has provided a new and intriguing paradigm to understand black cultural identity and self-understanding. Asante's strengths and weaknesses and their continuity and discontinuity in a historical perspective will be examined. Because so much of black identity, and subsequently how black folks enter into the political process, is shaped by our attitudes toward the African experience, the works of Cheikh Anta Diop will also be considered. While Diop has been a transformative intellectual figure in the black political thought across Africa, Europe, and Latin America, his ideas have received very little attention in America. One of the most pervasive legacies of slavery in America is that it not only taught black folks to hate themselves but also to hate each other and the very origins of who black folks are as African descendants. Everything black, and therefore African, was reviled—appearance, physical features, cultural practices, attitudes, music, language, history, religion, and thought. In American society, all areas of African life were rejected. In its place, *Eurocentrism* (its history, culture, language, and philosophy) was celebrated and allegiance to it was demanded.[9] What Diop and Asante offer is a corrective to the corrosive legacy of white supremacy in America, and a way forward in a context now informed to a large extent by the Obama presidency. By developing a proper understanding of what Asante means by Afrocentrism and what Diop proposes, we might gain a firm insight into these questions and others not presented.

Asante does not ignore the contributions of major African American historical figures that have helped shape the Afrocentric outlook. Among these are Booker T. Washington, Marcus Garvey, Martin Luther King, Jr., Elijah Muhammad, W. E. B. Du Bois, and Malcolm X (who's given the most consideration). Though it is problematic for some of Asante's critiques like Delores S. Williams, who points out the inherit sexism within Asante's Afrocentric proposal, Asante credits these men as paving the way for the Afrocentric outlook.[10] Each activist-scholar contributed in some way to its conception. For instance, Booker T. Washington's practical philosophy of economic independence and his emphasis on work and education are key elements to the African cultural project. Like Obama, Washington held mass appeal among both black and white audiences. He cast a dramatic vision of the American South in particular in a way that would sustain black survival while calming white fears of rebellion and retribution.

Though Washington was heavily critiqued by Du Bois for not being radical enough when it came to the immediate and unapologetic liberation of black people in the South, his legacy nonetheless contributed greatly to the conditions leading to Obama's historic win and the ongoing promise of racial equality in America. Washington's mistake, according to Asante, has been detaching economic independence from cultural independence. For Asante, the two are indivisible. "Economic freedom must always be connected to political and cultural freedom else freedom does not truly exist."[11] Without cultural power, economic power is meaningless in Asante's view.

Marcus Garvey and the Rise of "Afrocentrism"

Although there were many cultural and intellectual events in the African American experience, for our purposes we shall examine the contributions of Marcus Garvey, Malcolm X, and the Negritude movement alongside the Harlem Renaissance movements in relation to the Afrocentric perspective as presented by Asante. Here, it is not my intention to make comparisons between Obama and other black leaders like Garvey or consider how historical movements such as the Harlem Renaissance may have paved the way for his election. What I am doing here is simply offering a brief, albeit essential, exposition of major trends and movements in the historical development of black nationalism and their role in shaping black individual and collective identity.

Regarding Garvey, Asante proposes that "his vision foreshadowed the Afrocentric road to self-respect and dignity."[12] According to Asante, Garvey was consumed with seeing oppressed and downtrodden Africans respected and respecting themselves. He sought to do this by uniting African peoples of the world through his Universal Negro Improvement Association. In so far as Garvey expounded a collective consciousness that would bring African peoples together in the quest for liberation, there is continuity in Asante's position with Garvey. The concept of Nija, (the Way) for Asante, was already at work in Garvey's efforts from the beginning. As Asante examines Garvey's movement in retrospect, he observes, "We can say that Nija was the idea behind Garvey's impact on African people."[13] Afrocentrism is more than a nationalistic motif; it is a philosophical outlook that guides every aspect of our behavior. Through Garvey's movement a blueprint sketch of black nationalism was formed and provided the way for future nationalistic events as found with Malcolm X.

Malcolm X and Black Nationalism

Obama once remarked that he admired Malcolm X's passion and capacity for self-creation. He admired the ways in which Malcolm X was able to seize a sense of self-actualization in the quest for black liberation. While he disagreed with many of Malcolm X's basic ideas, he respected his unwavering commitment to help remake America into what it ought to be and to hold its leaders accountable to its democratic ideals. The contributions of Malcolm X are numerous in terms of ways to "fight for liberation" and his formulation of new creative ideologies that have challenged historical ignorance and political assertions of racial supremacy in America. Malcolm X, says Asante, knew what the Afrocentrist know, that is, "liberation could only come from a person's active will."[14] To place this in context, Asante offered these words about Malcolm X:

> In Malcolm's view, the United States owed African-Americans an enormous debt for the free labor rendered by our enslaved ancestors. The scandalous treatment of Africans existed, he said, because we had not stood up to demand our rights, to take our case to the World Court, to the United Nations. Malcolm, like Walter Rodney and Franz Fanon, was a commentator, an activist commentator on the revolutionary road to an Afrocentric viewpoint.[15]

Whether or not Malcolm X reached the destination of absolute Afrocentrism is unclear, what he did contribute was a "thousand ways to fight for liberation." This element of Asante's construct is significant in that it seems to provide a framework on the nationalistic landscape. Malcolm X's ideology provides ways to understand the varied class distinctions within the black community and ways of reexamining the practice of Eurocentric thought and behavior. The immense degree of consciousness stimulated through Malcolm X is what is most appealing to Asante's Afrocentric outlook. Both Diop and Asante seem to encourage this collective consciousness of a common historical experience of oppression and also a shared destiny. Obama used a similar strategy, as Diop and Asante seem to promote by appealing to a sense of shared "values" throughout the election. As he writes in *The Audacity of Hope*, "sometimes only the law can fully vindicate our values, particularly when the rights and opportunities of the powerless in our society are at stake."[16] Of course, Obama would not go as far as Diop or Asante in claiming a sort of Afrocentric perspective, he effectively was able to convince the majority of Americans that we all share common values beyond our particular racial, ethnic, economic, and cultural identities. For instance, as Obama frequently said throughout the campaign, many of the social changes that have taken place in America along race relations were brought about primarily through peaceful means by essentially appealing to this sense of shared values. According to Obama, efforts to end racial discrimination through such achievements as the Supreme Court decision *Brown v. Board of Education*, the Civil Rights Act of 1964, and the Voting Rights Act of 1965 were ultimately brought about through a deep and abiding commitment of many to envision a new, more free democracy for all. What Obama often ignores in his writings and speeches are the ways in which determined efforts by the collective protest of thousands of black folks by and large were responsible. Nonviolent passive resistance, as one of the chief instruments of protest, placed enormous social and economic pressures on local business and communities, in many instances, to force change. Very rarely was change brought about purely on the basis of moral suasion or appealing to common values, as Obama would often suggest. It took unified political action and protest, even the martyred lives of many like King, Malcolm X, and James Meredith to advance the kinds of changes we see today.

Diop proposes that this feeling of a shared past will be the glue that holds African peoples together and this knowledge is what provides us security against the ideological forces of Western imperialism. Asante holds that this shared history is what informs and directs our collective consciousness and leads to productive responses to political and social injustices. Asante states clearly that the substance of this consciousness in the Afrocentric outlook is found in recognizing the past and the realization of a common destiny:

> The particular nature of this consciousness expresses our shared commitments, fraternal reactions to assaults on our humanity, collective awareness of our destiny, and respect for our ancestors. When we come to acceptance, as surely we are coming, of this consciousness we will experience the rise of Afrocentricity. But consciousness is more than acceptance, it is response, it is action demonstrable and meaningful in terms of psychological and political actions.[17]

Since Afrocentricity is essentially a philosophical outlook determined by history, there is some discontinuity with Malcolm X's theoretical position. Malcolm X, at his nationalistic height, was a separatist and exclusivist. However, Afrocentrism appreciates and respects other cultures. The Afrocentric idea seems to suggest that one can live alongside a Eurocentric person. However, it is important for the Afrocentric person to be grounded historically and culturally. Malcolm X, especially in his earlier years, saw Eurocentric culture in American society as demonic. Hence, he believed that "Afro-Americans" should separate from that culture to form an independent state. Asante holds that Afrocentrism is a philosophical perspective that can exist within a multicultural setting and still thrive. Nonetheless, the contributions of Malcolm X and the black nationalist movement are immutable to Asante's intellectual and cultural project.

Negritude Movement

While black people in America are as American as all others, their experience in America has been one steeped in struggle, resistance, and resilience. In short, black folks in America have experienced history from "below" or the underside of American progressivism and rise as a global superpower in the world. A poem by Paul Laurence Dunbar offers a poignant image of what life has been like for the vast majority of black people in America,

> "We wear the mask that grins and lies,
> It hides our cheeks and shades our eyes—This debt we pay to human guile;
> With torn and bleeding hearts we smile,
> And mouth with myriad subtleties."[18]

Another key historical movement that has informed the Afrocentric outlook is the Negritude movement—a form of "black consciousness" and feeling of peoplehood among African peoples throughout the world. A term first coined by the Martinician poet and statesman Aimé Cesaire in Paris in the 1930s through discussions with fellow students Leopold Sedar Senghor and Leon Gontran-Damas, "Negritude" represents a historical movement in the African diasporic identity and culture. The meaning and themes found in Negritude are grounded in the thought of people like Martin Delany, William Blyden, and W. E. B. Du Bois. In the French-speaking Caribbean, some politicians early in the twentieth century like Hegesippe Legitimus, Rene Boisneuf, and Gratien Candace recognized the necessity for blacks to be seen as equals in the global community. This motivation led to exciting conversations among scholars and activists, especially in the Caribbean, about the true meaning of Negritude and its place in the black experience throughout the world.

Historically, "Negritude" has had two competing interpretations named after the two scholars who coined the term itself. First, Aimé Cesaire has designated the term as seeing the uniqueness and unity of African existence connected historically with contingent events of the African slave trade and the New World plantation system. Nick Nesbitt in his contribution to the *Africana Encylopedia* writes, "Cesaires developmental model of Negritude . . . continues to offer a model for the ongoing project of black liberation in all its fullness, at once spiritual and political."[19] For Cesaire, "Negritude" finds its meaning in the subjugation and exploitation experienced by the African peoples of the world. Through this common historical and cultural experience, the African people are bound together and "the compass of suffering" measures the richness of it.[20] The fact that blacks have suffered collectively throughout modern history and culture is the glue that binds us together as a people, as a nation. For Cesaire's counterpart Senghor Negritude represents the essence and core of unchanging African identity and black existence. Senghor's contribution did have a profound impact on value systems that had informed Western perceptions of blacks since the precolonial period.

In terms of language and its emphasis on African cultural identity, there is continuity with Asante's project. The language of Negritude in its profound literary expression is quite valuable to Asante's formulation of the Afrocentric perspective. Because Negritude lifted up the plight of the suffering African peoples and affirmed the inherent value of being black, Asante indicates that writings such as these are liberating and essential to Afrocentric outlook. Diop, on the other hand, finds the Negritude movement disconcerting when it suggests that blacks ought to embrace their emotional contribution to society alone. Diop argues that the Negritude poets lacked the scientific means to confront certain notions of black inferiority and accepted some of the views of Negritude. Indeed, the contribution of the Negritude movement to the Afrocentric idea is profound. Although Asante borrows heavily from Diop in his historical argumentation, he parts company with Diop in his support of movements such as Negritude as they provide an alternative cultural literary perspective—a necessary dimension of the Afrocentric position.

Harlem Renaissance

The Harlem Renaissance is a historical event in African American history that has helped form our understanding of cultural identity as well as provided some precedence for the notion of Afrocentrism. Unfolding during the 1920s and 1930s, the Harlem Renaissance was primarily a literary and intellectual movement involving a diversity of social and cultural expressions. Three essential literary works laid the foundation of what would become known as the "New Negro" movement. Claude McKay's volume of poetry *Harlem Shadows* (1922), Jean Toomer's *Cane* (1923), and Jessie Fauset's *There Is Confusion* were major works that were published and recognized not only by the black literary community but by many whites, who had to take note as well. From this new literary fervor, organizations like the National Urban League headed by Charles S. Johnson came into being to aid these efforts.[21] Through this mixture of intellectual and cultural expression, a new revised sense of identity and self-determination was forged into the fabric of the black experience in America. Alain Locke captures this understanding when he writes:

> The great social giant in this is the releasing of our talented group from the arid fields of controversy and debate to the productive fields of creative expression . . . But whatever the general effect, the present generation will have added the motives of self-expression and spiritual development to the old and unfinished task[,] making material headway and progress.[22]

Without question, the Harlem Renaissance has left an indelible mark upon the literary and intellectual landscape of African and African American arts and literature in the United States and abroad. The influences of the Harlem Renaissance have informed writers through history from Ralph Ellison and Richard Wright of the 1930s and 1940s to Alice Walker and Toni Morrison of the 1980s and 1990s and beyond.

In Asante's argument, there does appear to be some continuity with the Harlem Renaissance in terms of its reinterpretation of Africa as being the center of black literary artists' cultural understanding. Asante recognizes the achievements of the Harlem Renaissance as seen in the witness of Du Bois. Du Bois prepared the world for Afrocentricity, says Asante, yet was not Afrocentric himself. Nevertheless, the contributions of Du Bois and the Harlem Renaissance are indispensable to the Afrocentric outlook and what it means for us today. It would be a mistake to think that Obama's historic inauguration as the first black president of the United States has nothing to do with the vibrancy and cultural revolution of the Harlem Renaissance. The Harlem Renaissance and other efforts such as Garvey's Back to Africa Movement and the founding of the National Association for the Advancement of Colored People by Du Bois on February 12, 1909, all created the conditions under which Obama could build his campaign and eventually win the election.

Defining Afrocentrism in the Postmodern Context

Cultural identity is quintessential in such a changing and fragmented world as we see today. Without a strong sense of cultural identity, there is an increased likelihood of conflict, and intensification of the enormous challenges that continue to undermine black progress. Many poor black communities in America are now in a state of crisis. They are on the verge of establishing what the sociologist William Julius Wilson called a "permanent underclass."[23] Although Obama's presidency means a great deal as a source of cultural and racial pride, and as even a powerful source of hope that change might finally come to poor black communities, black folks themselves must recover a radical, affirmative sense of cultural identity to confront and overcome the burdens they face today. Asante and Diop, as sort of architects of contemporary thinking around black cultural identity, are helpful as we continue to reflect on what Obama's presidency means for the black experience, politics, and the American dream.

Asante and Afrocentrism

Although Obama has become the first black president of America, it is surprising how little American culture, broadly speaking, knows about the black experience in America and the world. This can be largely attributed to the history of systemic racism in America and colonialism throughout much of the developing world. For that reason, blacks have also suffered from a deficit of knowledge and understanding about the African experience.

Even in the age of Obama, blacks must anchor their sense of cultural identity in Afrocentric sensibilities if community organizing is to occur. In light of the history of black nationalism and cultural movements such as the Harlem Renaissance, Asante's description of Afrocentrism is helpful to further our understandings. Afrocentrism, Asante explains, is a "philosophical perspective" guided by African history that applies to all African peoples, diaspora, and the continent. For Asante, this takes on many dimensions—involving language, ideology, and cultural heritage.

Primarily a linguist, Asante places a considerable amount of attention on language and the use of it regarding how we communicate with others, how others communicate with us, and how we perceive ourselves. In short, Afrocentrism means reclaiming the language most familiar to us as a people and to our historical links. An example given by Asante is the way in which people communicate with their gods. Asante makes this assertion poignant when he states:

> If your God cannot speak to you in your language, then he is not your God. Your God is the God who speaks to you in your language. What is your language? It is the language with which you first got your consciousness. Thus, for African Americans, this would be Ebonics (the language of black Americans), for Yoruba, the language would be Yoruba, and for Asante, the language would be Twi. If you want to hear your God in the language of your ancestors, then learn an African language like Kiswahili or Yoruba. I implore you with every drop of blood in my veins to severely evaluate any and every idea that is contrary to your center; learning and speaking Arabic to become more spiritual is way off center.[24]

For Asante, many African Americans are confused and disempowered by the fact of not being able to communicate with their gods. Like the Islamic tradition that requires its members to communicate in the Arabic language when reading its holy writings, it is the same with African tradition and its peoples. If they are to communicate with their gods, they must know their language. However, Diop points out that there is no single African language; rather it must be rooted in the Egypto-Nubian language of antiquity. Because one doesn't know the language of one's gods, they cannot call on them in times of strife and trouble. Hence, what is necessary is to adopt African languages, like Kiswahili or Yoruba—at least being able to recognize and know them as well as European languages.

Language is also significant in how we understand symbols. To Asante, Afrocentrism places Africa at the center of our worldview and sociohistorical analyses. Thus, all linguistic symbols are interpreted through the lens of our African history and culture. Here, Africa becomes "subject, not object."

In the Afrocentric perspective we are taught to appreciate those places where the struggle for freedom and liberty has taken place. For instance, Afrocentrism is a perspective that places African and African American history at the nucleus of how we view the world. Asante offers examples of how this ideological perspective has been played out in the lives of people like W. E. B. Du Bois, Marcus Garvey, Malcolm X, Ron Karenga, and others. In the eyes of these men, Africa was not an "object" to be exploited or manipulated by imperial forces. Rather, it was and is at the center of human existence. It is this African-centered ideology based in a collective history that has the capacity to generate social, political, and economic empowerment among African peoples. Although Obama seems to have situated his identity firmly with the idealistic narrative of American democracy, where blacks and whites have found some sense of shared meaning and heritage, it is important that all Americans have a rich understanding of the significance and contributions of Africa in world history and culture. Obama must confront the stagnating racism of international and domestic policy as it relates to African descendants, which is chiefly due to the persistent denial of black humanity. As the Anglican Archbishop of Cape Town, Desmond Tutu, said repeatedly during the most volatile moments of the apartheid struggle in South Africa, which underscores the important message of Asante and Diop, "The only solution to South Africa's crisis is for whites to accept blacks as human beings."[25] When a realization of the other's humanity occurs, the brutality of poverty, economic exploitation, genocide, and other atrocities can no longer be tolerated, looked upon with blazon indifference, or morally and rationally justified.

Another dimension of Afrocentrism is the notion of collective consciousness that is rooted in a shared historical, cultural, and intellectual history. An important part of this, Asante asserts, is the concept of Nija, and the "teaching of Nija." "Nija" is the collective expression of the Afrocentric worldview grounded in the historical struggle of African people. Part of this formulation is the idea of collective consciousness. Before there can be unity, there must be collective consciousness, Asante asserts. Asante draws heavily on the experiences of Malcolm X and on the black nationalist movement as an illustration of his position. According to Asante, Malcolm X recognized the necessity of having a shared consciousness among black peoples—a consciousness guided and perpetuated by the masses.

Diop and Cultural Identity

Considered as one of the greatest scholars to emerge in the African world in the twentieth century, Diop was born in Diourbel, Senegal, a town on the west coast of Africa, in 1923. Diop arose to the heights of intellectual enterprise during the fervor of the Pan-Africanism movement led by America's Du Bois and the African Independence explosion, beginning with Ghana in 1958. Diop creatively used the disciplines of linguistics, cultural and physical anthropology, history, chemistry, and physics that his research required. Some of the creative pathways into developing a sound conception for Africa as the "cradle of humanity" were illustrated in other important works by Diop. Among these were *Black Africa: The Economic and Cultural Basis for a Federated State* and the comprehensive work on African history *The African Origin of Civilization: Myth or Reality*.[26] The former presented a blueprint for economic development in Africa through saving mineral wealth for unborn generations to come. This work was rarely read or understood. The latter is a one-volume translation of the major sections of two other books by Diop, *Nations negres et Culture* and *Anteriorite des civilisations negres*. This work challenged historical and cultural presuppositions, particularly held among Western scholars, about the place and contribution of Africa in world history and intellectual discourse. In doing so, Diop changed the landscape and attitudes about the place of African people in history in scholarly circles around the world.

It was this cultural and intellectual development that led to Diop's "magnum opus": *Civilization or Barbarism: An Authentic Anthropology*. This is considered the last of Diop's great contributions to the clarification of African history. The present work is in many ways a summation and an extension of his previous research; it is a refinement of his analyses and a final statement of his previous research, reflecting the completion of his mission. "Through this book he has left us an historical legacy that will inspire future historians and researchers who seek the truth about the role of Africa in world history."[27] Diop stated before his death that this would be his last scholarly work, and indeed this would be the case as Diop left a political and social master plan that would save Africa for the Africans.

The collective history is what connects a people to a shared past and thus renders a common destiny. Within history is a consciousness, a feeling of cohesion that provides security and a shield of cultural security for a people. Without this shared sense of history, there is nothing to draw or connect them in action or consciousness. Therefore, "*the essential thing, for people, is to rediscover the thread that connects them to their most remote ancestral past* [emphasis added]."[28] Historical continuity is perhaps the most viable weapon against outside aggression and disintegrating forces. Regardless of what that history might embody, what is important is the continuity of that history for the people who are part of it. Diop proposes that the feeling of historical unity and cultural identity through scientific research is capable of contributing to the African cultural consciousness. This reinforces the cultural identity of the "Negro African peoples" throughout the world. Diop goes on to write:

> It is by engaging in this type of investigative activity that our people will discover, one day, that the Egypto-Nubian civilization played the same role vis-à-vis African culture as did Greco-Latin antiquity in regard to Western civilization.[29]

The linguistic factor serves as a constituent of cultural personality and of cultural identity. For Diop, the language of a people is the hope of a people. Within the rhythms of language is a common denominator for communicating cultural identity and consciousness. Millions of Americans experienced this phenomenon as Obama and his campaign infused the language of hope and possibility at every level of the campaign. They were committed to the idea that what America needed more than anything was the rhetoric of hope, supported by strong policies and leadership. Montesquieu once wrote, "*As long as a conquered people has not lost its language, it can have hope* [emphasis added]."[30] Like Latin in Europe, there is ambiguity concerning African linguistic unity. In spite of the fact that Africa has more than 360 languages and dialects, what must be done is a recasting of the African educational programs and a centering of the many African languages and dialects to Egypto-Nubian antiquity, as with the Western educational system—having its foundation in Greco-Latin antiquity. This is the most powerful and effective method possible of reinforcing African cultural personality and cultural identity among Africans.

Unlike Asante who drew from a multitude of sources in order to formulate his version of Afrocentrism, Diop stands alone as a pioneer by establishing an intellectual and philosophical framework for understanding Africa and its place in the world. In Diop, we are armed with the scientific analysis necessary to questions related to African history and culture. The cultural identity of Africa and its peoples have been shaped by its history, and for Diop this history can no longer be marginalized outside the network of human civilizations. This is important to our understanding of the cultural identity of African peoples throughout the diaspora, particularly in the United States. The impact both Diop and Asante continue to have on our understanding of cultural identity is immutable to how we understand who we are as African peoples and ultimately where we are headed.

Conclusion

What I have tried to do in this chapter is to demonstrate the need for a black political and cultural identity rooted in the past—a history constructively shaped by voices in the black nationalist tradition and given expression in the contemporary movement of Afrocentrism. Barack Obama's presidency has meant and does mean a great deal to the continual unfolding of the black freedom struggle. It does not mark the end of that struggle. Overcrowded prisons, failing schools, the dilapidated houses of inner city Cleveland, Chicago, New York, Philadelphia, Oakland, and Memphis show that we still have a long way to go. However, the Obama presidency should give the black community pause, to once again consider what a collective commitment to struggle looks like in today's context—considering that the aforementioned perspectives and insights may shine light on a potential way forward in this process.

CHAPTER 6

Obama and the Changing Face of the Black Community

Unity is the great need of the hour—the great need of this hour. Not because it sounds pleasant or because it makes us feel good, but because it's the only way we can overcome the essential deficit that exists in this country . . . We have an empathy deficit in this country when we are still sending our children down corridors of shame—schools in the forgotten corners of America where the color of your skin affects the content of your education.

We have deficit when CEOs are making more in ten minutes than some workers make in ten months; when families lose their homes so that lenders make a profit; when mothers can't afford a doctor when their children get sick . . .

Brothers and sisters, we cannot walk alone. In the struggle for peace and justice, we cannot walk alone. In the struggle for opportunity and equality, we cannot walk alone. In the struggle to heal this nation and repair this world, we cannot walk alone. So I ask you to walk with me, and march with me, and join your voice with mine, and together we will sing the song that tears down the wall that divide us, and lift up an America that is truly indivisible, with liberty, and justice, for all. May God bless the memory of the great pastor of this church, and may God bless the United States of America.[1]

When Obama delivered this historic speech, entitled "the Great Need of the Hour," at Ebenezer Baptist Church in Atlanta, Georgia, on January 20, 2008, he was symbolically bestowed the official entry card into the elite ranks of black leadership and what Du Bois called the talented tenth of black America. The moment was tense when Obama spoke in the former organizing headquarters of the Civil Rights Movement and Martin Luther King, Jr., home church. During this time in the campaign, Obama and Hillary Clinton were neck and neck with delegates in the bid for the Democratic Party nomination. No one expected Obama to still be in the running at this time, much less in a dead heat with Washington, D.C.'s power couple for all times. In that moment, Obama moved from a marginalized, virtually unknown political figure to a premier leader in the black freedom struggle. Speaking before an audience of Atlanta's black elite and black political and economic leadership from across the nation, Obama directly linked his pilgrimage and efforts to King's prophetic vision of the beloved community and the broader quest for freedom and justice in America and the world. In doing so, Obama firmly situated himself within the trenches of the black community and its plight.

In the previous chapter, I talked about the relationship of Obama's political leadership to the broader quest for black cultural identity and black nationalism. But what do Obama's identity and sense of connection to the broader African diaspora tell us about the amazing changes taking place in the black community? Building on the problem of fragmentation in the black community as well as in the broader African diaspora, what does it mean to form vibrant black communities that can work together to form social and political transformation in both local and national spaces? One of the reasons that the Civil Rights Movement was successful, according to many historians like Lewis Baldwin, Clayborne Carson, Michael Eric Dyson, and Rosetta Ross, is that black folks held a shared narrative. Most blacks in the South could trace their ancestry to slavery in America. It was precisely because of the fact that blacks had come through the storm, through the trauma of years of racial struggle, that they could inhabit new spaces of solidarity, to work and even die together for the cause of freedom.

Beginning around the era of Obama's Kenyan-born father, the black community has experienced more and more fluidity, fragmentation, diversity, and pluralism. The rise in international travel, intermarriage, technological interconnectedness, and global communication has contributed to this emerging fluidity and to some extent fragmentation within the black community. Yet, Obama was able to claim over 90 percent of the black votes during the election. It conjures up memories of the Montgomery Bus Boycott when Rosa Parks almost instantly mobilized Montgomery's black community on December 1, 1955.[2] Obama's campaign, election, and presidency now present us with the occasion to consider those emerging ideas and perspectives on the complexity of black life today. All Americans must take seriously the nature of the black community because it has contributed so much to shaping American life and sharpening the image of the American dream as well.

Black Identity and the Quest for Community

I have, in this chapter, enlisted three figures, Cornel West, Edouard Glissant, and Stuart Hall, to help us think through the changes mentioned above, their relationship to the Obama presidency, and how they will further impact the capacity of black folks to continue to mobilize for social change. The ability of blacks in America to change their social and political situation has always hinged on the fulcrum of solidarity and collective consciousness. Electing Obama as president must not be the end of black political organizing and the pursuit of radical change. It has been a monumental achievement, but it would be a grave mistake to become simply content at this stage. As president, Obama will be able to do many things. At the same time, Obama is locked within a cultural system in Washington, D.C., that seems not at all concerned with the plight of poor blacks or the poor in general in America. Hence, it is essential to explore new ways of sustaining black unity and solidarity among various groups to forge change. In an age of globalization and the declining significance of nation-statehood, how do we begin to think of ethnic and political identity in shaping communities of resistance? At the "end of history," as described by Gianni Vattimo, the historical moment we now live in deeply complicates ideas about community and political identity. In considering the divergent views of West, Hall, and Glissant, perhaps we may shine more light on how to think about conceptions of community in a global economic and political system. While these thinkers focus much of their attention on the contradictions of modernity, their works take on significant meaning in a time of what West calls "monopoly capitalism." It is not my desire to develop a new paradigm for forging communities of resistance and cultural identity. Rather, the task is to explicate and critique conceptions of community that serve as viable models of responding to the oppressive and lingering structures of modernity. Indeed, a serious treatment of how to respond to the binary oppositions of the Western philosophical tradition is needed to understand the complex relationship between individual particularity and notions of group identity.

With Obama's historic win, it is easy to take for granted the achievement of an African American male being elected president. I do think, however, that understanding these complexities is critical to the ongoing struggle to advance black flourishing, to overcome the challenges of poverty, homelessness, educational disparities, the prison-industrial complex, homophobia, and other issues plaguing the black community. Obama made a similar point in *The Audacity of Hope* when he argued that Americans must go beyond the impulse to retreat to specific categories and personal identities, and find ways to connect on the basis of shared values, hopes, and dreams. Obama's life and the ways in which he constructed his campaign are excellent illustrations of kind of "fluidity" of ideas and racial difference that West, Hall, and Glissant allude to in their discussions. Harold Ford, Jr., in the *Newsweek* article "Black, White, Shades of Gray" observed that to "talk about the role of race in this presidential election, it becomes necessary to rehearse the life of Barack Obama."[3] Obama's life story is an illustration of the fluidity and complexity of racial differences today in a global world. As Ford indicates, by now everyone knows that Obama was a black boy, with a Kenyan father, raised by white women in Asian Pacific communities in Hawaii and Indonesia. These experiences reflect the ways in which identity, and subsequently the black community as well, is no longer limited to a homogonous, singular historical or cultural orientation.

West, Hall, and Glissant attempt to reflect on these themes from different perspectives. West's conception of community attempts to respond to the persistent nihilistic threat facing American civil society in the postmodern situation. The American social and political context becomes the chief preoccupation for West's delineation of nationhood and community. Although his thought has implications throughout the African diaspora, he is interested in critiquing both the nihilistic culture and the Western philosophical tradition that makes it possible. Presupposed in Glissant and Hall, however, is a broader diaspora sensitivity that places them in constant dialogue with the metropoles of France and Britain, in particular. Both Glissant and Hall evaluate the particularities of Martinican history and culture. In Martinique, Glissant is concerned with a sense of national identity that has historically been imported from the metropole (France). Cultural pillars such as language, musical expression, and even art and literature were "unconsciously" adopted by the people. Hence, the task for Glissant is to address the sense of "dispossession" caused by these dualistic cultural and psychological realities that undermine activism and the import of a shared political identity. Like Glissant, Hall looks closely at the Martinican situation, but in relation to Britain as the metropole. For Hall, the cultural exchange taking place in the African diaspora, particularly in London, produces a transient and continually evolving sense of identity. Here, I will examine the themes of community and postmodernity expressed in the unique perspectives offered by these thinkers. First, we will give attention to the presuppositions and contextual issues that inform their conceptions of community and identity. Second, our task is to understand exactly what is meant by community by these figures. Finally, a critical analysis is in order to show how these voices, when brought into conversation, help to further our understandings on how to think about individual and group identity in an ever-changing postmodern world.

Conceptions of Community

West, Hall, and Glissant all emerge from uniquely different cultural contexts, but they reflect the growing complexities and difference within the black experience today. Advancements in mass communication, cyberspace, the media, and global travel have now created conditions where people from all across the globe are constantly exchanging cultural ideas, values, experiences, and beliefs. West, Hall, and Glissant as leading thinkers of black cultural life might help shine light on the present state of affairs. While their perspectives are varied, they share a commitment to the cause of liberation of peoples of African descent. The particularities of the cultural issues they take up have greatly informed their views toward notions of community and cultural identity. West, drawing from the Afro-American religious experience, is specifically addressing the philosophical dimensions of how African Americans have historically responded to exploitation and entrenched subjugation in modernity. West was a major supporter of Obama throughout the campaign as he increasingly realized that Obama was genuinely committed to uplifting black life in America. West understood that Obama's life did not exactly mirror the kind of colonial experiences of Africans or blacks in Brazil or the Caribbean. He, nonetheless, recognized that Obama chose to identify himself as African American an identity that carries with it the long history of resistance to racism. Obama did not go the path of Tiger Woods, who described himself as "Cablinasian," thus distancing himself from blacks in particular, and the African experience in general. What Hall, West, and Glissant all underscore, which becomes apparent when looking at Obama's life and the election, is that "America has become a global society." Ford's assessment of the American racial and cultural makeup today speaks to Hall's and Glissant's insights directly when he writes:

> You can go to any large suburban high school in Los Angeles or Atlanta and see the proof. There are students from India and Peru and Laos and Egypt. They have come because the American Dream is potent. Sure there are separate cafeteria tables. But there is also flirting and unlikely friendships being formed. A young woman from Kansas falls in love with a visiting student from Kenya. In any American family I can name, there are cousins and in-laws of several races. There are grandchildren who do not look exactly like any of their grandparents. And many families have adopted a child from China or Guatemala. Or Bangladesh.[4]

Because of his incredible capacity to relate to all sorts of people, Obama was able to enter into the sacred space of communal identity. He went to painstaking lengths to show that he could relate to the experiences of whites as well as blacks, Latino and Asian, rich and poor, religious and secular. His campaign points to the challenge of deconstructing the problematic legacy of colonialism around the world, especially in places like the Caribbean and

Europe, which has tended to be places where blacks have struggled to find meaning and identity. Hall and Glissant both were concerned with the Caribbean experience of colonialism and cultural identity. While Glissant was preoccupied with the complexities of Martinican nationalistic expressions and consciousness, Hall locates the Caribbean situation within the larger context of black identity and modernity.

Steeped in the American pragmatist school of William James and John Dewey, West has described himself as "a Chekhovian Christian with deep democratic commitments."[5] Anton Chekhov, the noted Russian playwright and short-story writer, contributed to West the aesthetic insights into the human condition that he joined to his Christian religious sensibilities. West is essentially a philosopher of religion and social critic. In this manner, the Western philosophical tradition is laced all throughout West's work. However, some of West's strongest influences came from American pragmatism. In particular, the work of John Dewey, Charles Pierce, and William James has left an enduring imprint on West's philosophic outlook. West finds Dewey the most favored of the three insofar as Dewey emphasized a sense of historical consciousness and a concern for social and political matters.[6] From this perspective, West builds his intellectual arsenal to confront the critical question of how blacks have responded to the oppressive structures of the modern era. Unlike what we will find in Hall and Glissant, West is preoccupied with the American ideal and with conceptions of modernity. As he writes, "My Chekhovian Christian conception of what it means to be modern focuses on the night side of modernity, the underside of our contemporary predicament."[7] Although focusing on the particularities of the American situation, West attempts to address those expressions of "self-making" and "self-creating" demonstrated by those often overlooked in Enlightenment discourse. West determines to reconfigure modern philosophical claims about reason, human creativity, and consciousness from the perspective of those most severely victimized by the oppressive structures produced.

Like West, Hall attends to the contradictions posed by the modern experiment. However, Hall situates his discourse in the Caribbean social and political condition. The multilayered cultural exchange taking place constantly in Britain and the Caribbean forms the basis for how Hall understands community and cultural identity. Hall's work reflects such themes as "ethnicity" and "multi-accentuality."[8] In general, the African diaspora experience is the chief interest for Hall. He treats the cultural interactions of the West Indians and the British. for Hall, colonial subjects in the West Indies formed identity through the constant exchange of cultural ideas and experiences, creating a collage of cultural and ethnic difference. Hall was a founding member of the "New Left" in England and editor of the publication *New Left Review*. Grossberg describes Hall's thoroughgoing work in suggesting:

> For Hall, all human practices [including communication and communication theory] are struggles to "make history but in conditions not of our own making." He brings this Marxist maxim to bear upon at least three different, albeit related projects: (1) to offer a theory of ideology which sees communicative practices in terms of what people can and do make of them; (2) to describe the particular historical form of contemporary cultural and political struggle [hegemony]; and (3) to define a "Marxism without guarantees" by rethinking the "conjunctural" nature of society. At each of these levels, Hall connects, in complex ways, theory and writing to real social practices and struggles.[9]

The impact of globalization in shaping cultural and ethnic identity, in Hall's analysis, challenges the postmodern subject to think in new ways about questions of nationhood, political identity, and notions of an "imagined community." I think Hall's point here is particularly poignant because with the election of Obama, Americans are now challenged to rethink their own narrative. Since its founding, many, both within and beyond American borders, have maintained that being American was synonymous with being white. Obama's election in some ways disrupts what otherwise has been a stabilizing narrative that has given meaning for whites in America for decades. The black freedom struggle in America, to a large extent, was a radical indictment of attempts to alienate blacks from this historical claim on America and its dream. It has been this longing for freedom and justice, those fundamental Constitutional claims, that blacks have longed for through the echoing march of history. Perhaps it was this persistent conviction that led to Langston Hughes' masterful poem published on March 1, 1925, "I, Too, Sing America," where he writes:

> I, too, I, too, sing America.
> I am the darker brother.
> They send me to eat in the kitchen;
> When the company comes.
> But I laugh and eat well, and grow strong.
> Tomorrow I will sit at the table When company comes.
> Nobody'll dare say to me, "eat in the kitchen" then.

Hughes could only marvel in delight as the inauguration of Obama took place in January 2009, as Obama assumed office among the past 43 presidents in the White House.[10] While the world of Hughes is dramatically different from the kind of present situation Hall alludes to, there is still cause to see the powerful strand of freedom and justice at the heart of the long pilgrimage of black consciousness and formation of the black community. Even as this community becomes much more complex, diverse, multilingual, and multicultural, there is still a shared sense of togetherness emerging out of the historical fight against racism in America and in places like the Caribbean and Britain.

Hall speaks from the perspective of one having both Caribbean and British influences. Hall's "Caribbean discourse" supposes that the diaspora situation involves multiple identities. Drawing on Benedict Anderson and Mary Chamberlain, Hall attempts to confront notions of a stagnant form of cultural identity that negates difference and otherness. Although Obama did not emerge from the Caribbean experience, one can see his internal struggle to reconcile multiple identities. Obama was raised by his white mother, but as he reflects, her message came to embrace black people. He writes in his autobiographical work, *Dreams from My Father: A Story of Race and Inheritance*, how his mother would be intentional about exposing Obama to great black leaders in the Civil Rights Movement. Obama's mother also introduced him to black cultural icons like Mahalia Jackson, Lena Horne, and Harry Belafonte, in addition to figures like Fannie Lou Hamer and Thurgood Marshall. She wanted to impress upon Obama the richness of his cultural heritage as an African American. Obama's struggle with race would continue throughout much of his young adult life. He recalls coming across a picture in *Life* magazine of a black man who, because of the sting of racism and constant messages of racial inferiority, attempted to peel his skin off.[11]

Both Hall and Glissant, in this sense, help us to further illuminate the Obama presidency and what it means for race in America. As a mixed-race person, Obama's own experience with ethnicity will no doubt have implications on how he governs. It is critical that the Obama administration and the American population as a whole have an expansive view of racial difference, that racial differences are not stagnant, but continually changing. According to Thomas Sowell, in *Race and Culture: A World View*, there is a problematic tendency to grossly generalize racial and ethnic groups without recognizing the complexity and vast differences within groups.[12] Cultural differences are much more diverse, geographical, and particular than most people have ever imagined. As geographical and economic changes take shape, racial and ethnic differences also increase and become more prominent. In short, what Sowell surmised was that racial and cultural differences change as rapidly as demographical and economic transitions. Racial differences, then, assume a perpetual state of flux, especially in the context of a rapidly changing global world. That affects how individuals and groups (even nation-states) construct their realities and policies related to their countries. Hall, in his analysis of the Martinician situation under colonialism, may offer insights on how race and politics function amid the changing dynamics of the black community and America in general. Similarly to Glissant, Hall focuses on the Martinican situation. But Hall places more impetus on the interconnections and shared sense of difference encountered in the African diaspora. This leads Hall to a rejection of what he calls "foundational myths." For Hall, Caribbean peoples throughout the African diaspora have rested on Old Testament stories such as the Exodus in order to maintain a sense of hope in the face of oppression and injustice. Hall argues that these stories are not sustainable, especially for Caribbean people. These outlooks perpetuate fixed conceptions of community identity directed toward a distant and impervious past. From this perspective, Hall develops his conception of "hybridity," which as we will later observe, forms the basis for his understanding of community.

Glissant, like West and Hall, also serves as a major voice in the discourse related to black identity and modernity. Glissant was born in Sainte-Marie in 1928. Glissant's primary attention is paid to issues of cultural identity and nationalism in Martinique. Before leaving to study in France, Glissant was exposed to the work of Aimé Cesaire at the Lycee Schoelcher, along with the work of Cesaire's friend Andre Breton. Later, in Paris, Glissant became editor of the UNESCO journal *Courriere*. As J. Michael Dash points out, "what Glissant emphasizes is the structuring force of landscape, community, and collective unconscious."[13]

For Glissant, the colonial subject must challenge the temptations of colonial dependency with its economic and psychological implications. He argues that the "pre-Oedipal dependence on France" produces a sense of cultural and ideological dependency preventing the development of a collective consciousness among Caribbean people. In founding the Institut Martiniquias d'Etudes as a means to raise cultural and political consciousness, Glissant aimed at constructing a paradigm for cultural identity that would affirm the sense of personhood and consciousness stripped away by the Martinican position as a "department" of France.[14] The problem of the Martinican dependence on France, Glissant argued, stemmed from a psychic disintegration of the self. Rooted in history, the reality of "self dispossession" was the quintessential obstacle between individual identity and collective consciousness. Glissant observed that the people of Martinique were stifled in their individual activism and recognition of a common destiny because allegiances were greater to France than to their authentic selves as African descendant people. The implications of the suppositions offered in Glissant, Hall, and West become more apparent in considering their understandings of community and multiple layers expressed in those conceptions. What Obama and other black leaders in America must engage are the realities of multiple identities and understandings of communities in America and abroad. To draw on fixed, concrete conceptions of the black community in America or in other parts of the world like Iraq, Afghanistan, the Palestinian West Bank, or Central Europe would undermine the complexities and fluidity of groups in a time of rapid technological and geographical changes.

Ideas around what constitutes a particular community (who's in or who's out and why) have always been at the center of social and political transformation. The politics of race, especially in America but also abroad, has informed the way these questions have been addressed and discussed for decades. For instance, during the election, the *Chicago Tribune* reporter Kathleen Parker wrote that "mainly, an Obama presidency allows Americans to put a period at the end of a very long sentence. With a black president, the sins of slavery are not forgiven or forgotten, but we can move along. Nothing left to see here."[15] She also observes that "Obama smoothly, strategically and subtly mines the wells of white guilt."[16] All three figures (Glissant, West, and Hall) speak to Obama's challenge during the election, and even now as he attempts to advance vital legislation, to offer a narrative image of America that unites the black and the white experience. He also promoted an expansive vision of America that is inclusive of all races and cultures. In a similar fashion, Glissant, West, and Hall attempt to articulate a vision of community that is historically and culturally affirming and politically engaging.

Even with Obama's cross-racial appeal, there are yet major challenges to consider. According to Paul Street, in Barack Obama and the future of American Politics, there are essentially three reasons why Obama's presidency may pose major challenges for strengthening the black community and advancing race relations in America. For starters, Obama's broad appeal to different races may be related to the perception by many whites that Obama is not fully black. There is an unspoken assumption that the best of Obama is his whiteness. "Many whites who roll their eyes at the mention of the names Jesse Jackson or Al Sharpton—former presidential candidates who behave in ways that many whites find too African American—are calmed and 'impressed' by the cool, underplayed blackness and ponderous, quasi-academic tone of the half-white, Harvard-educated Obama," says Street.[17] As Street observes, Obama doesn't fit the traditional mold of black political leadership in the black community. He doesn't "shout, holler, or drawl. He doesn't rail against injustice, bring the parishioners to their feet, or threaten delicate white suburban and middle-class sensibilities."[18] Street argues that the racial attitudes of whites are not as progressive as they might seem in light of Obama's presidency. They may, in fact, reinforce certain deeply embedded racial attitudes and perceptions that whites hold by elevating the "kind" of black figure that most resembles their unspoken definitions of whiteness.

Street's perspective reinforces Cornel West's skepticism about the magical nature of Obama's rise to power very early on. I think West's observations are very poignant when he says that "it's hard for someone who came out of slavery and Jim Crow to call [the United States] a magical place."[19] There was nothing magical about the fact that, in this instance, Obama's mixed racial heritage worked in his favor as he was able to appeal to a massive and increasingly multicultural America. What the Obama campaign, and now in some ways his presidency, stands for is the radical movement beyond the stagnant, rigid racial categories that informed much of America's segregated past, from slavery to Jim Crow. It represents a movement toward multiple understandings of identity and community, a movement that must embrace difference and otherness as a fact of life and reality itself one that must make room for multiple perspectives, insights, ideas, histories, and beliefs.

Hall's ideas speak to what I think the Obama campaign and his administration speak to and its implications for how black folks and others construct understandings of community today. For instance, Hall's understanding of community as "hybridity" seems to be directly related to Obama's emphasis on the interrelatedness of races and cultures, that racial differences (for Obama) are not as sharp as they seem. That is not to say that there are not distinct differences among racial groups, but in reading Obama's *Audacity of Hope* and *Dreams from My Father*, it is clear he was to push us all to think more about what we share in common, instead of our differences. Hall's conception of community is seen as an ever-changing "hybridity" constantly in tension with past and present identities. Using Jacques Derrida's idea of *différance*, Hall argues for a conception of community devoid of permanent notions of cultural identity.[20] The binary oppositions, such as white/black, rich/poor, high/low, etc., produced exclusionary and oppressive hierarchical structures. Since the Caribbean constructions of cultural identity have been held hostage by "foundational myths" that promote continuity with an idealized past, a new understanding is needed, one that embraces difference. In Hall's analysis, the world is in a state of flux, primarily due to the reality of globalizations. The boundaries between nation-states are swiftly becoming devalued in light of transnational corporations and their demands for uniformity. Obama seemed to have an awareness of these realities in his inaugural address in Washington, D.C., on January 20, 2009, when he said:

> For we know that our patchwork heritage is a strength, not a weakness. We are a nation of Christians and Muslims, Jews and Hindus—and non-believers. We are shaped by every language and culture drawn from every end of this Earth; and because we have tasted the bitter swill of civil war and segregation, and emerged from that dark chapter stronger and more united, we cannot help but believe that the old hatreds shall someday pass; that the lines of tribe shall soon dissolve; that as the world grows smaller, our common humanity shall reveal itself; and that America must play its role in ushering in a new era of peace.[21]

In the speech, Obama goes on to talk about his commitment to reaching out across racial, ethnic, religious, and nationalistic lines. What Obama appears to be pointing to is a kind of universal humanitarianism that touches on some core values inherent in all cultures and with all peoples. He recognizes the fluidity of cultural values now taking place worldwide largely due to the expansion of global trade and technology. He also understands the tattered image of the United States in a post-Bush era and the need to repair that image in the world. He clearly seemed intentional in reaching out to the Muslim world, in particular, when he said, "To those who cling to power through corruption and deceit and the silencing of dissent, know that you are on the wrong side of history; but that we will extend a hand if you are willing to unclench your fist." In a very rare display of presidential humanity, when the nation is at war on two major fronts (Iraq and Afghanistan), Obama moved to situate America, not at the top of the world but at its center, as a reflection of the global world.

Obama's speech, and his commitments to dialogue and diplomacy, reflects the current postmodern climate that has created the need to rethink notions of cultural identity and nationhood. Hall's description of the Caribbean is a good illustration in these changing trends and its implications on building and sustaining a sense of shared identity in the black community. The Caribbean, for Hall in this regard, becomes the chief recipient of this imagined community. He creatively illustrates those forces attempting to undermine the sustained development of conceptions of black identity.[22] A Marxist critique helps us to see the disintegration of identity due in part to the fact that cultural subjects are shaped by social and historical conditions beyond their control. In this regard, history has to be seen as a continuous dialectic relationship between the past and future. Notions of identity are also displaced because of the psychic unconscious realities at work in the everyday lives of cultural subjects. One cannot disassociate the psychological processes of the mind from the damaging social images of degradation. The nature of language and linguistics, in the Saussurian sense, shapes constructions of community and even cultural identity, as Hall purports. Language, in Saussure's appraisal, is always a function of the relationships operative within the language. All language is somehow related to formerly existing linguistic structures of the sort. Of course, Hall establishes the fragmentation of identity to set the foundations of his conception of cultural identity as "hybridity." Hall's recognition of the challenges of identity and community in today's ever-expanding postmodern context is very telling. It offers dramatic insight to the continuous problem of decoding the language of race and racism, especially when, as Hall observes, cultural identity is becoming so mixed and in a state of flux.

Years ago, the black-power activists Stokely Carmichael and Stanley Hamilton struggled with these issues at the height of America's black power movement in the mid-to-late 1960s. They observed in their book *Black Power* that "racism is both overt and covert. It takes two, closely related forms: individual whites acting against individual blacks, and acts by the total white community against the black community."[23] The forces of both individual and institutionalized racism seek to establish and maintain systems of white privilege and power, often reinforced by language.

Glissant will also take up this theme of community but focus on the particularities of the Martinican experience. The polemics of community for Glissant are observed in the form of nationalism and collective consciousness. Unlike Hall and West, Glissant places more emphasis on the aesthetic dimensions of cultural identity and its implications toward nationhood. He posits a sense of community that situates individual identity in relation to national bonds associated with struggle and liberation. Inasmuch as West and Hall seek to overcome the modern predicament in primarily linguistic and philosophical terms, Glissant wishes to develop an aesthetic epistemology that will liberate the mind and body of the Martinican. Glissant maintains that art, music, and novelic literature described as "cross-cultured poetics," have the ability to communicate beyond traditional structures of modern linguistic discourse. Glissant made this observation in the Haitian experience. Because of the massive illiteracy of the population of the day, the use of language was rendered unintelligible in developing a sense of cultural identity. It had to be seen, heard, and felt. Glissant's assertion speaks to Obama's ability, during the election, to draw in voices from all sectors of the black community, from hip-hop artiste like Jay Z, Beyonce, 50 Cent, Naz, and P Diddy to artists, actors, and musicians from around the nation. Certainly, this does not negate the importance of language to Glissant's agenda. On the contrary, Glissant attempts to reinterpret the meaning of language in light of the Martinican experience. Glissant opts for a "Caribbean discourse" that is in touch with lived experience.

For Glissant, the Martinican community was unconscious, numb to the forces of dispossession at work in their social and political reality. Glissant saw that the mixture and bringing together of different ethnic groups were favored over the "totalizing" claims of historicism. The role of history in shaping imaginative constructs of nationhood and cultural identity cannot be denied for Glissant. Glissant's reading of history appears to be a reactionary response to the hegemonic construal of Hegel and the materiality of Marx. Georg Friedrich Hegel was a nineteenth-century thinker whose work informed a great deal of Western understandings about history and culture. His work was also painfully racist as he called Africa the "dark continent" devoid of civilization and culture. It was Hegel's work that paved the way for European exploitation of indigenous peoples around the world. For Hegel, Europe stood at the center of history as a mythical and idealized community destined for world domination and as the culmination of human civilization. Because history has been interpreted and explained in a systematized and hierarchical fashion, it produces progressivistic narratives and mythical stories of redemption and triumph.

Though drawing from different sources, Glissant and Hall seem to share a common reading of history as "mythical" stories that, instead of liberating, serve to perpetuate oppression and resistance to difference and the other. History, for Glissant as well as Hall, informs cultural identity and conceptions of nationhood. As Martinique, and much of the Caribbean for that matter, has received most of their history from the metropole of France, it is in a state of "nonhistory." The lack of a shared story and consciousness leads to a condition of "disintegrated self"—having a double consciousness, caught between the "fallacy of the primitive paradise, the mirage of Africa, and the illusion of a metropolitan identity." The influences of Cesaire are apparent in these sentiments. In conceiving his understanding of "Negritude," Cesaire recognizes these competing identities.

Du Bois and Frantz Fanon also made similar observations in their own particular contexts. Du Bois, whom West was heavily influenced, articulated his form of double consciousness out of the dismal legacy of racial slavery in America among blacks. Fanon's memorable account of the psychological dimensions of colonialism in Africa, in *Black Skins, White Masks*, explicates these themes as well. An attempt to overcome this dichotomy has been at the root of cultural identity, consciousness, and nationhood, according to Glissant. Of course, this paradox is not easily overcome, but must require serious treatment of the particularities of the Martinican experience and the generality of New World strivings for "the ideal of a history." As mentioned earlier, Glissant believes that the flexibility and creativity deriving from the arts offer the tools necessary to overcome such a quagmire. Glissant's *Caribbean Discourse* may be illustrative in this regard. Traditional constructions of plot, characterization, and chronology, for Glissant, cannot contain the truths and meanings accessible through the multiple levels of meanings and ambiguities he has observed. West seems to employ the same method in his depiction of American jazz music, particularly the artistry and person of John Coltrane, as demonstrating meanings too "funky" to be encased in modern notions of form and structure.

Conclusion

Interpreting the nature of the black community in today's global world, a world now shaped by an "African" and "African American" president, means thinking critically about the multiple strands of the black experience today. If black people are to ever be able to organize effectively to forge change in their communities, it must begin with an awareness of our differences as well as our common struggle. Hall, West, and Glissant point to this complexity but also assert new understandings of blackness and the capacity to mobilize communities of resistance and protest as well. I have attempted to explore conceptions of community in Hall, West, and Glissant with the hopes of advancing understandings on how we are to think about notions of community in a postmodern era. Bringing Obama's presidency and the current racial situation in America in dialogue with these thinkers may yield new insights into the underlying cause of fragmentation and division in the black community that continue to present obstacles for coalition building.

CHAPTER 7

Race, Power, and Technology in the New Millennium

The ruling of men is the effort to direct the individual actions of many persons toward some end. This end theoretically should be the greatest good of all, but no human group has ever reached this ideal because of ignorance and selfishness. The simplest object would be rule for the Pleasure of One, namely the Ruler; or of the Few—his favorites; or of many—the Rich, the Privileged, the Powerful. Democratic movements inside groups and nations are always taking place and they are the efforts to increase the number of beneficiaries of the ruling.[1]

We can't have a situation in which the corporate duopoly dictates the future of the Internet and that's why I'm supporting what is called Net Neutrality. And part of the reason for this is companies like Google and Yahoo might never have gotten started had they not been in a position to easily access the Internet and do so on the same terms as the big corporate-companies that were interested in making money on the Internet.[2]

For the first time in our nation's history, a presidential candidate was able to raise millions of dollars with a grassroots fundraising strategy. First introduced by Howard Dean in the 2000 election season, Obama was able to draw on the tools of the Internet, text messaging, e-mails, and web logs to create one of the most powerful political machines in American history. Sure, people will talk about Obama's nearly angelic rhetorical capacities, his charisma and debating strengths, but his community organizing skills translating into political campaigning were truly remarkable. What I'd like to talk about in this chapter is the connection between technology and constructions of power that is now shaping political life in America and what it means for each of us in participating in political processes locally, nationally, and globally. The critical question taken up in this chapter is: how has technology introduced new ways of thinking about power, community, and race in light of Obama's run for presidency and his new tech-savvy administration?

Lani Gunier, the former candidate for U.S. attorney general under the Clinton administration, published the classic and controversial book *Tyranny of the Majority* where she eloquently outlined the ways in which minority communities in America would never truly be afforded significant political power or influence in a "one vote/one person" democratic structure.[3] For as long as the majority community held sway over the entire political system, controlling the way congressional districts are drawn and the overall electoral system, she argued that black folks would be incessantly doomed politically and economically unless dramatic changes occurred. Needless to say, Gunier was not confirmed, but her ideas live on. They offer compelling insights to the problems of political power and the awesome influence of race in the electoral process. Since the 1968 Democratic Convention in Chicago, which essentially led to the fracturing of the Democratic Party, and which took nearly thirty years to repair, the politics of racial divisiveness (under the guise of the GOP's "values" platform) has continued to be a controversial yet effective tool of black subjugation from the political process.

Barack Obama, as yet the first bona fide black president of the United States, in spite of these incredible odds, was able to not only seize the Democratic nomination but emerge victoriously in a decisive win over a longtime, well connected senator and war hero—John McCain. This was not by accident or a fluke of nature. Postmodernists, from Michel Foucault, Gilles Deleuze, Slavoj Zizek, Jacques Derrida, Cornel West, and even Martin Luther King Jr. forecasted a coming age when power would be decentered, when the power of technology as a means of connecting individuals and communities could be used to defeat the mighty forces of aristocracy and oligarchy in the world. Indeed, Obama, along with his gifted colleagues David Axelrod and David Plouffe, used technology as a strategic method of mobilization, fundraising, and political maneuvering, the likes of which have never been seen in human history, let alone American history. Sarah Lai Stirland, writing for the online magazine Wired.com early on in the primaries, observed:

> The use of technology like blogs, mass texting and online phone banks has been key to Sen. Barack Obama's surprise sweep of recent primaries.
>
> The Illinois senator's campaign has been making use of a range of technologies—from ringtones to SMS—to inspire Obamamania. And it's working. Obama's recent parade of victories in the primaries has given him a slight lead over Sen. Hillary Clinton for the Democratic presidential nomination.

"They've been using [texting] to get out the vote, which is incredibly smart because it gives people a way to take immediate political action," says Julie Germany, director of the Institute for Politics, Democracy and the Internet. "It's just what mobile technology is suited for."[4]

What Stirland recognized early on was that technology as a means of relating empowers the rugged individualistic world of a new technocratic generation while at the same time drawing individuals into this broader communal consciousness. Because the very essence of technology is inter-connectedness, being linked up through electronic pulsations and digital monitors (large and small), Obama tapped into a new way of constructing ideas about political mobilization. Power became communal, a matter of connectivity (literally and figuratively). To be plugged in, as it were, meant becoming an agent of change in ways never possible before. The old system of political power was based solely on longstanding networks and a small handful of wealthy supports from which to draw. By expanding his base of support, though seemingly insignificant at first, Obama was able to not only build a broad coalition of financial contributors but also workers and volunteers who would beat the pavement in their local communities. They would now be invested and connected to a political process that, for many years had been totally off limits. One young lady, only known as Kimberlee, had this to say about the campaign on one of Obama's online blogs:

> I learned I could ask total strangers to vote for a candidate they may never even have heard about. I learned about great strength with local union vol-unteers. I learned about solidarity and teamwork. I learned that the voices of a few can change a city or a country. I learned how to get past my fears and call people and ask for a vote or donations. I learned you can love total strangers, even some from a different state. I learned how to persuade many people. I learned about sacrificing and donating money to a cause bigger than myself. I learned that change is possible. I learned I could survive eating doughnuts and pizza . . .
>
> I learned I had a family on a blog who was always there and where we could pump each other up or just vent. I learned I helped in change . . . I learned that I could get and liked working in politics. I learned politics wasn't only for my parents.
>
> I learned a lot about myself.[5]

Whether one holds to the view that the internet or digital technology can foster any true sense of community or not, the fact does remain that an eager generation steeped in technological enculturation find relating digitally both liberating and transformative. The Obama campaign used online blogs and photo galleries like Flickr.com to make the campaign and Obama's message personal and interactive. Its aim was to provide a feel of being an active and close member of the campaign, to journey with Obama and the core staff as they moved from phase to phase throughout the election. In addition to online banking pools, supporters were contacted with text messages encouraging them to get out the vote, providing contact information for polling places and help calls. Even well-established online groups like Moveon.org helped raise over $500,000 by appealing to their members.

Moveon.org also developed a program called Endorse-o-thon widgets that promoted an online peer-to-peer endorsement among its members in which individuals were able to dialogue directly with other members to build support one person at a time. This was really a compelling strategy considering that most political campaigning in the last few decades was based primarily on winning key voting blocks and constituent groups. Getting big endorsements was the aim and leveraging major financial contributions from big donors were the foundational strategies. Technology helped Obama to directly connect to his supporters in near real time. So the often hectic and politically volatile news cycle became an ally as Obama's team quickly responded to problems in a corrective yet constructive manner. But his team's ability to create an opportunity of engaging in the political process at multiple levels and in a deeply personal way was not only empowering, it captivated millions.

Technology, in spite of its many limitations, created an opportunity for people to connect and reconnect in ways that were virtually impossible. The capacity to mobilize and organize millions of people in almost real time efficiency was nothing short of amazing. Through this complex matrix of digital relationality, race became a reality but not the central feature in how people related. They were relating based on a common cause, a shared commitment, a shared vision and hope. I would reject the notion that this kind of relating somehow translates into a "post-racial" world experience. On the contrary, race never went anywhere, as it never will. But the fact that people were able to celebrate their differences and appreciate the beautiful tapestry of diversity is what made Obama's election so awe inspiring. It made many of us realize that we may, in fact, hold much more in common than we do different. Technology allowed people the space to share much more about themselves than their racial features.

Through online blogs, chatrooms, YouTube, Flickr, and text messages, they were able to also share their ideas, thoughts, dreams, hopes, fears, and general perspectives in ways that caused them to meet each other as they were—simply human. I do not at all mean to paint a rosy picture of the entire process.

Technology also presented a number of problems. It was also used to spew very dangerous racist venom, myths about Obama's identity, incendiary claims about black people, and what it would mean for Obama to become president.

It is quite evident that Obama has ushered in a new era of what I would call techno-politics. It is a radical engagement with technology in a way that decentralizes power, deemphasizes racial and ethnic difference, and fuses collective consciousness with individual aspiration and desire. Obama's historic campaign for presidency was, indeed, what the online blogger and journalist Soren Dayton called the "Obama Campaign's Tech-Savvy Revolution."[6] Obama was not able to transcend race with his use of technology. At every stage of the campaign, the issue of race was played out in graphic detail online and in the media. What Obama was able to do was to resituate race, not as an obstacle of coalition building, but an asset in constructing a multicultural vision for America. Multiculturalism became a lynchpin toward an ideological construction of hope and change.

Hope and change, in a strange and curious way, became synonymous with multiculturalism and difference. Obama's campaign drew on the Internet as a fundamental space for social networking, community building, and subsequently fundraising as well. Technologists or those who tend to envision a world in which technology plays a crucial role favored Obama 6–1, according to Wired Magazine's Technology Scorecard. While the Republicans used technology only as a way of enhancing their traditional strategies and processes, Obama's campaign viewed technology as a central tool to winning the election and building a multicultural and diverse socioeconomic coalition.

The Internet allowed Obama to "lower the barrier to entry for medium and low-dollar donors" in a way that brought in new voices and energy to the campaign.[7] For decades, many blacks and the youth have felt locked out of the political process in part because much of the attention in political campaigns was directed toward large individual donors and powerful constituent groups. Communication—with donors, volunteers, logistical support persons, and the general public—allowed Obama to connect in real time with all types of constituents in a way that created urgency and reduced anxiety and distance. Obama was able to intervene in an otherwise treacherous and divisive news cycle that could have easily encouraged fragmentation and division among his supporters time and time again. This was certainly the case during the Jeremiah Wright drama played out during the primaries, but repeated over and over again with the constant attacks by the McCain/Palin camp on Obama's racial and religious identity.

Obama wanted to train an army of organizers, who with the support of others through a complex web of cyber connections, could be recruited and take on leadership roles swiftly and efficiently. They could also be empowered to recruit and train others. As Dayton observed, "political organizations grow exponentially when you improve the organizers," which is exactly what Obama was able to do through the use of technology.[8] One of the most important features in Obama's campaign was to use technology to make organizers more effective and efficient at the local level, but connect these individuals and groups to the larger campaign headquarters. In short, technology connected Obama to his organizing base—a base that is incredibly multicultural, socioeconomically diverse, and eager to make a difference.

The Internet favors the "outsider" or the mysterious "other" according to Steve Schifferes of the BBC News.[9] Schifferes argues that part of Obama's dramatic rise to prominence and the groundswell of support came from his use of technology and his willingness to allow others to participate in an organic process of growth and development. Before Obama announced his bid for president in Springfield, Illinois, he already had a fully developed Internet site with plentiful resources available for his supporters. Obama's technological might also translated into economic power. No national campaign has ever been successful without an effective fundraising strategy. In drawing on his rapidly expanding base of supporters, Obama was able to call upon them to give and give again (and again). Because the donations were small, they could continue to give to the campaign, investing in a process that encouraged them to also volunteer in their local communities, with no worries of maxing out on the legal limit of individual donors. Before even announcing his campaign, Obama supporters had generated over 160,000 supporters who were signed up on MySpace, an online networking community.[10] Supporters were also able to make a public statement by joining Obama's facebook network—a social networking site widely used by college and university students across the nation and the world.

What was quite compelling is that Obama, through the use of the Internet, appealed not only to blacks, but to the youth in general (of a broad range of racial, ethnic, and socioeconomic backgrounds). As Harvard University professor Thomas Patterson observed, Obama's use of "social networking" online opportunities helped him surpass Hillary Clinton during the primaries and on to presidential victory in November. Karen Tumulty makes a fascinating observation when she says:

> It's a buzz that Obama is finding new and creative ways to fuel, adapting to a world in which the concept of community has grown to include MySpace and Facebook. No campaign has been more aggressive in tapping into social

networks and leveraging the financial power of hundreds of thousands of small donors. Nor has any other campaign found such innovative ways to extend its reach by using the Internet—more than 10 million of Obama's second quarter contributions were made online, and 90% of them were in increments of $100 or less.[11]

Since less than 20 percent of Americans hold 80 percent of the wealth, the strategy to go after small, yet numerous, donors was nothing short of brilliant. Decentralizing his donor base was in many ways the culmination of a growing trend of community activists to challenge traditional power structures by connecting individuals and communities. Obama recognized that by connecting individuals, neighborhoods, resources, and ideas through technology, he would be able challenge and even overtake those systems of power that had long held sway in American geopolitical spaces. Many of the popular African American websites and blogs like Blackamericaweb.net, Thinkpolitics.com, AfricanAmericanOpinion.com, TheRoot.com, and Netrootsnation.org have been able to mobilize a broad and diverse constituency. Obama's campaign was able to intensify the emergence of a new integrated technological global, economic, and political age where economics, as it courses through digital pulsations, places the battle squarely in the realm of information and exchange of information to the general populous. It is, in short, a battle for the very hearts and minds of the public, with digital information and technology as the chief weapons of choice.

Don Tapscott, author of *The Digital Economy*, offers a dramatic picture of the rapidly changing political dynamics brought into being through the digital age.[12] The new global situation, he observes, is revolutionizing the world economy and politics in America precisely because of the interrelatedness of people and business in America and abroad. The following offers some compelling insights when he writes:

> The economy for the Age of Networked Intelligence is a digital economy. In the old economy, information flow was physical: cash, checks, invoices, bills of lading, reports, face to face meetings, analog telephone calls or radio and television transmission, blueprints, maps, photographs, musical scores, and direct mail advertisements.
>
> In the new economy, information in all its forms becomes digital—reduced to bits stored in computers and racing at the speed of light across networks. Using this binary code of computers, information and communications become digital ones and zeros. The new world of possibilities thereby created is as significant as the invention of language itself, the old paradigm on which all the physically based interactions occurred.[13]

In addition to this new digitally based economic and political system, knowledge becomes as effective as power. In fact, knowledge becomes power because it provides a basis of entrance into the vastly global, multicultural, and multidimensional digital networks. Through networking sites like YouTube, godtube, flickr, Facebook, and others, individuals and groups who have the capacity to inject fresh ideas, as subversive or revolutionary as they might be, are enabled to advance their agendas through progressive and far reaching connections. The radical shift from the industrialized economy spawned at the turn of the twentieth century brought with it the big corporate barons who could easily and readily influence the working class and politicians at all levels. The factories and massive systems of mechanization militated against connections. Connections were dangerous and information was not nearly as important as the equipment and machinery needed to produce and distribute goods. According to Tabscott, "The factory of today is as different from the industrial factory of the old economy as the old factory from the craft production that preceded it."[14] I agree with Tapscott when he observes that networks (multifaceted connections of individuals, groups, ideas, and information) are the foundation of the new digital economic and political age.

Obama was effectively able to tap into this reality and use it as a political force. He drew on the imaginative and fearless energy of a largely youthful (and technically savvy) generation hungry for change and meaning. Who would have thought that the Internet, created by the U.S.-led 1969 Advanced Research Projects Agency (ARPA) by the Department of Defense to be able to exchange information globally, could be used for such dramatic political change? E-mail, which we now know is considered one of the most used and dynamic forms of communication, was considered a minor addition for sharing information among researchers.

Regardless of its origins, now that this digital age is upon us, and now that Obama has clearly demonstrated the massive power of its resources, the political implications are enormous and enduring. Several years ago, the Aspen Institute produced a study that spelled out a number of areas that would promote democratic participation. Some of those areas included: representation, reorganizing, intermediaries, and mutual understanding.[15] Technology has a way of increasing representation because of the ability to connect limitless persons together and engage multiple perspectives and insights in almost real time. Throughout the campaign, David Plouffe and David Axelrod (Obama's chief strategists) sent numerous emails and text messages to communicate with supporters. They also maintained 24-hour web logs, constantly inviting input and contributions from the field. Geographic boundaries, to communicate or strategize, were removed. They could organize coast to coast meetings with ease thanks to virtual tele-presence that allowed the Obama administration to maximize its resources and to continue to inspire and recruit new supporters.

Challenges of Techno-Politics and Race

Obama's willingness to engage technology also comes with many dangers. Kalle Lasn, founder of Adbusters Magazine, joined together with other activists of what he calls a consumer based "postmodern spectacle." In *Culture Jam: How To Reverse America's Suicidal Consumer Binge—And Why We Must*, Lasn makes a very compelling case on why technology and the ways in which it has been co-opted by the massive marketing and corporate industries should be looked upon with suspicion and fear.[16] On the one hand, technology, as Obama has been able to appropriate it, presents an opportunity to resituate politics as a decentralized process that is both multicultural and multidimensional in scope. On the other hand, technology creates the space for near mind control, manipulation, and corruption because what one encounters with technology still arrives through the pulsating portals of electric energy. Information arrives through digital screens, along with a constant and massive bombardment of advertisements—all meant to do nothing but make you and I consume more and more. So the world of reality, of truth, of justice, of hope, is easily blurred with the world of fantasy, sensation, and magic. Throughout the campaign, Obama was repeatedly cast as a "celebrity" and "rock star" by John McCain. The McCain campaign even ran scathing advertisments comparing Obama to Paris Hilton. It would seem that the McCain campaign wanted to manipulate the ways in which the media and pop culture in general has a way of merging the world fantasy and reality to advance political agendas. Lasn describes the problematic dimensions of today's media and consumption-obsessed culture in this way:

> Living inside the postmodern spectacle has changed people. Figuratively, most of us spend the majority of our time in some ethereal place created from fantasy and want. After a while, the hyperreality of this place comes to seem normal. Garishness, volume, glitz, sleazy excess—the American esthetic H. L. Mencken called "the libido of the ugly"—becomes second nature.[17]

The real problem here is that if the sensationalism of the mass media and fragmentation quite typical of a technological age contributed to President Obama's success, then it could also have dire effects on his ability to continue to advance and sustain change and transformation. Lasn has effectively lined the problematic dimensions of technology with consumerism. The relationship between politics and consumerism is as ancient as time. Most of us are quite familiar with the connections between money or economic influence and the political process. After the election, even while Obama was still measuring the curtains in the White House, the Illinois governor Rob Blagojevich was accused by the attorney general of Illinois of selling Obama's senate seat to the highest bidder. It comes as no surprise that the interest of the rich and powerful, because of their stake in the systemic policies of government legislation and activity, remains a central force in how political decisions are made, who gets into office and who stays in.

The interconnectedness of technology (especially related to the media), politics, and economics has received far less attention. Historically, there has been the assumption (which many unfortunately still maintain) that the media, as well as news and information generated through Internet blogs and reporting, is unbiased and legitimate. The emergence of nonstop 24-hour info-tainment has left many puzzled and downright baffled at the competing narratives, almost always ideologically driven, guiding most of what we see, hear, and process. How do you navigate such a pervasive abundance of news and information in a way to make informed decisions as agents in the American political process?

The Media's Love Affair with Obama and Its Political Implications

Since the very beginning, President Obama had a love affair with the media. And the media (including Internet bloggers and progressive online media like the Thehuffingtonpost.com), including news stations such as CNN, MSNBC, CBS, and NBC, had a love affair with Obama as well. His handsome and intelligent presence exuded images of a Hollywood blockbuster star. David Mendell chronicled Obama's rise to prominence as senator of Illinois in the book, *Obama: From Promise to Power*.[18] Obama's message of inclusivity and brotherly compassion, says Mendell, struck a cord with the public. His humble story and optimism made compelling connections with a wide range of people throughout the state and eventually would find appeal across the nation. He observed that "not since the days of Jack and Bobby Kennedy, and their luminous political Camelot, had a politician captured so quickly the imagination of such a broad array of Americans, especially the significant voting bloc of black Americans." Mendell's insights about Obama are very accurate, given the repeated media comparisons between Obama and John F. Kennedy throughout the campaign. Since 2006, Obama drew crowds in the thousands and plastered the covers of major national magazines. David Axelrod, Obama's chief media strategist, was even concerned that his torpedic rise to prominence could be setting him up for a huge and painful fall. Axelrod described that working with Obama was like carrying a priceless piece of porcelain through a crowd of people.[19]

Obama drew heavily on his media persona. He used marketing to package his "brand" as the candidate of change. Marketing, as one of the chief instruments of capitalism to manufacture desire and the need to consume, became Obama's top weapon to project his image, not as an African American, but as an embodiment of the change so desperately called for in the current American political climate. Karen Tumulty of *Time* Magazine said during the beginning of the Obama/McCain presidential campaign, "No campaign has been more aggressive in tapping into social networks and leveraging the financial power of hundreds of thousands of small donors."[20] Obama's campaign was well aware of the tools of marketing and branding strategies and their ability to shape public life and discourse.

The more Obama became popular in the eyes of the public, the more those around him (including David Axelrod and David Plouffe) became protective of his image. In addition to Peter Wynn Thompson of the *New York Times*, Claire Cain Miller also made some compelling observations about Obama winning the nomination early on and subsequently clenching the presidency. Whereas John F. Kennedy was able to seize upon the budding technology of the modern television in the 1960 election, Obama was able to draw on the Internet.[21] In his discussion of politics, in his second autobiographical work, *The Audacity of Hope: Thoughts on Reclaiming the American Dream*, Obama said:

> From the time that I announced my candidacy for the Senate to the end of my first year as a senator, I was the beneficiary of unusually—and at times undeservedly—positive press coverage. No doubt some of this had to do with my status as an underdog in my Senate primary, as well as my novelty as a black candidate with an exotic background. Maybe it also had something to do with my style of communicating, which can be rambling, hesitant, and overly verbose (both my staff and Michelle often remind me of this), but which perhaps finds sympathy in the literary class.[22]

Conclusion

It is clear that even Obama had an awareness of how to use technology and the way he was projected in the media, some of which had to do with his identity as a black American immigrant and gifted orator. He also points out the problematic growth of the partisan nature of the press. The style of what Obama called the "opinion journalism" of trading insults, accusations, gossip. and innuendos speaks to the troubling ways in which information is received and disseminated today. Obama's experience has been in sharp contrast to the traditional portrayals of black males in the media. Earl Ofari Hutchinson so eloquently alluded to the fact, in *The Assassination of the Black Male Image,* that since the days of slavery, black males have been negatively projected as shiftless, lazy, undisciplined, dangerous, and sex crazed. These kinds of depictions, according to Hutchinson, make it much more easy to dismiss or diminish the contributions of black males in American society, and also perpetuate racist policies and practices related to black males in public life (from prisons to educational institutions).

Obama was different. Obama understands that mass media, the Internet and television, as he says, "coarsens the political culture."[23] The sensationalism of today's media culture is meant to fuel conflict, prick the emotions, enrage, and petrify. It is meant to ignite the fires of our deepest fears and unearth our rawest of sensitivities. For this reason, Obama was embroiled in many controversial exchanges, from his links to his former pastor (Jeremiah Wright), speculations of being Muslim and a socialist, undertones of Obama having ties to terrorists, and more. "To make the deadline, to maintain market share and feed the cable news beast, reporters start to move in packs, working off the same news releases, the same set pieces, the same stock figures," says Obama. Indeed, the new interconnectedness of print, online, and visual media speak to both the possibilities and pitfalls of technology and political power.

CHAPTER 8

Obama's Economic Vision and Black America

But the American experiment has worked in large part because we guided the market's invisible hand with a higher principle. A free market was never meant to be a free license to take whatever you can get, however you can get it. That's why we've put in place rules of the road: to make competition fair and open, and honest. We've done this not to stifle but rather to advance prosperity and liberty. As I said at Nasdaq last September, the core of our economic success is the fundamental truth that each American does better when all Americans do better.[1]

There should be little doubt in anyone's mind, naysayers alike, that the Obama presidency has changed American society, and subsequently left an indelible imprint on world politics. Expectations are high for Obama all around the world in terms of the leadership he can provide to take on some of the world's most persistent challenges. Even Desmond Tutu, a huge fan of Obama, extended a word of caution amid all the Obama hype when he said, "Obama too could easily squander the goodwill that his election generated if he disappoints."[2] Tutu expresses how America, in overcoming the travesty of the Bush years, has a lot to make up for. Obama can certainly be a part of restoring that tattered image. As Tutu observed, "Going forward, as we strive to create a stable, prosperous world for all, we need to work together with other nations for justice, equality and peace. We need to believe that the values of fairness and compassion are not only yours and mine; they are shared by all humanity."[3] It would be critical for Obama, and American citizens as a whole, to seize upon Tutu's words in urging the kind of social, political, and economic changes that forge friendships and a deeper sense of community in the world. Obama cannot and will not be able to do it alone. Everyday citizens must continue to be actively involved with the same level of intensity during the campaign if positive, more equitable, social change is to continue to take shape.

The Obama/McCain presidential campaign was as much about the ideological dimensions of the Iraq/Middle East conflict as it was about the potential economic policy shifts from the Bush administration. Perhaps Obama recognizes, as King did a generation ago, that the plight of black folks will only improve when connected to the broader economic realities of poor and working class whites. Their destinies are intertwined. With that in view, I would like to provide the reader with a critical appraisal of the economic vision of the Obama presidency, bringing him in conversation with movements such as the Poor People's Campaign and the persistent problem of poverty in America.

Obama's Bottom-Up Economics, Race, and America

John R. Talbott offered the first serious treatment of Obama's approach to economic issues. Obama's perspective on economics matters, at this moment in history, because it may very well be the first opportunity since King's Poor People's Campaign in the late 1960s to pursue sweeping economic changes on behalf of the poor and working class. Senator John Edwards was the most outspoken in actually calling for an end to poverty in America. Edwards, unlike Obama and Clinton, used the language of "poverty" and called for domestic policies that would directly address the needs of the poor and working poor. Obama, however, did make repeated references to understanding economics from the bottom up. Talbott's book, *Obamanomics: How Bottom-Up Economic Prosperity Will Replace Trickle-Down Economics*, injected a blasting critique of the normative political and economic ideology that has long dominated American domestic and international policy. Talbott illuminates the problem of wealth disparities in America, where "wealthiest Americans live in 20,000+ square foot homes, while millions of Americans are risking losing their homes to foreclosure."[4] Talbott observes how the very rich are living lavish lives of luxury, on private mega boats, sipping champagne, and living the "good life" in the midst of incredible poverty, housing disparities, a declining middle class, and record growths in unemployment. He points out some very gripping statistics: 113 million are victims of chronic illnesses, 47 percent have no health insurance, and nearly 37 million may be facing what sociologist William Julius Wilson calls a permanent underclass.[5]

The American culture of consumerism has led to a world that celebrates uncontrollable and profligate consumption, individualism, and materialism, and at the same time demonizes the poor. The "free market" trickledown economics of John Maynard Keynes and Ronald Reagan has gone unchecked for several decades in spite of mounting trade deficits and an exploding national debt.

The current international trade deficit has reached $700 billion annually. At the same time, the housing crisis has reached epic proportions with the wave of foreclosures in communities across the nation from 2007 to 2009, in addition to an ineffective healthcare policy and stagnating educational system. All of these conditions point to the desperate need for change, a new economic vision that appreciates the creativity and innovation of a free market system, yet affirms some safety nets for the poorest among us as a fundamental core value.

What Talbott points out is that Obama, from the very beginning of his campaign, was not so much concerned about the macroeconomic approaches of his colleagues in the senate or presidential hopefuls of the past, but a more grassroots economic agenda that looks at economic justice for working families as a point of departure. His often-repeated phrase during the campaign centered on attending to the people and institutions on "main street" not just "wall street." On February 13, 2008, Obama gave one of his more prominent economic policy statements before workers at the General Motors Assembly Plant in Janesville, Wisconsin. Here, Obama established in bold language the ways in which the constitution spoke to the ideal that all life has meaning, that every single human being, in spite of socioeconomic status, ought to have a say in the political process. By doing this, Obama was breaking with his predecessors. He was introducing a new economic agenda, disengaging from potential allegiances among America's wealthiest elites and multinational corporation lobbyists with big money and big influences in Washington, D.C. He was intentional about appealing to the masses of poor, working-class Americans.

Obama's main focus in terms of economics, according to Talbott, is "fairness." Obama's reversal of Reagan's mantra by emphasizing "bottom-up" economics underscores Obama's concern for the working class. As Talbott observes, "The power of bottom-up economics . . . is that it is an economically just system that encourages everyone to work hard, to educate themselves, and to be their most productive, because it fairly rewards those who do so."[6] He suggests that "a white man, a black man, a woman, an Arab, a Jew, a Muslim, and yes, even a poor person, all have the same opportunities, and thus all are equally motivated to excel, because they know the system will treat them fairly and reward their hard work and effort."[7]

Obama and the Unfinished Work of the Poor People's Campaign

Of course, Obama's economic sensitivities are not new. He is drawing from a long line of African American political leaders who have been committed to elevating the plight of the poor in mainstream debate. Although Obama did not explicitly speak to the issue of poverty in his campaign, his policies reflect strong commitments to making life better for the nation's poor and working poor. Specifically, the Obama campaign affirmed the need to take a comprehensive approach to ending poverty, including creating new jobs, rehauling social security, establishing some form of universal healthcare, investing in early childhood education, and reforming housing. In a sense, his economic policy agenda conjures up thoughts of King's vision of economic justice. Martin Luther King Jr., especially toward the end of his life, fought to inject new meaning into economic justice in America. He moved progressively from a civil rights agenda to its connectedness to economics and labor issues. Before his assassination in Memphis, Tennessee on April 4, 1968, King was organizing in support of better working and economic conditions for sanitation workers. He was simultaneously planning his most aggressive and confrontational protest with the Poor People's Campaign. He believed that lives of the poor in America would never improve unless there was a total transformation of the economic situation of American society. He recognized that capitalism, as traditionally conceived and practiced, was fundamentally flawed and intrinsically bankrupt.

The core mission of the Poor People's Campaign was to establish, in bold and unapologetic terms, a "Bill of Rights" for the poor. The initiative lost traction after King's tragic death, but the idea remains the most powerful ever conceived in the American prophetic imagination. In the mid-1960s, King began to aggressively shift his attention from Civil Rights and Voting Rights to the broader question of human rights and poverty. He began to realize with dangerous precision that poverty stood as one of the greatest obstacles to realizing the beloved community. In 1964, King published his first proposal calling for a "Bill of Rights for the Disadvantaged." Racism, he said, was a tenacious evil, but not immutable. He saw something happening on the horizon among both poor whites and poor blacks in the South and across the country. As he wrote, "White supremacy can feed their egos but not their stomachs. They will not go hungry or forego the affluent society to remain racially ascendant."[8] He also declared:

> The curse of poverty has no justification in our age. It is socially as cruel and blind as the practice of cannibalism at the dawn of civilization, when men ate each other because they had not yet learned to take food from the soil or to consume the abundant animal life around them. The time has come for us to civilize ourselves by the total, direct and immediate abolition of poverty.[9]

After winning the Nobel Prize in November 1964, King began exploring northern cities like Chicago, New York, Boston, Detroit, Cleveland, and

Philadelphia. The words of his acceptance speech were still lingering in his mind when he said:

> I have the audacity to believe that peoples everywhere can have three meals a day for their bodies, education and culture for their minds, and dignity, equality and freedom for their spirits. I believe that what self centered men have torn down men other-centered can build up. I still believe that one day mankind will bow before the altars of God and be crowned triumphant over war and bloodshed, and nonviolent redemptive good will will proclaim the rule of the land.[10]

Although there is very little evidence that Obama has sought to draw on King's radical vision of the Poor People's Campaign as a source of inspiration or strategic insights for his policy agenda, the similarities are quite apparent and compelling. Early on in his presidency, in February 2009, Obama had to past "swiftly and boldly" his economic plan to rebuild the American economy. He took a very different approach than his predecessor. Perhaps Obama recognizes, as King did more than forty years ago that the destiny of black folks in America is wrapped up in the plight of all poor people in the country and the world. Perhaps Obama sees that unless he helps to advance policies for all persons on the bottom, then black Americans will continue to be economically disenfranchised and politically excluded. In addition to providing support for the struggling financial banking industries and major U.S. corporations like General Motors, Chrysler, and Chevy, Obama was also deeply attentive to the poor and working class. He has vehemently challenged the outdated presuppositions of "free market economy" ideologies, exchanging it for an economic vision for the common good. In his work on the Southside of Chicago, Obama has no doubt seen the painful pitfalls of free-market capitalism as did King toward the final days of his life. Claude McKay's wonderful poem "A Capitalist at Dinner" offers a dramatic image of the insidious problems of Americanized capitalism as traditionally conceived. As McKay observes:

> An ugly figure, heavy, overfed,
> —Settles uneasily into a chair;
> Nervously he mops his pimply pink bald head,
> Frowns at the fawning waiter standing near.
> The entire service tries its best to please
> This overpampered piece of broken-health,
> Who sits there thoughtless, querulous, obese,
> Wrapped in his sordid visions of vast wealth.

> Great God! if creatures like this money-fool,
> Who hold the service of mankind so cheap,
> Over the people must forever rule,
> Driving them at their will like helpless sheep—
> Then let proud mothers cease from giving birth;
> Let human beings perish from the earth.[11]

Why Capitalism Does Not Work for Poor Blacks

The classical problem with capitalism is that it does not account for those perishing souls who do not have the means to participate in the capitalist process. All these souls have to offer up, as Karl Marx observed, is their fledging bodies that continue to be a source of exploitation and manipulation in the quest for increased profits. As I inferred in the previous chapter, economics (and Obama's economic philosophy in general) will play a pivotal role in the Obama administration. The critical question is: what is the nature of his economic philosophy and what impact will it have on Black America in particular?

Black leaders, historically, have always critiqued and celebrated, both at once, the American capitalistic imagination. On the one hand, black leaders have reflected the black desire for material wealth and prosperity, modeled on the lifestyles of their majority white kindred. On the other hand, black leaders have decried the oppressive nature of capitalistic exploitation of black labor, the inability of upward mobility in high level management and corporate ownership. Du Bois, as early as the turn of the century, observed the challenges of black life in navigating the "Veil" or gap between the world of black consciousness and white America. Du Bois knew all too well that capitalism historically has roots profoundly embedded in America's slave past. In the blood-drenched fields of wealth and prosperity among many of the wealthiest Americans are investments, generational inheritances that were built on the backbones of enslaved Africans. A failure to recognize the connections between wealth and America's political might today apart from the great cornerstones of slavery would mean to obfuscate America's responsibility to all those on the bottom (the laborers, nannies, sanitation workers, nurses, police officers, and farmers) who continue to sustain the American and world economy.

Randall Robinson has written prophetically about searing connections between politics, the American economy, and the history of slavery. In both of his books, *The Debt* and *Quitting America*, he raises the controversial and imperative concern that America and the global economic superpowers in general have a debt—economically and politically—to pay to America's predominately poor blacks. He also demonstrates how poor blacks in America are simply examples of how the wealthy elite (and the current capitalistic structures that sustain their existence) have ignored and exploited the poor of the world to gain more wealth and centralized political power.

Robinson repeatedly argued that U.S. wealth was a product of the common wealth. For decades, politicians have ignored the economic and political plight of black folks, not only in America but across the African diaspora. The economic policies of the World Bank, G8 (world's wealthiest eight nations), the International Monetary Fund and other global institutions have virtually excluded the voices and interest of blacks. When one considers the desperate conditions of many inner-city African American communities, Robinson's claims have dramatic appeal. Since the decline of American industrialization beginning in the late 1960s, global trade grew more prominent as corporations looked for cheaper products and labor in overseas postcolonial markets.

In the radical shift from industrialization to information technology, the U.S. government, working in partnership with American corporations, abandoned the cities, leaving many to die in their own sea of hopelessness and despair. Factories and shops closed down permanently in cities like Flint, Michigan; Buffalo, New York; Camden, New Jersey; and East Saint Louis, Missouri. The unfortunate aftermath was painfully depressed neighborhoods, deteriorating schools, and an emergence of a secondary labor market in drug culture and gang life. Needless to say, given the fact that Obama was very active on the south side of Chicago as a community organizer, he was well aware of the social and economic (systemic) dynamics concerning black poverty in the city.

Obama's resounding refrain throughout the campaign, in suggesting that Wall Street cannot thrive without the flourishing of Main Street, asserts a major critique of free market capitalism, which is what many activists and social critics have been saying for years. According to Talbott, Obama understands all too well that the markets have little regard for the poor because they do not have the capital to inject economic influence.[12] The market, as an economic system, only respects more and more capital. More capital means more power. The market is not, nor can it ever be, moral in and of itself. It requires moral people of goodwill; it involves the character and compassion of a neighbor to institute regulatory processes, protect the poor, and create conditions for human flourishing even among the weakest and most vulnerable.

Transforming the market place will be a real challenge for the Obama administration. The plight of black folks hinges on his success. His communal sensitivities were very prominent in his speeches and economic policy statements. Although he rarely explicitly names his concern for black folks in his economic policy agenda, it comes through abundantly clear that Obama seems deeply committed to serving the interest of the poor, even as he recognizes that these conditions affect people of all races and ethnicities. During the October 2008 Presidential Debates on the campus of Belmont College in Nashville, Tennessee, Obama made reference to his mother dying of cancer at the hospital while still having to argue with insurance companies about the procedures. He also referred to his family's history with food stamps and public assistance.

Because African Americans absorb less than half of 1 percent of the nation's wealth, Obama's economic plan, as it relates to poverty, must be front and center in evaluating his economic vision for America. As Douglas S. Massey and Nancy A. Denton surmised in *American Apartheid: Segregation and the Making of the Underclass*, the persistent reality of segregated communities in America has reinforced conditions of ghettoization, discriminatory practices, and economic exploitation at all levels. Racial segregation in housing practices continues to sustain disparities in wealth and income along racial lines. According to Massey and Denton, it is precisely because of the history of segregation and its ongoing legacy that we still see the pervasive maintenance of the black underclass, or communities in a perpetual state of poverty, struggle, and survival. Residential segregation, they write, "is the principal organizational feature of American society that is responsible for the creation of the urban underclass."[13] Segregated neighborhoods are often falsely perceived as a function of individual economic choices. However, a closer analysis reveals, as Massey and Denton show, that whenever there are slightly increased levels of poverty among residentially segregated groups, there is an automatic geographical increase in the concentration of poverty in a given area. It subsequently affects property values, access to needed resources, and public transportation. Through his campaign, Obama touted that his economic plan would center on three areas: a tax cut for working families, tax relief for small businesses and startups, and advancing (not free trade) but fair trade. Obama and Joe Biden said that if elected they would provide tax cuts for 95 percent of "working Americans," while pushing for capital gains taxes for businesses and opening up foreign markets in a way that is equitable for all parties involved. He certainly broadcasted a very powerful and sweeping economic vision, but rarely directly engaged the issue of poverty as did his former presidential opponent, John Edwards. Perhaps this was sophisticated political maneuvering on behalf of Obama, recognizing that he most likely would not get elected if he talked about the poor a bit too much. Or perhaps, as many sociologists have observed over the years, in spite of how poor Americans might be, there is a propensity to want to identify with the language of the "middle class," representing values of hard work, traditional family life, home ownership, and a tendency to identify with the Judeo-Christian tradition.

In either case, it is quite clear that the issue of poverty, both in urban centers as well as in rural settings, is one of the most pressing matters affecting black life across the nation. Out of poverty springs a well of other debilitating concerns in the black community: from gang violence, deteriorating schools, depressed economic communities, poor housing, and fracturing of general family life. As William Julius Wilson observed in both *The Declining Significance of Race* and *When Work Disappears*, economic hardships in predominately black communities is coming perilously close to establishing a permanent "underclass" in America—which is largely black, hopeless, desperate, and crying out for help. Even Obama reflected some deep sense of insight when he said that in many of the nation's urban cities, quiet rebellions are brewing. Obama must be aware that in many black communities across the nation, survival is all that matters. The depth of poverty, exacerbated by the renewed interest in urban gentrification, is being felt in an enormous way.

While the language of middle class is a wonderful political slogan that holds broad and enduring appeal for Americans, the problem of poverty (where individuals and families do not have access to even the most basic of human needs) is literally a matter of life and death. The heart of Obama's plan for confronting poverty is job creation. He has maintained that sustaining and building jobs must be the fulcrum upon which all other economic matters are addressed. He is wise enough to understand, as well, that issues of war, education, healthcare, and housing are all profoundly interrelated. For instance, the billions of dollars, which have been and continue to be spent in Iraq and Afghanistan, could be directed to infrastructural development in America: to build roads, bridges, update schools, and expand transportation systems.

Obama's Response to Poverty

On paper, Obama's economic plan to "combat poverty" is very compelling. Recognizing that more than 37 million Americans are in poverty, Obama sees work as the answer to many of the woes affecting the poor. Because Obama has been very careful not to particularly address the issue of poverty among African Americans, it is difficult to get a sense of how he will respond to the complex interrelatedness of poverty and racism in America. Job creation in America does not always translate into jobs for African

Americans. In fact, African Americans usually end up claiming the short end of the stick primarily because the systems and structures in the housing market tend to reflect deep racial disparities that undermine black progress. In *Black Wealth/White Wealth*, Massey and Denton offer some reflections on the nature of economic disparities and their causes. These are incredibly important factors in advancing any economic agenda. Black folks, historically, have been the last hired and first fired. It is systematically true that blacks with equal education and experience as their white counterparts are paid less and are much less likely to be hired for the same jobs. So, I am not convinced that job creation alone will somehow help end the nightmare of black poverty in America. Obama must go further by dealing with the systemic ills of racism intrinsic to the very fabric of economic life in America.

Here is a brief summary of some of Obama's strategies for dealing with the issue of poverty:

> Help Americans Grab a Hold of and Climb the Job Ladder: Obama and Biden will invest $1 billion over five years in transitional jobs and career pathway programs that implement proven methods of helping low-income Americans succeed in the workforce.
>
> Create a Green Jobs Corps: Obama and Biden will create a program to directly engage disadvantaged youth in energy efficiency opportunities to strengthen their communities, while also providing them with practical skills in this important high-growth career field.
>
> Improve Transportation access to Jobs: As president, Obama will work to ensure that low-income Americans have transportation access to jobs. Obama will double funding for their federal Jobs Access and Reverse Commute program to ensure that additional federal public transportation dollars flow to the highest-need communities and that urban planning initiatives take this aspect of transportation policy into account.
>
> Reduce Crime Recidivism by Providing Ex-Offender Supports: Obama and Biden will work to ensure that ex-offenders have access to job training, substance abuse and mental health counseling, and employment opportunities. Obama and Biden will also create a prison-to-work incentive program and reduce barriers to employment.[14]

What Obama offered throughout much of his campaign and continues to offer are promising possibilities for ending the cycle of poverty in such a wealthy country as the United States. These initiatives, if his administration does in fact follow through with them, could have a significant impact on working-class families nationwide. On the one hand, what is good for the nation as a whole is good for black folks. Black people will no doubt benefit greatly from the symbolic and political nature of Obama's administration. As the first black president, African Americans from coast to coast can boast of a new badge of cultural pride, knowing that from their ranks a president was born. The ancestors are rejoicing and the elders are bursting with pride. They celebrate the Obama administration as a testimony to those brave resisters during the abolitionist movement, the cultural architects of reconstruction and the early twentieth century, and the magnificent freedom fighters of the Civil Rights Movement. Obama's mere presence in the White House will shine new light on the plight of black folks in America and throughout the African diaspora. The world will be invited to look upon black folks in America and throughout the world in a different light. They will, in some ways, be forced to acknowledge the genius and potentiality of blackness in the world.

On the other hand, black people in America and the diaspora have particular issues rooted in a history of slavery, colonialism, and racial struggle. Addressing the economic situation for black people will also require a particular response. For instance, the problem of HIV/AIDS among black populations in America, Africa, Brazil, and the Caribbean has been largely linked to poverty. The magnitude of poverty felt by many African descendants across the globe is unparalleled in human history. So, Obama will need a progressive and intentional plan for responding to the needs of African Americans around issues of housing, education, incarceration, healthcare, and employment. Of course, Black Americans do share in common many of the same social ills as other Americans. However, given the historical, economic, and political system, deeply engrained with racist meaning and practices, Obama will need to do more than what Bill Clinton attempted to do with his Commission on Race. Clinton's Commission on Race reported that while racism in America has declined, the reality of white privilege still remains. What Clinton's commission failed to do was to speak plainly and openly about the persistence of racism, its implications for Black suffering, and what it will take to move beyond the nightmare to the dream.

Speaking of Obama's plan for the economy, the CEO and Chairman of Berkshire Hathaway, Inc., Warren Buffett, said, "I believe that Barack Obama has the right understanding of the fundamental challenges we face and the right vision for where we need to go as a nation. When my secretary pays taxes at a higher rate than I do, it's clear we need to restore that sense of fairness to our economy that allows all Americans a chance at the American Dream."[15] Buffett, as America's most prominent billionaire, shines light on these searing disparities. The problem is quite clear. The question remains of how Obama will respond and whether he will attend to the particular needs and concerns of Black folks. Indeed, there will be challenges if Obama does not continually link the economic needs of Black Americans with all Americans. He must forever resist being tainted as "too black," or as someone who could be perceived as playing "favorites" when it comes to black people. Obama may recognize, as Martin Luther King did toward the end of his life, that transforming the economic plight of Black folks in America must be connected to the broader, systemic issues of poverty caused by the very system of capitalism itself. Toward the end of his life, beginning in 1966 with Operation Bread Basket in Chicago, King understood that poverty in America was the real enemy of human flourishing. He argued that racism and militarism (twin evils) were divisive tools that perpetuated the suppression and suffering of poor people around the world for the benefit of the elite wealthy few.

There has always been a struggle within the black experience over how best to approach economic and social change. Obama stands squarely in this tradition. His grounding in community organizing is firmly rooted in the history of the black freedom struggle, as expressed in the lives of individuals like Sojourner Truth, Henry Highland Garnett, Frederick Douglas, Booker T. Washington, W. E. B. Du Bois, A. Philip Randolph, Martin Luther King Jr., Joseph H. Jackson, Adam Clayton Powell, and many others. The problem has always centered on how best to bring about the change needed. Changes, nevertheless, were imperative and inevitable, given the continual outcry of destitution. Black leaders have long since recognized the interconnectedness of poverty, politics, and race in America. Labor relations, social service benefits, housing reform, and healthcare were never apolitical or colorblind concerns. They were always laded with racial messages, themes, and innuendos. What many black leaders, historically, were able to do was to unveil the nakedness of racial politics and its impact on black poverty.

According to Peter Paris in *Black Leaders in Conflict*, during the time of his assassination in Memphis, Tennessee, in 1968, King was planning the Poor People's Campaign. King had a very dialectical and integrative mind. He saw connections others were not able to see. Even during the Montgomery Bus Boycott in 1955 and 1956, King voiced the connections between racial segregation and black poverty. As Paris assesses, "Segregation, he believed, deprived Blacks not only of their civil and political rights but also of the opportunity to acquire economic security."[16] Paris goes on to suggest that "early in his life, he was bewildered by the affluence of the few and the poverty of the many. Although he never became a Marxist, his study of Marxism caused him to see the dangerous problems inherent in traditional capitalism."[17]

King expressed his reading of Marx, and in many ways the feeling of many black people in America during the time, with the following:

> My reading of Marx also convinced me that truth is found neither in Marxism nor in traditional capitalism. Each represents a partial truth. Historically capitalism failed to see the truth in individual enterprise. Nineteenth-century capitalism failed to see that life is social and Marxism failed and still fails to see that life is individual and personal. The Kingdom of God is neither the thesis of individual enterprise nor the antithesis of collective enterprise, but a synthesis which reconciles the truths of both.[18]

Obama seems to hold a common view as King, though there is little evidence that Obama had any exposure to dialecticalism in his development. During his days as president of the Harvard Law Review, Obama was known by his peers as a consensus builder. He had a way of bringing, and keeping, people together. When it comes to economics, however, Obama will surely have his hands full. The gross disparities in our country are so overwhelming that they are even leading to crumbling financial markets across the world. Millions of Americans who have been living off of debt for years are now topped off. They no longer have the capacity to sustain the kind of debt and consumerism that they have grown accustomed to and that the financial markets have build their industries upon.

Andrew Hacker, author of the bestselling book *Two Nations: Black and White, Separate, Hostile, Unequal,* argues very persuasively that the societal disparities we see in America, to which Obama will have to respond, come from a fundamental flaw in the economic systems that order American society.[19] Hacker argues that every year over $4 trillion changes hands and gets introduced into the U.S. economy. The question, says Hacker, is not whether money is available. Indeed, wealth and money are plentiful in our society. The question is: who gets it? What kinds of economic philosophies inform how money is allocated, which programs get funded, who regulates these funds, and how are they regulated, if at all? From Franklin Roosevelt's New Deal, Lyndon Johnson's Great Society, and Ronald Reagan's supply side credo of "trickle-down economics," the role of policy and politics has been irreducible to shaping a culture that leaves millions hungry, broke, and destitute, while others sip champagne in mansions, secluded gated communities, and yacht clubs. James Madison, described by some as the father of the Constitution, wrote The Federalist Papers, a series of papers around the time of the American Revolution, where he emphasized capitalism and private enterprise as most consistent with human nature. He thought that unbridled capitalism and celebrating private enterprise would provide the space for human innovation and creativity in a way that honors the many gifts and insights within a given society. The real problem with the kind of Madisonian understanding of capitalism, as Hacker rightly points out, is that it assumes there are persons within a given society that hold the "faculties of acquiring property" and are therefore inherently entitled to their wealth and elite social status.[20] Their perception of wealth in American society, drawing on the likes of Madison and Adam Smith, is that the rich somehow deserve to be rich (perhaps because of their skills, talents, education, or abilities).

Conversely, the poor deserve their plight as well, according to this position, making it that much easier to justify their impoverished conditions. As Hacker observes, "his reasoning, simply, was that the good fortune of the nation depends on the prosperity of its business community." He also argues that Madison viewed the nation as divided into a rigid line of "those who hold and those who are without property."[21] By property, Madison was speaking about those who owned more than the usual possessions of a personal home and some land. He was referring to large business owners, those who controlled the means of production, factories, commercial farming, and the like. Throughout the campaign, John McCain referred to himself and his position repeatedly as "federalist." Very few media outlets picked up on this very controversial position, which essentially walks directly in the paths of Madison and Adam Smith. Going all the way back to the founding of the constitution, federalists were those who supported a strong centralized government. However, McCain's use of the term conflicts with its historical meaning. On the one hand, McCain would say, "I am a federalist," while at the same time he pushed for more regional autonomy and state rights. For McCain, the Constitution simply issues a license for individual states to do as they wish in accordance with its citizenry. In this sense, a strong federal government simply ensures the capacity for individual states to determine their own realities. This perspective seems to be in total contradiction with how the term has been historically understood. McCain's perspective has also come to reflect some of the most conservative views on justifying free market capitalism, even at the expense of the nation (and the world's) poor.

Conclusion

The paradoxical situation Obama now finds himself in is between a capitalistic economic system that allows for the few to absorb the vast majority of societal wealth and his socialist sensibilities that affirms care and concern for all citizens. Obama's critics accused him of wishing to advance socialism because of his call for "bottom-up" economics. It has yet to be revealed what Obama's "bottom-up" economic agenda will look like, but one cannot deny the significance of this position, its resemblance to Karl Marx's conception of socialism and communism, and the economic dimensions of King's vision of the beloved community. The fact is that for poor people, socialism (in general) doesn't look so bad. It speaks to the deep and abiding concern that the needs of the poor, the worker, the disabled, and marginalized of American society be addressed. Hacker's assessment of Karl Marx is helpful as we think about what Obama's economic vision might mean for Black America. He writes:

> His theories of socialisms and communism aside—witness the demise of regimes bearing his name—Marx's insights into market economies still inform our thinking . . . he stressed that the pursuit of profits depends on new technologies. Thus the leading players in the capitalist drama are entrepreneurs and engineers. It is their interplay that shapes the configuration of classes, determining the distribution of income and the contours of careers.
>
> This system, [says Marx] "cannot exist without constantly revolutionizing the instruments of production, and with them the whole relations of society."[22]

Marx's analysis was right on target, especially when we think about today's rapidly intensifying consumer culture in which black people seem to be the primary targets. Urban centers are inundated with advertisements bent on getting black people to consume more and more. Although blacks do have the spending power, their debt/credit ratio is more problematic than any other group. What Obama must address is both the culture of consumption we have come to know, and upon which the U.S. economy is built, and the oppressive conditions that make the extreme disparities in wealth possible.

CHAPTER 9

Why Obama's Presidency Will Change the World

Even so is the hope that sang in the songs of my fathers well sung. If somewhere in this whirl and chaos of things there dwells Eternal Good, pitiful yet masterful, then anon in His good time America shall rend the Veil and the prisoned shall go free. Free, free as the sunshine trickling down the morning into these high windows of mine, free as yonder fresh young voices welling up to me from the caverns of brick and mortar below—swelling with song, instinct with life, tremulous treble and darkening bass. My children, my little children, are singing to the sunshine, and thus they sing:

Let us cheer the weary traveler . . . Cheer the weary traveler; Let us cheer the weary traveler A long the heavenly way.[1]

There is a kind of weariness in the midst of hopeful desperation sweeping across the face of humanity. Things cannot go on as they have been in the past decades. Human poverty and deprivation is intensifying, the environment is in a tailspin out of control, and countries are more fragmented than ever before. The human soul, as Langston Hughes once wrote, has "grown deep like the rivers." The human soul seems to be growing weak, drowning in a turbulent sea of suffering with no rafts to be found. Something strange is happening on this lonely little planet. In this chapter I want to survey what Obama's presidency means for the international community, its hopes and fears, as well as the challenges he will face in the process. Obama's interaction with the international community is also metaphoric of how every American must contend with issues of difference and otherness in our time. No longer can Americans, black or white, rich or poor, male or female, afford to retreat into silos of isolation and exclusivism. Their world of difference is in our midst more than ever before. Whether in small towns, mega cities or the suburbs, each of us are now interacting and relating to peoples and cultures from across the globe. Obama's life experience is an example of the difference embodied in each of us. So the question is not whether or not we must address issues of difference, the question is how individuals and the public responds to and practices difference. This chapter also focuses on Obama's presidential campaign, his presidency, and what it means for a global world of difference and its ramifications for domestic and especially international policy.

I called my doctoral dissertation advisor just days after Obama had clinched the Democratic nomination and was eager to get his thoughts. While strolling across a golf course in Wilmington, North Carolina, he simply said, "I see King all over him." As one who served as a student activist during the Civil Rights Movement and experienced firsthand a number of speeches by King, he was implying a kind of historical continuity between King and Obama in proclaiming a language of unity, equality, and social harmony in a way which transcends barriers of race, class, and ideology. As I argue in this chapter, the Obama presidency makes little sense and finds modest historical merit apart from King and the Civil Rights Movement, and Du Bois's theory of the color line in America. Looking at Obama's place in the continuing unfolding of racial politics in America, I chart a course on the prospects and limitations of his presidency in light of Martin Luther King's dream and vision of racial progress. Langston Hughes's poem speaks well on this growing sentiment and need for change, felt not only by black people but by much of the world as well:

> I've known rivers:
> I've known rivers ancient as the world and older than the
> flow of human blood in human veins.
> My soul has grown deep like the rivers.[2]

What Obama's Presidency Could Mean for All of Us

However Obama's presidency plays itself out, whether he experiences a successful presidency with high approval ratings throughout or not, the fact is that the political process in the nation will never be the same after his inauguration. Like the signing of the Emancipation Proclamation, the *Brown v. Board* Supreme Court ruling, the March on Washington, and Reagan's famous immortal speech to tear down the Berlin wall, a fundamental paradigmatic shift has taken place in the American geopolitical theater. So the question really concerns what it means for all Americans in our times and in the years to come. Blacks, whites, Asian Americans, Latino/Latinos, Native Americans, immigrants, all others will be affected by in a number of ways. One of those ways relates to a shift in perceptions toward minority communities and their capacity for top leadership. At first glance, this sounds like an incredibly overly optimistic claim about Obama's administration. After all, he still belongs to a massive, historic, and powerful political machinery of which he is beholden to as he seeks to reform it from within. But there is a sense in which his mere presence causes us to rethink what it means to be "American" and that ownership of the American constitutional promises doesn't just belong to good gun toting white folks, but to all Americans, perhaps even to those who desire to share in its future and treasures.

The Power of Hope

It is important to talk about why hope, as a religious, political, and social construct, has meaning for each person's capacity to bring about change in local spaces, from family life to public policy. The idea of "hope" is not new, but must always be recontextualized in every generation. Obama has been able to capture the essence of what hope may mean in today's era of war, global ecological crisis, poverty, terrorism, and nuclear proliferation.

This is a conversation that has been going on since the beginning of the Obama campaign. We now have occasion to reflect seriously on both the challenges and promises of Obama's election when it comes to the persistent reality of race and racism in America. Racism is still, of course, alive and well. But what the election does tell us is that the way we think about race in America has forever changed. Perhaps blacks, in general, will not be nearly as suspicious about whites, viewing them categorically as merely an extension of a racist past. Whites might be able, through the gifted leadership of Obama, to see black people as human, embodying the same dreams, hopes, and aspirations as them. Or perhaps the demons of racism, fear, and hatred will reappear, regroup, and react in more insidious ways, invoking the kind of white backlash not seen since the later years of the Civil Rights Movement during the rise of Black consciousness and youth rebellion.

Even as the Obama administration has become fully engaged with its domestic and international policy agenda, I find it rather daunting that after centuries of racial turmoil in America, many mainstream politicians, religious leaders, and academics have yet to make critical connections between the brutal history of racism in this country and foreign policy impacting black and brown peoples of the world. There seems to be a pervasive desire to forget those historical atrocities like genocide of Native Americans, the slave trade, Hiroshima and Nagasaki, segregation, lynching, and most recently the atrocities of a post-hurricane Katrina debacle.

The Obama presidency holds exciting possibilities precisely because he may bring sensitivities about race and the ways in which racial attitudes are infused in the formation of policies and practices. Even with the greatness of Abraham Lincoln, America has never experienced this kind of leadership. We do not yet know how Obama will engage policy with an awareness of race and racism. We do hope that as an African American, with an African American wife and African American children, he will bring to his leadership an awareness of how race has shaped the U.S. policy agenda. His pragmatic approach is very appealing and I think will be well received. It will also, perhaps, lead to new conversations about policies that are grounded not in white supremacist nationalistic ideologies, but in sound thinking and wisdom.

The connection between America's history with racism and its foreign policy has been overlooked for far too long. The nation's approach and dealings with other nation-states is often mediated through the lens of false notions of superiority and imperialistic ideals. Those devising and implementing both foreign and domestic policy have been conditioned in a eurocentric culture that has historically viewed whiteness as divinity and blackness as its negation or that which is antiwhite, antigood, antihuman. As the country heads towards the general elections, particularly the Democratic convention, the real test for "redeeming the soul of America" begins.

During his presidency, Obama will have the opportunity to push forth sweeping changes related to the environment, terrorism, technology, global poverty, militarism, and social and political conflicts across the world. Indeed, he will have his work cut out for him. The problems facing the globe are staggering. Bob Goudzwaard, Mark Vander Vennen, and David Van Heemst in their groundbreaking book, *Hope In Troubled Times*, offer perhaps the most in-depth and comprehensive treatment of the crises facing the world to date.[3] These thinkers recognize that the problems are interrelated, vast, and localized all at once. No longer can local communities and even small towns like Vidalia, Georgia; Louisville, Kentucky; Baton Rouge, Louisiana; Wilmette, Illinois; and the like ignore what is happening in the larger global context. Though the implications are local, the problems we face are global and will require global solutions. According to Goudzwaard, Vennen, and Heemst, the insidious impact of greenhouse gases in the atmosphere, along with the uncontrollable advances in technology, seems to be leading the world on a collision course with catastrophe. The 2005 report by the United Nations, "Millennium Ecosystem Assessment," made it very clear that many of the most significant large natural ecosystems are close to collapsing.[4]

These are systems that furnish natural resources and habitats that supply food, oxygen, water, and material resources throughout the world. The United Nations report does, however, point to human agency as both the culprit and the hope for redemption. The study argues that "it lies within the power of human society to ease the strains we are putting on the natural resources of the planet."[5] Sir Martin Rees in *Our Final Century: Will Civilization Survive the Twenty-first Century?* raises the provocative concern that human technological development is far outpacing human moral development. His words are illustrative of the magnitude of the problems facing not only black people but all of humanity:

> Science is advancing faster than ever, and on a broader front: bio-, cyber-, and nanotechnology all offer exhilarating prospects; so does the exploration of space. But there is a dark side: new science can have unintended consequences; it empowers individuals to perpetuate acts of megaterror; even innocent errors could be catastrophic. The "downside" of twenty-first century technology could be graver and more intractable than the threat of a nuclear devastation that we have faced for decades . . . humanity is more at risk than at any earlier phase in history.[6]

Rees' observations, with the pitfalls of twentieth-century nuclear warfare, point to the gravity of the situation. Martin Luther King Jr.'s *Where Do We Go From Here: Chaos or Community* made a similar claim by saying, "Either we will learn to live together as brothers or perish as fools." King understood, like Rees, that unless human beings and government institutions that serve human societies channel their technological advances to the flourishing of all human life, all of us are doomed. Obama's global experiences seem to have taught him a wise lesson as a leader that humans, regardless of their socioeconomic and political context, have some of the same basic fundamental needs and hopes for the future. It is often the loss of understanding that inflames hostilities and fears toward others that leads to the kinds of tragic death of innocents seen in previous wars and natural disasters.

The Italian philosopher Gianni Vattimo expressed in his book *The End of Modernity* that the perception of progress now appears through the guise of technological advances. Especially in American society, the public is constantly given messages that with the introduction of every new technological gadget (IPod, cell phone, super thin laptop, plasma television, sleek appliances or tools), human social and moral progress is being made. It is as if using new technology makes you a better person. Clearly, that is not the case. On the contrary, the danger imminent in this escalation of new technology is precisely because human beings are so prone to destructive, abusive, and exploitative behavior. As Cornel West has so rightly observed, what we are now seeing is a profound sense of nihilism (hopelessness) setting in. The meaninglessness of technological advances, innovation, and consumption when detached from human flourishing leads only to a continuum of hopelessness and despair. In addition to Vattimo's work, books such as *The End of History, The End of Ideology, The End of Faith, The End of Nature,* and *The End of Science,* as well as apocalyptic movies such as *The Matrix Trilogy, Lord of the Rings, The Day After Tomorrow,* and the *Day the Earth Stood Still,* all point to the current human fascination and bewilderment with nonexistence.[7] What is, in fact, the meaning of life and why is it worth living? Rick Warren, pastor of the popular Saddleback Church in California, tried to address this question in his book, *The Purpose Driven Life.* Though his book leaves much to be desired in terms of theological substance and social analysis, he does tap into some of the most basic human yearnings—the meaning and purpose to our existence. But that does not mean one needs to fear or be ambivalent about innovation. Innovation, while being celebrated, needs to be managed, regulated, and monitored for the common good, and put to the service of promoting human freedom and community for all.

The fact that corporations and even governments have been reluctant to put technology to the service of ending poverty is another graphic example of human neglect in the face of amazing technological growth. Since 2005, leaders of the Millennium Project sought to at least provide basic education for all children, cut child and maternal mortality rates, and reverse the spread of HIV/AIDS and malaria.[8] Government leaders from 189 countries in the year 2000 agreed to these goals, but little progress has been made precisely because the wealthiest nations have been slow in their response and support of the initiative. Jeffrey Sachs has argued that the wealthiest countries, including the United States, must "increase their development assistance to 0.7 percent of their gross national product (GNP)."[9] What these problems translate into is a problem of political will. In the last three decades, U.S. politics has been especially dominated by corporate interests with very little regard for the poor and marginalized. Urban centers which once based good-paying factory jobs for many inner-city black families dried up like the desert in the late 1960s and early 1970s due to expanding global markets, deregulation, and the corporate search for cheap labor overseas. The collapse of the banking industry in the fall of 2008, during the heated moments of the presidential campaign, encouraged new questions about the ways in which our economic system is structured. The following observations concerning global poverty are staggering:

> In 1969 the incomes of the wealthiest 20 percent of the world's population were 30 times higher than those of the poorest 20 percent of the earth's people. By 1990 that gap had doubled: the incomes of the wealthiest 20 percent were 60 times higher than those of the poorest 20 percent. The difference factor is now 83. Jeffrey Sachs reports that not only does half of Africa's population live in extreme poverty, but also "this proportion has actually grown worse over the past two decades as the rest of the world has grown more prosperous."[10]

As Sach points out, the reality of global poverty is felt most severely on the African continent. The aftermath of slavery, colonialism, and now neo-colonial economic exploitation is still one of the greatest human travesties of our time. Many are, in fact, wondering how Obama will respond to the issue of global poverty at home and abroad, given his own struggles with poverty in his upbringing and his ancestral connections to Kenya. In the *Audacity of Hope*, Obama expresses his commitments to both individual autonomy and communal responsibility. On a visit to Kenya with his wife, Michelle, he talks about the wonderful experience of meeting with relatives, walking the streets of Nairobi, camping in the Serengeti, fishing off the island of Lamu, and taking in all of the majestic qualities of his father's homeland. At the same time, he was disturbed by a lack of core "values" similar to those reflected in the Bill of Rights, grounding the social and political environment in Kenya. Obama observed that many Kenyans feel as if their lives are not in their hands. There is a strong absence of self-realization or agency in the consciousness of ordinary Kenyans. He believes that individual freedom is an important quality of what it means to be American, one which many of us take for granted.

Obama does have a good grasp of the complexity of balancing individual freedom and autonomy with the necessity of communal responsibility (ensuring that the basic needs of all people are met). He seems to be aware of the fact that one of the greatest obstacles to ending global poverty, in terms of the need for contributions from the wealthiest nations) is the lack of commitment on behalf of wealthy and middle-class individuals to sacrifice some of their abundance for others. Taxation, which has been one of the chief means to address this problem, has been at the forefront of political debate and controversy. With explosive language like "big government" or "tax-and-spend democrat" the debates almost always lead to nowhere. Obama seems interested in challenging the very radical distinctions (individual/communal, rich/poor, democrat/republican, liberal/

conservative) often postulated around these issues in the quest for some larger metanarratives of values and commitments. He poignantly expresses these sentiments when he writes:

> If we Americans are individualistic at heart, if we instinctively chafe against a past of tribal allegiances, traditions, customs, and castes, it would be a mistake to assume that this is all we are. Our individualism has always been bound by a set of communal values, the glue upon which every healthy society depends. We value the imperatives of family and the cross-generational obligations that family implies. We value community, the neighborliness that expresses itself through raising the barn or coaching the soccer team. We value patriotism and the obligations of citizenship, a sense of duty and sacrifice on behalf of our nation. We value faith in something bigger than ourselves, whether that something expresses itself in formal religion or ethical precepts. And we value the constellation of behaviors that express our mutual regard for one another: honesty, fairness, humility, kindness, courtesy, and compassion.
>
> In every society (and in every individual), these twin strands—the individualistic and the communal, autonomy and solidarity—are in tension, and it has been one of the blessings of America that the circumstances of our nation's birth allowed us to negotiate these tensions better than most. We did not have to go through any of the violent upheavals that Europe was forced to endure as it shed its feudal past. Our passage from an agricultural to an industrial society was eased by the sheer size of the continent, vast tracts of land and abundant resources that allowed new immigrants to continually remake themselves.[11]

Conclusion

Ultimately, Obama knows that values are bound to collide. Values often translate to self-interest, racism, greed, dangerous forms of nationalism, and other expressions of exploitation. Obama does not give serious treatment to the historical atrocities of slavery, genocide of the American Indians, internment of the Japanese during World War II, and exploitation of immigrants and children during the Age of Industrialization. However, the mere fact that Obama is interested in having a conversation around values at all is a momentous achievement from previous administrations. If he is true to his own stated beliefs and commitments, Obama will indeed address issues around global poverty as well as other challenges concerning terrorism, global warming, public education, incarceration, and a host of other issues.

His interest in going beyond rigid distinctions and strategies informed by binary (either/or thinking) seems apparent in, for instance, his stance on education. In the promotional book put out by his campaign, Obama claimed he will help transform education by emphasizing social responsibility and values at home. Some of the things Obama intends to do is enjoin schools to have clear goals and expectations for student performance if they are to receive government funds, encourage close relationships between schools and parents, call on parents to turn the television and video games off, and create opportunities and expectations for community service work from all students. Though simple, these are huge steps in the right direction. Educators have been saying for years that the problems facing America's schools require a comprehensive response. Neither the school system nor parents alone can solve the desperate challenges ahead. It involves a holistic agenda that speaks to what happens in the classroom and at home.

Indeed, Obama's historic bid for presidency and his administration will leave an indelible impact on America and the entire world. It will not be simply because he overcame insurmountable odds to become the first black president of the United States or that he was able to take on domestic and global challenges not seen since World War II and the Great Depression. It will be because of his ability to inspire, to provide a vision, and to induce hope to the lives of millions all over the globe. His acceptance speech delivered on a massive platform in Grant Park on a brisk Chicago evening on November 4, 2008, illuminates the likely impact of Obama for many years to come.

With the resounding familiarity of Martin Luther King Jr., just a generation ago, Obama said, "If there is anyone out there who still doubts that America is a place where all things are possible; who still wonders if the dreams of our founders is alive in our time; who still questions the power of our democracy, tonight is your answer."[12] While Obama could have used the moment as an opportunity to critique America's painfully divisive past with its history of exploitation of women, African Americans, Asians, and Latino/Latina populations, he instead called for a recovery of the most compelling dimensions of America's democratic history. He linked himself as a continuum of a much larger historical legacy of freedom, justice, and opportunity (however flawed and mangled it might be). As *New York Times* reporter Nancy Gibbs observed, "Some princes are born in palaces. Some are born in mangers. But a few are born in the imagination of scraps of history and hope." Gibbs argues that inasmuch as Obama himself has been quick to admit his own humanity and limitations, it was the urgent need of the hour, of the current moment in history, that created the conditions where over 120 million pulled the lever and mailed in their ballots to elect someone like Obama. Barack "Hussein" Obama, says Gibbs, did not win "because of the color of his skin. Nor did he win in spite of it. He won because at a very dangerous moment in the life of a still young country, more people than have ever spoken before came together to try to save it. And that was a victory all its own."[13] Political pundit Joe Klein even goes as far as saying that Obama's election was about the "ratification of an essential change in the nature of the country."[14] It was about reconceptualizing what it means to be "America" and subsequently ushering in a new direction for both domestic and international policy in the world. By becoming the first black president, championing the heritage of Martin Luther King Jr., Abraham Lincoln, the Founding Fathers, and others throughout history, Obama helped pave the way for a new mode of discourse, language not simply grounded in compartmentalized rhetoric that breeds corruption and conflict, but words of collaboration, dialogue, respect for difference, hope, and possibility.

Of course, the challenges before the Obama administration and the nation are riveting. It will take incredible effort, focus, and concentration from all involved to help maneuver the country out of these treacherous waters. Whether it is the stalwart problem of Russian President Dmitry Medvedev's invasion of Georgia, Pervez Musharraf's transition in Pakistan's fragile democracy, the regrouping of the Taliban in Afghanistan, or even the political crisis in Zimbabwe over Robert Mugabe and Morgan Tsvangirai's power struggle, there is indeed a lot of work to do. However, there is good reason to be hopeful and excited about the possibilities that lie before the nation and the world in these troubling times. Indeed, each of us can celebrate the ways in which this election has revealed the marvelous capacity for individuals to transcend their immediate social and historical circumstances to imagine something greater, more compelling and transformative at work in our world. Obama has simply served as an agent in the quest for social change for our time and for those disquieted generations to come that continue to beckon us onward.

CHAPTER 10

Obama's Presidency and the Black Agenda

Have you ever seen a cotton-field white with the harvest,—its golden fleece hovering above the black earth like a silvery cloud edged with dark green, its bold white signals waving like the foam of billows from Carolina to Texas across that Black and human sea?[1]

In this passage, W. E. B. Du Bois looked out upon the vast wealth of the many southern white landowners and was mystified at the fact that the wealth was a product of black labor that made "Cotton King." From the construction of the White House to the hard labor of working the massive steel industries at the turn of the twentieth century, black people have worked arduously to make America what it is, and perhaps what it can be. Now is the time to work harder than ever before to settle the debt of injustice and racial inequality born out of centuries of pain and struggle. Now is the time to passionately push for sweeping policy changes for the betterment of black life, and in doing so, enhance the lives of all Americans. Now is the time to issue a call to action, to continue to form multicultural and multiracial coalitions to attend to the lives of the poor and disenfranchised. The black experience in America is ultimately the indicator of the greatest challenge and greatest promise for the American dream. In this final chapter, I issue a call to action, a call for all Americans, especially black people (individually and collectively) to labor more feverishly than ever before to enact sustainable transformation in all areas of life, from education and healthcare, to housing, political engagement, and the arts. Because of the deeply rooted racial realities of America, as I have attempted to sum up in these brief pages, the Obama administration may very well be the closest opportunity to move toward a more economically and politically equitable climate in America since the Lyndon B. Johnson administration more than forty years ago. Obama will not be able to do it alone. It will require the sacrifice of millions and a groundswell of support in local communities across the nation to see change occur.

In many ways, as reflected in the eloquent words of Du Bois, black people are still making cotton king. Considering the ways in which African Americans have made an enduring contribution to all sectors of American society, what does it mean for Obama, now the commander in chief, to have a critical dialogue with the black agenda for our time? In short, what is the black social and political agenda and how does it coincide with the Obama administration?

Just a few years ago, some of the leading voices in the black community came together to produce the *Covenant with Black America*. The book, largely led by scholars, activists, and the journalist Tavis Smiley, did a remarkable job of outlining a number of key issues that are particularly important to the African American community. These contributors did a fine job of outlining the problems of black America in very simple terms. They also offered solutions and responses at all levels, from the perspective of responsible personal citizenship to advancing national legislation. Drawing on this wonderful resource would be an important guide in providing a blueprint in the kinds of changes that need to take place. Shortly after the election and inauguration, Smiley published another important text, *Accountable,* in which he calls on all Americans, especially blacks, to hold its elected leaders (including Obama) responsible in representing their interests. Here I would like to establish a dialogue between what Obama has said he will do as president and the black agenda as expressed in recent years. The black community is not a monolithic community. One would search in vain to find a singular vision, perspective, or understanding of what even constitutes the black community, let alone what the black agenda should be. The gamut of perspectives on the black community ranges from the anti-Civil Rights agenda of Ward Connerly to the radical street walking buoyancy of Reverend Al Sharpton. It absorbs wealthy black elites like Oprah Winfrey, Bill Cosby, and Will Smith to rappers like 50 Cent, T-Pain, and Lil' Wayne.

The black community also incorporates the over 1 million black men in prison, the thousands of black children without healthcare, black soldiers, and countless others. So, when I speak of the black agenda, I am speaking of a comprehensive, fluid, and diverse social, economic, and political plan that will lead to black flourishing in all its forms. Lest this be construed as a black nationalist agenda with little concern for the "other," I don't believe that advancing black flourishing negates the desire for all human beings to flourish. Because of how black folks have historically suffered unduly in America for no other reason that the color of their skin, centering in on black suffering serves as a case study of the human quest for freedom and fulfillment in the modern era. The black struggle represents, in many ways, the human struggle to overcome what Martin Luther King Jr. described as "man's inhumanity to man."

It has not been since the desolate days of reconstruction that black folks have come together in this manner. As blacks, as the historian John Hope Franklin describes, came "up from slavery" in the pursuit of justice, dignity, and community, we now hear, like the beat of a thousand drums, the voices of the masses of our people crying out in the shadows of the depth of their suffering and the yearning for human fulfillment.

The present moment calls for a progressive social agenda for the black people, moving beyond reactionary, kneejerk, temporary responses to the complex and difficult issues confronting our people. A progressive agenda takes into account the comprehensive dynamics of social, political, economic, spiritual, and religious forces involved in the creation of flourishing black communities. We are invited to share in the prophetic legacy of Martin Luther King, Jr., who once observed that "any religion that professes to be concerned by the souls of men, but is not concerned by the slums that cripple the soul, the economic conditions that may damn the soul, is a dead, dry, do nothing, religion in need of new blood."

Globalization and the African American Community

Dealing with the problems of economic globalization and how it impacts black life must be at the center of Obama's agenda. Globalization has been a troublesome and pervasive problem, especially in black urban centers since the late 1960s and early 1970s. As multinational corporations and the United States economy in general moved from an industrial-based society to a more information-based society shortly after the demise of the Civil Rights Movement with King's death, black inner-city communities were devastated as work essentially disappeared. As well-paying industrial jobs in factories, shipping, and large-scale commercial activity were either dismantled or relocated to foreign developing nations for cheap labor, millions of black folks in inner cities across the northeast and mid-west, were economically abandoned and socially alienated. The escalation of gang violence, the breakdown in the family, and explosion of the crack epidemic in the mid to late 1980s was an inevitable bi-product of these larger, albeit global, economic shifts taking place. No president, since Lyndon Johnson, has introduced a progressive urban agenda for America's cities, of which blacks have unduly paid the price.

The economic problem posed by globalization by the nature of the term implies a kind of distance, emotional and special, from immediate experiences, especially when it comes to the American context. I would agree with Dwight Hopkins in his interpretation of globalization as a positioning of the United States as the "sole superpower throughout the earth and in outer space programs."[2] Recognizing globalization as a religious system, not simply economic or even political in orientation, it speaks to the religious drive toward monopolization of finance and capitalist wealth where global wealth becomes concentrated in the vaults of a small group of elite families on a global scale. As a black theologian, Hopkins speaks with strong sensitivities concerning the African American religious experience and history of pain and suffering in America. He illuminates the fact that the ravages of globalization are not limited to Asia, Africa, Latin America, or the Caribbean, but also touches ground on American soils in the industrial abandonment of inner cities and stagnating displacement of many rural communities across the United States.

Since the groundbreaking work of William Julius Wilson in the book *The Declining Significance of Race* the kind of critical social analysis of the urban poor has claimed serious attention. Wilson makes clear that the economic disparities being generated across the globe are deeply interwoven with the disappearance of work and its consequences to social, economic, and cultural life in inner-city ghettos.[3]

America is now in the shadow of the 400th anniversary of the Jamestown settlement and the 40th anniversary of the Poor People's Campaign, the final pilgrimage of hope envisioned in the prophetic leadership of Martin Luther King, Jr. King, in particular, saw emerging on the horizon a radical decentralization of Europe as the seat of power in the world to America and the thrust of free market capitalism. The intensification of technological advances and the promulgation of mass media and access to travel, for King, meant that the world must begin to radically reorganize its economic commitments concerning the poor. He introduced the concept of a "bill of rights for the poor" as a step toward a democratic socialist vision of society, which he believed lay at the heart of the Judeo-Christian faith. The challenge before us today is to contextualize King's vision as we forge a progressive urban agenda for the African American community today. This means, we must begin to affirm the reality that God is concerned with all areas of human life, including the social, political, economic, and cultural dimensions of our experience. Working toward a just public policy is as essential to the worship of God within the context of the church on Sunday morning. The Holy Spirit, according to the Latin American theologian Gustavo Gutierrez is at work wherever the activity of justice, mercy, and human freedom abide.

King's legacy also offers a way of framing up various modes of resistance, or ways of addressing the many problems affecting the black community. The first mode of resistance means reclaiming the prophetic tradition of the

African American religious and cultural experience. A growing temptation and disturbing trend in many churches, black social groups, and historical political organizations today is to acquiescence to capitalistic desire and assume an uncritical obsession with wealth and material prosperity. By prophetic I mean seriously considering and responding to the systemic forces at work in the lives of the poor. Second, resistance requires curtailing the lure of capitalistic desire. Daniel Bell offers an instructive approach as he draws a distinction between those "technologies of desire" created by the massive economic marketing machinery of Madison Avenue and the like and the "disciplines of desire" displayed in the biblical call to self-denial and living for the other.

One model of a constructive response to globalization and poverty, particularly concerning African Americans, has come from the late Rev. Dr. Leon Sullivan, expressed in what has come to be known as the Sullivan Principles. In 1977, Rev. Sullivan, then pastor of the historic Zion Baptist Church in Philadelphia, Pennsylvania, introduced the Sullivan Principles and later the Global Sullivan Principles as a way of promoting and advocating for corporate social responsibility and equality.[4] Rev. Sullivan began by working with corporations such as General Motors in the late 1970s to invest in job training and equity in hiring practices and to encourage companies to call for an end to apartheid in South Africa. His principles included equal and fair employment practices, training development programs at all levels, enhancing all areas of black life (including housing, transportation, schools, recreation, and healthcare), and also an end to laws and customs that militate against social, economic, and political justice.

Although Sullivan introduced his ideas more than thirty years ago, his work still has considerable relevance today. Like Sullivan, Obama worked directly in inner-city neighborhoods and understands the challenges of black urban life in America. His work as a community activist on the South Side of Chicago may offer some powerful insights into the complex interconnections of housing, unemployment, incarceration, and education that now seem to plague poor black communities across the nation. Sullivan focused his attention on black youth in the city, which is where Obama must concentrate his efforts if the impact is to be long lasting and sustained. As with Sullivan's agenda several decades ago, Obama must establish a comprehensive social and political agenda that attends to the challenges of black youth as well.

Confronting the Youth Crisis

All black youth, males and females, are very vulnerable in today's context. They are at risk not only because of the social structures that often make it difficult for black children to thrive in school but also due to the pervasive psychological forces of negativity in the media and popular culture bearing down on them as well. Black males, in particular, have been especially susceptible to these forces. Even as a youth, Obama struggled with his father's absence and his identity, leading him to experiment with drugs and alcohol. As Obama experienced himself as a youth, black males in American society have felt the brunt of national neglect of the poor over the last thirty years. In addition to focusing on all youth, there must be an intentional effort to attend to the needs of young black males within today's context of growing gang violence, excessive drop-out rates, and high suicide rates. Indeed, black males in American society in general are in crisis, however, for our purpose we will examine the issue as it relates to the most vulnerable group, and at the same time the group in the best position to be ministered to—in particular black males between 10 and 15 years of age.

In an important study by Ronald Mincy, *Nurturing Young Black Males*, he identifies the nature of this crisis and pathways to respond proactively.[5] Mincy proposes the groups most in need are black males between 10 and 15 years of age. In outlining a series of programs, Mincy delineates the urgency of the matter. Mincy focuses on the developmental concerns that black males are confronted with. These concerns center on a complex web of social, historical, and economic issues. That racism and socioeconomic disadvantage come together to have a negative impact on the development of black males, merely the normal challenges of development are compounded and overwhelmed with "extreme environmental stress during the crucial early years of life."[6] The questions that arise are: what exactly is the extent of this dilemma and its implications regarding black males? What is the black church's stance on these issues? Are there programs and insights that may challenge this crisis? What are the implications of this crisis regarding the black family and ultimately the future of the black community as well?

The popular media has bombarded the public with news about black men either on their way to prison, serving in prison or jail, and newly released from prison. The popular columnist and scholar Earl Ofari Hutchinson writes, "The image of young blacks prone on the ground, handcuffed against walls and over the hoods of police cars make better copy anyway."[7] Negative images overwhelm our culture about the nature of this problem. Is there really a crisis? While the idea of "crisis" implies a temporary deviation from a more suitable norm or that a more secured condition preceded the current state, for black males evidence suggest that the present situation is not at all temporary; in fact the severity of the problem is increasing.

We must be aware of the interconnectedness of problems facing black males at every age level. Pedro A. Noguera, in his "Reconsidering the 'crisis' of the Black Male in America," points primarily to economic strains as the most urgent problem. For instance, black males earn on average 73 percent of the income of white males.[8] In almost all areas of the professional job market, black males are highly underrepresented and even considered "less desirable employees," and are thus less likely to be hired. Moreover, despite laws designed to prevent discrimination, racism and discrimination in hiring practices still persist.[9]

Issues of discrimination are intertwined with the education system in America. Black males are more likely to be suspended and/or expelled from school, and there is an even greater probability that this group will be placed in special education classes. Noguera links these trends in education to the historical legacy of slavery and Jim Crow segregation where separation and different treatment was rationalized by notions of "innate inferiority." Although there was some increase in college enrollment during the mid-1970s, from 1977 there has been a continuous decrease in college enrollment of black males. In fact, black males are more likely to be destined to the prison halls rather than college halls. As Noguera indicates, "In 1995, one out of every three black males (versus one out of 10 white males) between the ages of 18 and 30 were either incarcerated or in some way ensnared by the criminal justice system."[10] This reality is even more severe in some places. In our nation's capital, Obama's own backyard, the District of Columbia, 91 percent of the prison populations are black males, while 5.9 percent are black females. Factors such as racism, discrimination, and economic inequality are also major factors in the challenges faced by young African American males.

Other problems such as health issues also plague the black male presence in America. In the article "Dying is No Accident" clinical scholars report that "for the last 10 years, black males have been the only group within the U.S. population to record a declining life expectancy."[11] The homicide rate for black males aged 15 to 24 is seven to eight times higher than that of white males in the same age group.[12] Noguera also maintains that "black males are also at greater risk of substance abuse, of dying during infancy, or of dying prematurely due to heart disease, hypertension, diabetes, and AIDS."[13] Amid these alarming facts, it is evident that a "crisis" truly exists concerning black males, particularly as it relates to young black males in America.

Perhaps the greatest crisis involves the issue of nihilism. West, in his acclaimed *Race Matters,* submits, "The major enemy of black survival [particularly among black males] has been and is neither oppression nor exploitation but rather the nihilistic threat—that is loss of hope and absence of meaning." [14] Many of our young people feel as if there is no cause worth living for, more accurately a cause worth dying for. There seems to be a pervasive absence of meaning with black youth. The problem of hopelessness and lack of confidence in a better day is very real and truly a problem. Because of Obama's unique gift to inspire and the fact that black males might be able to look upon Obama as an example of what might be possible in their own lives, there is now an opportunity to once again renew the struggle to liberate the hearts and minds of black male youth and all youth in general.

The Agenda: Developing a Comprehensive Response

Whether the focus is on youth or economics, the response must be comprehensive. Black leaders and communities must articulate a language of solidarity that expresses the deep yearning and prophetic urgency that we now feel as a community in responding to these pressing issues. As Tommie Shelby writes in *We Who Are Dark: The Philosophical Foundations of Black Solidarity*, black folks have cause to work together, even with other historically oppressed groups, because of "the shared experience of racial oppression and a joint commitment to resist it."[15] He also surmises that "the practicality and scope of black solidarity depends on a diagnosis of the complex forces that constitute black oppression and on the extent to which blacks suffer specifically because of antiblack racism, past and present."[16] I agree with Shelby's assessment that any effort to rally black folks toward some kind of progressive social agenda must draw on that history of common struggle as a basis of black unity and political cooperation.

It was and has been this renewed commitment to the particular dimensions of black racial oppression that has led to a conversation around a proactive, comprehensive agenda for the black community. In the *Covenant*, Smiley called together leading voices from across the country and outlined a provocative proposal for developing a progressive social agenda. The book, however, did not address the unique contributions and role black churches play in establishing meaningful change. Our black churches are in the trenches, in the crucible of suffering in our communities. The black church still holds the moral authority on shaping the lives of black folks across the country. Indeed, it is still the black preacher that African Americans look to for spiritual guidance, constructive vision, and passionate leadership on issues of social justice, healing, and political action. Beginning with the "cradle-to-prison" crisis, I offer a critical appraisal and perspective on how to move forward toward a progressive agenda for our time. Drawing on the Covenant, below are highlights of what a progressive urban agenda for the African American community must take into account.

As has historically been the case, the black church, in particular, and its friends in other faith communities, has the grand opportunity of advancing these efforts through the mighty army of God's people who are also citizens of these United States of America, as well. The statistics in all of the areas below are daunting and for our purposes, I won't revisit those here. Below is a synopsis of what can be done among policy makers to improve these areas. That does not mean that personal responsibility is essential. Many of our leaders have always and continue to call for responsible personal behavior. However, forging an urban agenda for the African American community means holding public leaders accountable and pressing forward some of the following initiatives.

Ending the "Cradle-to-Prison" Crisis: Addressing the Problem of Mass Incarceration

An overwhelming chorus of voices both within the corrections system and among politicians and community activists is calling for radical change in current jailing/corrections policies. Many are now becoming painfully aware that the present system is not working. Simply incarcerating individuals for lengthy sentences is not effective as a deterrent and does not contribute to a reduction in crime. Many of the current policies and practices that reflect strict sentencing policies and no-holds barred policing and incarceration were fueled by the late 1980s and 1990s politically motivated "Get Tough on Crime" and "War on Drugs" policies.[17] To his credit, Obama's campaign went on record saying they will introduce a number of programs that are focused on prevention and reduction of recidivism rates. They have also said they will help take back black neighborhoods from drugs by focusing on what is known as "Weed-and-Seed initiatives."[18] These initiatives seek to "weed out" the most violent offenders while investing in preventive and rehabilitative programs in the community. Obama's campaigns have also committed to increasing the number of law enforcement personnel on the street, supporting "CeaseFire" programs, and expanding "Promise Neighborhoods" for urban youth across the country.[19] These programs and initiatives are essential to begin stemming the tide of racial disparities in prisons and in the broader legal system in America.

The dramatic shift from rehabilitation to retribution as paradigms for addressing criminality and jailing/corrections developed largely out of the desire for politicians to use public fear as a campaign platform for election and also the sensationalism of television and media in covering violent crimes. A common slogan in many news rooms is, "If it bleeds, it leads."

In order to increase and sustain ratings, television and the media often intensify public fears and anxieties, especially among suburbanites, despite the reality that most crimes occur in the community where individual offenders live.

The problem with the current system is that it does not address the ravaging of communities when individuals (fathers, brothers, mothers, sisters, uncles, etc.) are taken out of the community for long periods of unproductive time. The present system also does not address the more complex system issues of poverty, unemployment, housing, the cultural particularizes related to mentoring, social and religious life, and the nearly 70 percent of single-female led households. William Julius Wilson, in his groundbreaking book *When Work Disappears* makes a compelling case for the connections between poverty in the urban setting and high levels of arrest and subsequent incarceration. According to Wilson, it is dangerous and socially/economically irresponsible to continue to incarcerate individuals without looking at the searing problems of poverty that continue to plague the African American community. By investing in the development and economic foundations of predominately poor African American males, says Wilson, we will not only ensure public safety but contribute to a vibrant and flourishing community for all.

Political scientists, sociologists, and criminologists are not the only ones concerned with the Corrections systems. The Criminal Justice and Corrections systems, as a function of the public good, impact all aspects of the community. Social and religious leaders are continuing to call for a *restorative* understanding of policing and incarceration. In *Beyond Prisons: An Interfaith Paradigm for Our Failed Prison System*, Laura Magnani and Harmon L. Wray offer a thought provoking analysis of the present policing and corrections systems. By adopting a *restorative justice* approach, they argue, the public experiences not only a reduction in crime and violence, but also saves millions of dollars that could be used for education and/or economic development for all. Magnani and Wray, in reflecting on the present system observe:

> Present prison policy demonstrates that we do not believe that prisoners can repent, show remorse, and work toward healing themselves and their relationships. When the weakest or most impoverished among us does not experience the support or sustaining balance of a healthy society, we are not a just society. Just as when survivors of serious crime are unheard, marginalized, or exploited, when offenders suffer the unending isolation of our prisons [and jails] we can hardly lay claim to justice.[20]

The Children's Defense Fund, in recent years, has launched an all-out war against what they describe as the "cradle to prison pipeline."[21] The report has called for a radical and immediate end to childhood and adult mass incarceration, especially among nonviolent offenders. They have called for more programs and initiatives geared toward prevention and rehabilitation. As the study points out, there is a direct correlation between the concentration of African American and Latino/Latina populations and poverty in urban and rural areas alike. It translates to disparities in education opportunities, job training, and access to information and technology that might expand opportunities and choices as well. Both activist and criminal justice officials alike are calling for a reclaiming of the restorative-justice/rehabilitation model, especially for nonviolent offenders. This model recognizes the complexity of issues regarding the factors and influences contributing to arrests, incarceration, recidivism, etc.

By approaching the corrections/jailing process from the restorative justice perspective, we are empowered to further ensure public safety while also reducing the financial burden to taxpayers, and also contributing to the restoration of families and communities. Programs such as the Alternative to Incarceration (ATI) Program of the Division of Probation and Correctional Alternatives in the New York State Counties and the City of New York offer some helpful resources as to what can be done at many levels to confront what James Bell calls the "cradle-to-prison superhighway" (CPS).[22] Reforming outdated and unjust drug policies is essential. Written in the very law code are disparities that particularly disenfranchise black people. Also there must be an effort to dismantle those mandatory sentencing programs that often deny or diminish the complexity of individual cases and persons involved. It often leads to gross abuses by the legal system as a whole. Some of the other matters that should be addressed are helping women in prison maintain family ties and improve parenting skills and increasing educational and counseling opportunities for juveniles in the Juvenile Justice system.

But the prisons are simply one aspect of a larger, more comprehensive program, which also relates to issues such as healthcare. In the area of healthcare, there is a need to improve data collection at all levels and establish a real universal healthcare program for all children. Another often overlooked dimension of the healthcare crisis is providing adequate places for children to play and providing access to healthy food markets in local communities. Of course, education is also an essential part of the problem.

The Bush administration's "No Child Left Behind" act left a painful sore on the body of the American public educational system. The act contributed to massive school closings, placed undue pressures on local schools to meet testing requirements, yet was grossly underfunded and ill-supported by the Department of Education. There is a need to repeal the "No Child Left Behind" Act and revise the legislation to include a much more comprehensive approach to education. Some of those measures could include investing in child and parental development, pushing for federal support at all levels of education, including teachers, administrators, support staff, and incentives to encourage parental involvement.

Introducing ethics and life-skills training into the curriculum, as well as culturally-oriented materials is also critical to meet the specific challenges affecting black children. Often those who set policies in the educational system do not have black children in mind. It has been assumed, for instance, that issues around ethics and morality should be left to parents and the child's household. It is true that parents must be actively involved in the lives of their children, especially when it comes to ethical teachings. However, the reality of breakdown in many African American families suggests the need for teachers and schools to also be involved in holistically shaping the lives of children—not just their minds, but their bodies and souls as well. Many black youth are forced to navigate the harsh realities of poor housing, drug-infested communities, insufficient nutrition, and traumatic experiences with violence before even entering the doors of their local schools on a daily basis. Treating a host of issues related to housing, education, healthcare, and employment are indispensible for moving toward an effective, long lasting agenda for the black community for years to come.

Conclusion

Together, we can coordinate and develop a comprehensive strategy to help strengthen African American communities for today's context. Obama's administration is presented with an awesome opportunity to lead long term, generational changes. It will require a high degree of courage, moral persuasion, and indefatigable determination from the Obama administration and the nation to confront this present crisis. By renewing our commitment to the collective struggle in the black community, we also bear witness to the struggle of other communities, including women, gays and lesbians, voices in developing nations, the elderly, and the disabled as well. Whether black, white, Latino/Latina, Asian, or Pacific Islander, we all have a stake in the flourishing of the black community. Their story reflects the plight of all who suffer and seek to overcome the weight of historical dehumanization. In joining hands together, as many did throughout the Obama campaign, we might be able to sing anew that great song African American forebears called the "Black National Anthem":

> Lift ev'ry voice and sing,
> Till earth and heaven ring,
> Ring with the harmonies of Liberty;
> Let our rejoicing rise
> High as the list'ning skies,
> Let it resound loud as the rolling sea.
> Sing a song full of the faith that the dark past has taught us,
> Sing a song full of the hope that the present has brought us;
> Facing the rising sun of our new day begun,
> Let us march on till victory is won.[23]

Notes

Introduction

1. W. E. B. Du Bois, *The Souls of Black Folks* (New York: Penguin Books, 1995; originally published in 1903), 47.
2. Townsend Davis, *Weary Feet, Rested Soul: A Guided History of the Civil Rights Movement* (New York: W. W. Norton, 1998), 9–10. The Congress of Racial Equality (CORE) was a peace group founded in Chicago in 1943 that initiated the Freedom Rides of the early 1960s. CORE also aided in coordinating the activities of the NAACP and SNCC. FOR was founded after World War I as an organization committed to the work of peace and reconciliation. Figures such as James Lawson and Glenn Smiley led the organization at its high points during the civil rights movement. The MFDP was established in the state in 1964 to combat the all-white state Democratic Party to serve as an alternative organization to reflect the needs of blacks in Mississippi. The SCLC was founded by Martin Luther King Jr. and Ralph Abernathy shortly after the Montgomery Bus Boycott in Atlanta primarily to give young ministers a forum to advocate and demonstrate around issues of segregation and voting rights in the South. Other organizations such as the NAACP, the Montgomery Improvement Association (MIA), and many historically black Church denominations were actively engaged in the civil rights struggle of the 1950s and 1960s.
3. Du Bois, *Souls of Black Folks*, 227–28.
4. Thomas C. Battle and Donna M. Wells, Moorland-Spingarn Research Center, eds., *Legacy Treasures of Black History* (Washington, D.C.: National Geographic Society, 2006; originally published by Howard University), 123.
5. David Mendell, *Obama* (New York: HarperCollins, 2007), 143.
6. Randall Kennedy, *Sellout: The Politics of Racial Betrayal* (New York, Pantheon, 2008).
7. World Health Organization Report 2008, "Primary Healthcare Now More Than Ever"; http//www.who.int/mediacentre/news/releases/2008/pr38/en/index.html.

Chapter 1

1. An American Negro Spiritual.
2. Martin Luther King Jr., "Mountaintop" speech, Memphis, TN, April 1968.

3. The following passage appears on a monument in front of the National Civil Rights Museum outside the historic Lorraine Hotel in Memphis, Tennessee, where King was killed on April 4, 1968. The passage is taken from the King James Version of Genesis 37. The passage speaks of the story of Joseph, son of the promise, who was sold into slavery by his elder brothers, only to become royalty later in Egypt. Because of Joseph's gift of interpreting dreams, he was elevated in Pharaoh's court. In the story, Joseph eventually saves his family, who had formerly betrayed him, and all his people from famine and disease by giving them refuge in Egypt.

4. Kenneth L. Smith and Ira G. Zepp, Jr., *Search for the Beloved Community: The Thinking of Martin Luther King, Jr.* (Valley Forge, PA: Judson, 1998), 42.

5. Ibid.

6. David J. Garrow, *Bearing the Cross: Martin Luther King, Jr., and the Southern Christian Leadership Conference* (New York: Vintage Books, 1986), 83.

7. Stephen Mansfield, *The Faith of Barack Obama* (Nashville, TN: Thomas Nelson, 2008), xv. Mansfield has also written *Never Give In: The Extraordinary Character of Winston Churchhill, Then Darkness Fled: The Liberating Wisdom of Booker T. Washington, Forgotten Founding Father: The Heroic Legacy of George Whitefield, The Faith of George W. Bush, The Faith of the American Soldier,* and *Benedict XVI: His Life and Mission.*

8. Barack Obama, *The Audacity of Hope: Thoughts on Reclaiming the American Dream* (New York: Three Rivers, 2006), 208.

9. Martin Luther King, Jr., "Nonviolence and Racial Justice," *Christian Century* 74 (February 6, 1957): 165–67; also in James Melvin Washington's *A Testament of Hope: The Essential Writings and Speeches of Martin Luther King, Jr.* (New York: HarperCollins, 1991), 5–9.

10. Ibid., 7.

11. Townsend Davis, *Weary Feet, Rested Souls: A Guided History of the Civil Rights Movement* (New York: W. W. Norton, 1998), 22.

12. David J. Garrow, *Bearing the Cross: Martin Luther King, Jr., and the Southern Christian Leadership Conference* (New York: Vintage Books, 1986), 12.

13. Ibid., 13.

14. Ibid.

15. King Speeches and Sermons, "Address to the Initial Meeting of the Montgomery Improvement Association," December 5, 1955.

16. William B. Whitman, ed., *The Quotable Politician* (Guilford, CT: Lyons, 2003), 170.

17. Highlander Center Records, Record Group 2, box 2, series I, folder 38, transcript pp. 6–9.

18. Townsend Davis, *Weary Feet, Rested Souls: A Guided History of the Civil Rights Movement* (New York: W. W. Norton, 1998), 22.

19. Martin Luther King, Jr., *Where Do We Go from Here: Chaos or Community?* (Eugene, OR: Wipf and Stock, 2002; previously published by Harper & Row, 1991), 200.

Chapter 2

1. W. E. B. Du Bois, *The Souls of Black Folks* (New York: Penguin Books, 1995; originally published 1903), 43.
2. Barack Obama, *Dreams from My Father: A Story of Race and Inheritance* (New York: Three Rivers, 1995), 50–51.
3. Du Bois, *Souls of Black Folks*, 43.
4. Evans Thomas, "A Memo to Senator Obama," *Time*, June 2, 2008, 22–27.
5. John Hope Franklin, *The Color Line: Legacy of the Twenty-First Century* (Columbia, MO: University of Missouri Press, 1993), 7.
6. Basil Davidson, *The Black Man's Burden: Africa and the Curse of the Nation-State.* (New York: Three Rivers, 1992).
7. Ibid.
8. Barack Obama, *The Audacity of Hope: Thoughts on Reclaiming the American Dream* (New York: Three Rivers, 2006), 231.
9. Obama, *Dreams from My Father*, xiv.
10. Ibid., 6.
11. Ibid., 9.
12. http://www.glpinc.org/Classroom%20Activities/Kenya%20Articles/Struggle%20for%20Independence.htm.
13. Ibid.
14. Obama, *Dreams from My Father*, 10.
15. Ray Stannard Baker, *Following the Color Line: American Negro Citizenship in the Progressive Era* (New York: Harper & Row, 1964; originally published by Doubleday, 1908).
16. Ibid., 7.
17. Michael K. Brown, Martin Carnoy, Elliott Currie, Troy Duster, David B. Oppenheimer, Marjorie M. Shultz, and David Wellman, *Whitewashing Race: The Myth of a Color-Blind Society* (Berkeley, CA: University of California Press, 2003), 1.
18. Ibid.
19. Townsend Davis, *Weary Feet, Rested Souls: A Guided History of the Civil Rights Movement* (New York: W. W. Norton, 1998), 313.
20. Ibid., 315.
21. http://www.huffingtonpost.com/2008/03/18/obama-race-speech-read-t_n_92077.html.

Chapter 3

1. John Hope Franklin, *The Color Line: Legacy for the Twenty-First Century* (Columbia: University of Missouri Press, 1993), 31. See also A. Leon Higginbotham, Jr., *In the Matter of Color: Race and the American Legal Process* (New York: Oxford University Press, 1978).
2. Barack Obama, *The Audacity of Hope: Thoughts on Reclaiming the American Dream* (New York: Three Rivers, 2006), 232.

3. Ibid., 233.
4. Ibid.
5. W. E. B. Du Bois, *The Souls of Black Folks* (New York: Penguin Books, 1995; originally published in 1903), 54.
6. Ibid., 4.
7. Ibid.
8. Ellison, Ralph, "What America Would Be Like without Blacks" (Times Essay, April 6, 1970).
9. Martin Luther King, Jr., *Where Do We Go From Here: Chaos or Community?* (New York: Harper & Row, 1967).
10. Laura Magnani and Harmon L. Wray, *Beyond Prisons: A New Interfaith Paradigm for Our Failed Prison System* (Minneapolis, MN: Fortress, 2006), 30.
11. Leonardo Boff, *Global Civilization: Challenges to Society and Christianity* (London: Equinox, 2005).
12. Martin Luther King, Jr., "Letter from Birmingham Jail" in *Why We Can't Wait* (New York: Harper & Row, 1963, 1964)..
13. All of the United States armed forces (including the U.S. Army, Navy, Air Force, and Marines) are governed by the Uniform Code of Military Justice, which also establishes guidelines on the treatment of prisoners of war in accordance with the Geneva Convention.
14. Earl Ofari Hutchinson, *The Assassination of the Black Male Image* (New York: Simon & Schuster, 1997).
15. Bruce Wright, *Black Robes, White Justice: Why Our Legal System Doesn't Work for Blacks* (New York: Kensington, 1987; reprinted in 1993).

Chapter 4

1. W. E. B. Du Bois, *The Souls of Black Folks* (New York: Penguin Books, 1995; originally published in 1903), 265.
2. Barack Obama, "On Africa," in *Barack Obama: In His Own Words*, edited by Lisa Rogak (New York: Carroll and Graf, 2007), 6. This quote appeared in the October 2006 issue of the magazine *Essence* as well.
3. Barack Obama, *Bearing the Cross: Martin Luther King, Jr., and the Southern Christian Leadership Conference* (New York: Vintage Books, 1986), 114.
4. Ben Wallace-Wells, "Destiny's Child," *Rolling Stone*, February 22, 2007.
5. Ibid., 26.
6. Aimé Cesaire, *Discourse on Colonialism*, trans. Joan Pinkham (New York: Monthly Review Press, 2000; originally published as an essay in 1950), 31.
7. Ibid., 32.
8. Ibid., 39.
9. Wallace-Wells, "Destiny's Child," 25.
10. Barack Obama, *The Audacity of Hope: Thoughts on Reclaiming the American Dream* (New York: Three Rivers, 2006), 279.
11. Ibid., 280.

12. Ibid., 303.
13. Frantz Fanon, *A Dying Colonialism*, trans. Haakon Chevalier with introduction by Adolfo Gilly (New York: Grove, 1994), 1. The book was originally published in France as *L'An Cinq, de la Révolution Algérienne* in 1959 by François Maspero.
14. Ibid.
15. Howard Winant, *The New Politics of Race: Globalism, Difference, Justice* (Minneapolis, MN: University of Minneapolis Press, 2004), 44.
16. Ibid., 97–98.
17. Ibid., 98.
18. Ibid., 45.
19. Ibid., 137–38.
20. Obama, *Audacity of Hope*, 320.
21. Obama, "On Africa," 6.
22. Ibid. Obama, "On His Multicultural Heritage." The former appeared in a speech at the Aspen Institute (July 2, 2005) and the latter in *Washington Post* (July 27, 2004).
23. http://www.rebirth.co.za/AIDS_in_Africa_1.htm.

Chapter 5

1. Barack Obama, "US Senator Barack Obama on Black Student Politics," *Black Collegian*, October 2006.
2. Barack Obama, "When It Comes to Race, Obama Makes His Point—With Subtlety," *Chicago Tribune*, June 26, 2005.
3. Michael C. Dawson, *Black Visions: The Roots of Contemporary African American Political Ideologies* (Chicago: University of Chicago Press, 2003).
4. Sterling Stuckey, *The Ideological Origins of Black Nationalism* (Boston, MA: Beacon, 1972).
5. Robin D. G. Kelley, *Race Rebels: Culture, Politics, and the Black Working Class* (New York: Free Press, 1996), 9.
6. http://www.trinitychicago.org/index.php?option=com_content&task=view&id=20 (accessed on May 19, 2009).
7. http://www.trinitychicago.org/index.php?option=com_content&task=view&id=20 (accessed on May 19, 2009).
8. Paul Street, *Barack Obama and the Future of American Politics* (Boulder, CO: Paradigm, 2009), 78.
9. I define *eurocentrism* as a privileging of Western European history, culture, and language over against all others. Eurocentrism purports to the originators of human civilization, above all others, where, for instance, classical music might be viewed as a more evolved, sophisticated art form over Jazz or Hip Hop. Like Afrocentrism, Eurocentrism is a cultural orientation, a perspective through which to view the world. In the academic world, it informs (whether knowingly or unknowingly) what courses are taught, what texts are used, and what interpretations are given and approaches taken to disciplines and research as well.

10. Roberts, J. Deotis, *Africentric Christianity: A Theological Appraisal for Ministry* (Valley Forge, PA: Judson, 2000), 4. Cf. Cheryl Sanders, ed., *Living the Intersection: Womanism and Afrocentrism in Theology* (Minneapolis, MN: Augsburg Fortress, 1995), 43–56.

11. Molefi Asante, *Afrocentricity* (Trenton, NJ: African World, 1988), 9.

12. Ibid., 12.

13. Ibid.

14. Ibid., 19.

15. Ibid.

16. Barack Obama, *The Audacity of Hope: Thoughts on Reclaiming the American Dream* (New York: Three Rivers, 2006), 62–63.

17. Ibid., 26.

18. Paul Laurence Dunbar, "We Wear the Mask," in *The Complete Works of Paul Laurence Dunbar*, ed. W. D. Howells (New York: Dodd, Mead, 1922), 71.

19. Henry L. Gates and Kwame Appiah, *Africana* (New York: Basic Civitas Books, a division of Perseus Books, 1999). See also Norman R. Shapiro, comp., *Negritude; Black Poetry from Africa and the Carribean*, bilingual ed. (New York: October House, 1970); Albert H. Berrian, comp., *Negritude; Essays and Studies* (Hampton, VA: Hampton Institute Press, 1967); Irving L. Markovitz, *Leopold Sedar Senghor and the Politics of Negritude*, 1st ed. (New York: Atheneum, 1967; originally published in 1934); Richard Long, *Negritude: Philosophy of Culture*, CAAS Occasional Paper, No. 7 (Atlanta, GA: Atlanta University, Atlanta Center for African-American Studies, 1971; originally published in 1927); Colette Verger Michael, *Negritude: An Annotated Bibliography* (West Cornwall, CT: Locust Hill, 1988); Julio Finn, *Voices of Negritude: With an Anthology of Negritude Poems Translated from the French, Portuguese and Spanish* (London: Quartet, 1988).

20. Aimé Cesaire, "*Cahier d'un retour au pays natal*" [Notebook of a return to my native land] (Nigeria: New Horn, 2005, originally published 1939).

21. On March 21, 1924, Charles S. Johnson of the National Urban League hosted a dinner with the black and white literary community to introduce young writers to the white literary establishment. As a result, the *Survey Graphic*, a magazine of social analysis and criticism that was interested in cultural pluralism, produced a Harlem issue in March 1925. The National Urban League was founded in 1910 to help black Americans address the economic and social problems they encountered as they resettled the urban North. The Harlem issue of *Survey Graphic* was later expanded and edited by the philosopher and literary scholar Alain Leroy Locke, a Rhodes scholar and Harvard graduate quite similar to Du Bois in his intellectual orientation.

22. Alain Locke, "The New Negro," in *Afrocentric Christianity,* by J. Deotis Roberts (Valley Forge, PA: Judson), 22.

23. William Julius Wilson, *When Work Disappears* (New York: Random House, 1996). Wilson is also author of several critical studies on the plight of black people today, including *The Declining Significance of Race: Blacks and Changing American Institutions* (Chicago: University of Chicago Press, 1978). Some of his recent publications include "Social Theory and the Concept 'Underclass,'" in

Poverty and Inequality, ed. David B. Grusky and Ravi Kanbur (Palo Alto, CA: Stanford University Press, 2005), 103–116; *There Goes the Neighborhood: Racial, Ethnic, and Class Tensions in Four Chicago Neighborhoods and Their Meaning for America* (with Richard Taub) (New York: Knopf, 2006); *Good Kids from Bad Neighborhoods: Successful Development in Social Context* (with D. Elliott, S. Menard, A. C. Elliott, B. Rankin, and D. Huizinga) (New York: Cambridge University Press, 2006); "Speaking to Publics," in *Public Sociology: Fifteen Eminent Sociologists Debate Politics and the Profession in the Twenty-first Century*, ed. Dan Clawson, Robert Zussman, Joya Misra, Naomi Gerstel, Randall Stokes, Douglas L. Anderton, and Michael Burawoy (Berkeley, CA: University of California Press, 2007), 117–23; "A New Agenda for America: Ghetto Poor," in *Ending Poverty in America: How to Restore the American Dream*, ed. John Edwards, Marion Crane, and Arne L. Kalleberg (New York: New Press, 2007), 88–98.

24. Asante, *Afrocentricity*, 4.

25. This quote appears in the dedication page of James Melvin Washington's *Testament of Hope: The Essential Writings and Speeches of Martin Luther King, Jr.* (New York: HarperCollins, 1986).

26. Cheikh Anta Diop, *Nations negres et Culture* (Paris: Presence Africaine, 1954; Pocketbook edition, 1979); *Anteriorite des civilisations negres: Mythe ou verite historique?* (Paris: Presence Africaine, 1967); *L' Antiquite Africaine par l'image* (Dakar: IFAN, 1976); *L'Afrique Noire precoloniale* [Precolonial black Africa] (Paris: Presence Africaine, 1960). See also by Cheikh Anta Diop, *Parente genetique de l'egyptien pharaonique et de langues negro-africaines* (Dakar: IFAN, 1977); *L'Unite culturelle de l'Afrique Noire* (Paris: Presence Africaine, 1959).

27. *Nations negres et Culture.*, xiv.

28. Ibid., 222.

29. Ibid., 214.

30. Ibid.

Chapter 6

1. Barack Obama, "The Great Need of the Hour," address at Ebenezer Baptist Church, Atlanta, Georgia, Sunday, January 20, 2008.

2. Townsend Davis, *Weary Feet, Rested Souls: A Guided History of the Civil Rights Movement* (New York: W. W. Norton, 1998), 22. According to Davis, E. D. Nixon, the lawyer Clifford Durr, and his wife, Virginia, bailed Parks out of jail. But the spark had already been ignited. Of course the anger and frustration over Jim Crow segregation had been mounting for years, but the ways in which blacks in Montgomery were able to mobilize speak to their sense of connectedness and understanding of a shared narrative in their experience with segregation and desire for change.

3. Harold Ford, Jr., "Black, White, Shades of Gray," *Newsweek*, June 2, 2008, 28–30.

4. Ibid., 30.

5. Cornel West, *The Cornel West Reader* (New York: Basic Civitas Books, 1999), xv.

6. Ibid., 146.

7. Ibid., xix.
8. Lawrence Grossberg, "History, Politics, and Postmodernism: Stuart Hall and Cultural Studies," *Journal of Communication Inquiry* 10 (2): 61–77.
9. Ibid., 62.
10. Thomas C. Battle and Donna M. Wells, Moorland-Spingarn Research Center, *Legacy: Treasures of Black History* (Washington, D.C.: National Geographic, 2006), 158. The poem was published on March 1, 1925, in the *Survey Graphic* magazine, in a special issue devoted to the arts and the black Renaissance. The volume was edited by Alain Locke, a close friend of Hughes. Hughes wrote a letter to his good friend Locke, sharing his poem and his desire to want to be judged by his internal merit and not by the color of his skin.
11. Barack Obama, *Dreams from My Father: A Story of Race and Inheritance* (New York: Three Rivers, 1995), 51.
12. Thomas Sowell, *Race and Culture: A World View* (New York: Basic Books, 1994).
13. Edouard Glissant, *Caribbean Discourse: Selected Essays* (Charlottesville: University Press of Virginia, 1999), xiii.
14. Ibid., xvi.
15. Kathleen Parker, "Obama Has U.S. Hooked on a Feeling," *Chicago Tribune*, January 11, 2008. This quote also appeared in Paul Street's *Barack Obama and the Future of American Politics* (Boulder, CO: Paradigm, 2009), 73.
16. Ibid.
17. Paul Street, *Barack Obama and the Future of American Politics* (Boulder, CO: Paradigm, 2009), 82.
18. Ibid., 82.
19. Richard Wolffe and Darren Briscoe, "Across the Divide: Barack Obama's Road to Racial Reconstruction," *Newsweek*, July 16, 2007.
20. Stuart Hall, "Thinking the Diaspora: Home-Thoughts from Abroad," *Small Axe* 3, No. 6 (1999): 1–18>
21. Barack Obama, Inaugural Address, January 20, 2009, Washington, D.C..
22. Stuart Hall, "Ethnicity: Identity and Difference," *Radical America* (Oct–Dec., 1989), published June 1991, 10ff.
23. Stokely Carmichael and Charles Hamilton, *Black Power: The Politics of Liberation in America* (New York: Vintage Books, 1967), 4. See also Stephen Steinberg, *Turning Back: The Retreat from Racial Justice in American Thought and Policy* (Boston, MA: Beacon, 1995), 75–76.

Chapter 7

1. W. E. B. DuBois, *Darkwater: Voices from Within the Veil* (New York: Schocken Books, 1969; first published in 1920), 134.
2. Barack Obama, "On the Internet," in *Barack Obama: In His Own Words,* ed. Lisa Rogak (New York: Carroll and Graf, 2007), 63. This quote also appeared in a segment as "Network Neutrality," podcast, June 8, 2006.
3. Lani Gunier, Tyranny of the Majority (New York: Free Press, 1994).

4. Sarah Lai Stirland, "The Tech of Obamamania: Online Phone Banks, Mass Texting and Blogs," *Wired.com*, February 14, 2008.

5. http://my.barackobama.com/page/content/hqblog (accessed on October 15, 2008).

6. Soren Dayton, "The Obama Campaign's Tech-Savvy Revolution," Pajamasmedia. com. The article was posted on November 14, 2008, 9:00 a.m. in Blogosphere, Computers, Elections 2008, Internet, Media, Money, Politics, Science and Technology, US News.

7. Ibid.

8. Ibid.

9. Steve Schifferes, "Internet Key To Obama Victories," BBC News, June 12, 2008. See http://news.bbc.co.uk/go/pr/fr/-/2/technology/7412045 (accessed on October 10, 2008).

10. Ibid.

11. Karen Tumulty, "Obama's Viral Marketing Campaign," *Time*, July 05, 2007. See www.time.com.

12. Don Tapscott, *The Digital Economy: Promise and Peril in the Age of Networked Intelligence* (New York: McGraw-Hill, 1996).

13. Ibid., 6.

14. Ibid., 7.

15. The Promise and Perils of Emerging Information Technologies, *A Report on the Second Annual Information Roundtable,* The Aspen Institute, 1993. See also a paper on the subject by John Seely Brown, Paul Duguid, and Susan Haviland, titled "Towards Informed Participation: Six Scenarios in Search of Democracy in the Electronic Age." These themes were also reflected in Tabscott's discussion in *The Digital Economy*, pages 303–309.

16. Kalle Lasn, *Culture Jam: How To Reverse America's Suicidal Consumer Binge— And Why We Must* (New York: Quill, 1999).

17. Ibid., 7.

18. David Mendell, *Obama: From Promise to Power* (New York: HarperCollins, 2007).

19. Ibid., 11.

20. Karen Tumulty, "Obama's Viral Marketing Campaign," *Time*, Thursday, July 5, 2007.

21. Claire Cain Miller, "How Obama's Internet Campaign Changed Politics," *The New York Times*, November 7, 2008.

22. Barack Obama, *The Audacity of Hope: Thoughts on Reclaiming the American Dream* (New York: Three Rivers, 2006), 120.

23. Ibid., 122.

Chapter 8

1. Barack Obama's economic speech at Cooper Union in New York on "Renewing The Economy." This speech also appeared in the New York Times, March 27, 2008.

2. Desmond Tutu, "A Word of Caution to Obama," Lecture at the 75th Anniversary of the British Council, February 2009. Tutu is the first black archbishop of Cape Town in South Africa, winner of the Nobel Peace Prize, and champion in the anti-apartheid struggle. See also Johnny Bernard Hill, *The Theology of Martin Luther King Jr., and Desmond Mpilo Tutu* (New York: Palgrave Macmillan, 2007).

3. Desmond Tutu, "A Word of Caution To Obama."

4. John R. Talbott, *Obamanomics: How Bottom-Up Economic Prosperity Will Replace Trickle-Down Economics* (New York: Seven Stories, 2008), 13. See also Barack Obama, Keynote Address, 2004 Democratic National Convention, July 2004, http://www.americanrhetoric.com/speeches/convention2004/barack-obama2004 dnc.htm (accessed on August 12, 2008); Speech by Barack Obama, "Keeping America's Promise," Janesville General Motors Assembly Plant, February 13, 2008, http://my.barackobama.com/page/community/post/samgrahamfelsen/ Cmzm; and Obama Campaign, "The Blueprint for Change: Barack Obama's Plan for America," Obama for America, http://www.barackobama.com/pdf/ ObamaBlueprintForChange.pdf.

5. Talbott, *Obamanomics*, 14.

6. Ibid., 34.

7. Ibid.

8. King, *Where Do We Go From Here?*, 179.

9. Ibid., 194.

10. Martin Luther King, Jr., "Nobel Prize Acceptance Speech," in *A Testament of Hope: The Essential Writings of Martin Luther King, Jr.* (New York: HarperSanFrancisco, 1988), 224.

11. Claude McKay, "A Capitalist At Dinner," in *Selected Poems*, ed. and with an introduction by Joan R. Sherman (New York: Dover, 1999), 25.

12. Talbott, *Obamanomics*, 36.

13. Douglas S. Massey and Nancy A. Denton, *American Apartheid: Segregation and the Making of the Underclass* (Cambridge, MA: Harvard University Press, 1993), 9.

14. These initiatives are drawn from the Obama-Biden Campaign website, http:// www.barackobama.com/issues/poverty/. Several other initiatives were mentioned, including measures related to "Making Work Pay for All Americans," "Strengthen Families," "Increase the Supply of Affordable Housing," "Tackle Concentrated Poverty," "Ensure Community-Based Investment Resources in Every Urban Community," and "Invest in Rural Areas."

15. Obama for America, *Change We Can Believe In: Barack Obama's Plan To Renew America's Promise*, with a Foreword by Barack Obama (New York: Three Rivers, 2008), 27–28.

16. Peter J. Paris, *Black Leaders in Conflict: Joseph H. Jackson, Martin Luther King Jr., Malcolm X, Adam Clayton Powell Jr.* (New York: Pilgrim, 1978), 104.

17. Ibid., 104–105.

18. Martin Luther King Jr., *Stride Toward Freedom* (New York: Harper & Row, 1958), 77.

19. Andrew Hacker, *Money: Who Has How Much and Why* (New York: Scribner, 1997), 31. Hacker is also author of *Two Nations: Black and White, White, Separate and Unequal* (New York: Ballatine Books, 1995), 31.

20. Hacker, *Money*, 32.

21. Ibid., 33.

22. Ibid., 44.

Chapter 9

1. W. E. B. DuBois, *The Souls of Black Folks* (New York: Penguin Books, 1995; originally published 1903), 276–277.

2. Langston Hughes, "I've Known Rivers," *The Collected Poems of Langston Hughes*, (New York: Alfred A. Knopf, 1994).

3. Bob Goudzwaard, Mark Vander Vennen, and David Van Heemst, *Hope In Troubled Times: A New Vision for Confronting Global Crises* (Grand Rapids, MI: Baker, 2007).

4. The report is available at http://www.millenniumassessment.org. Statement from the board of the Millennium Ecosystem Assessment, "Living beyond Our Means: Natural Assets and Human Well-Being" (Board of MEA, 2005; available via World Resources Institute, Washington, D.C.), 23. This also appeared in Goudzwaard, Vander Vennen, and Van Heemst, *Hope in Troubled Times*, 16. See also Stephen Lewis, *Race Against Time* (Toronto: House of Anansi, 2005).

5. Lewis, *Race Against Time*, 23.

6. Martin Rees, *Our Final Hour: A Scientist's Warning: How Terror, Error, and Environmental Disaster Threaten Humankind's Future in This Century on Earth and Beyond* (New York: Basic Books, 2003, repr., 2004), vii, 188.

7. Francis Fukuyama, *The End of History and the Last Man* (Toronto: HarperCollins, 1993); Daniel Bell, *The End of Ideology* (Cambridge, MA: Harvard University Press, 2000); Sam Harris, *The End of Faith* (New York: PenguinBooks, 2005); Bill McKibbon, *The End of Nature* (New York: Anchor Books, 1997); John Horgan, *The End of Science* (Toronto: HarperCollins, 1998).

8. Goudzwaard, Vander Vennen, and Van Heemst, *Hope in Troubled Times,* 18.

9. Ibid., 18. This quote was also published in *Time Magazine*, March 14, 2005, 35. See also Jeffrey Sachs, *The End of Poverty: Economic Possibilities for Our Time*, Foreword by Bono (New York: Penguin Books, 2005). For issues around global trade and poverty, read Bob Goudzwaard and Harry de Lange, *Beyond Poverty and Affluence: Towards a Canadian Economy of Care*, trans. and ed. Mark Vander Veenen, with Forward by Maurice F. Strong (Toronto: University of Toronto Press, 1994), 85–86. The book was also published as *Beyond Poverty and Affluence: Toward an Economy of Care* (Wm. B. Eerdmans and WCC).

10. Goudzwaard, Vander Vennen, and Van Heemst, *Hope In Troubled Times*, 20. For more on the problem of global poverty, read George Soros, *The Crisis of Global Capitalism: Open Society Endangered* (New York: Public Affairs, 1998), xix–xx. See also John A. Coleman's *Globalization and Catholic Social Thought*,

ed. John A. Coleman and William F. Ryan (Maryknoll, NY: Orbis Books, 2005), 12.

11. Barack Obama, *The Audacity of Hope: Thoughts on Reclaiming the American Dream* (New York: Three Rivers, 2006), 55.

12. Barack Obama, Acceptance Speech, delivered on November 4, 2008, at Grant Park, Chicago, IL.

13. Nancy Gibbs, "This is Our Time: Barack Obama—President Elect of the United States," *Time Magazine*, November 17, 2008, 34–40.

14. Joe Klein, "Passing the Torch: Obama's Victory Heralds a New Generation of Leaders—and an America That is Still Taking Shape," *Time Magazine*, November 17, 2008, 26–27.

Chapter 10

1. W. E. B. DuBois, *The Souls of Black Folks* (New York: Penguin Books, 1995; originally published in 1903), 162.

2. Dwight Hopkins, *Heart and Head: Black Theology—Past, Present, and Future* (New York: Palgrave Macmillan for St. Martin's Press, 2002), 130.

3. William Julius Wilson, *The Declining Significance of Race*. See also by Wilson, *When Work Disappears: The World of the New Urban Poor* (New York: Vintage Books, 1996).

4. Leon H. Sullivan, *Moving Mountains: The Principles and Purposes of Leon Sullivan* (Valley Forge, PA: Judson, 1998).

5. Ronald B. Mincy, *Nurturing Young Black Males: Challenges to Agencies, Programs, and Social Policy* (Washington, D.C.: Urban Institute Press, 1994).

6. Cf. A. G. Hilliard, "A Framework for Focused Counseling on the African American Man," *Journal of Non-White Concerns in Personnel and Guidance* 13 (1985): 72–78. H. F. Myers and L. M. King, "Youth of the Black Underclass: Urban Stress and Mental Health," *Fanon Center Journal* 1 (January, 1980): 1–27.

7. Earl O. Hutchinson, *The Assassination of the Black Male Image* (New York: Simon & Schuster, 1994), 125.

8. National Research Council, *A Common Destiny: Blacks and American Society* (Washington, D.C.: National Academy Press, 1989).

9. J. R. Feagin, and M. p. Sikes, *Living with Racism: The Black Middle-Class Experience* (Boston, MA: Beacon, 1994); Andrew Hacker, *Two Nations: Black and White, Separate, Hostile, Unequal* (New York: Scribner, 1992); D. Massey and N. Denton, *American Apartheid* (Cambridge, MA: Harvard University Press, 1993). Cf. Julius W. Wilson, *When Work Disappears* (New York: Alfred A. Knopf, 1996); and A. Wilson, *Understanding Black Adolescent Male Violence* (New York: Afrikan World Infosystems, 1992).

10. Pedro Noguera, "Reducing and Preventing Youth Violence: An Analysis of Causes and An Assessment of Successful Programs," *Wellness Lectures* (Oakland, CA: University of California Office of the President, 1995).

11. H. Spivak, D. Prothrow-Stith, and A. Hausman, "Dying Is No Accident," *Pediatric Clinics of North America* 35, no. 6 (December, 1988).

12. Cf. W. Roper, "The Prevention of Minority Youth Violence Must Begin Despite Risks and Imperfect Understanding," *Public Health Reports* 106, no. 3 (May–June, 1991).

13. Noguera, "Reducing and Preventing Youth Violence," 2.

14. Cornel West, *Race Matters* (New York: Vintage Books, 1993), 23.

15. Tommie Shelby, *We Who Are Dark: The Philosophical Foundations of Black Solidarity* (Cambridge, MA: Belknap Press of Harvard University Press, 2005), 11.

16. Ibid., 12.

17. Andrew Black, "'The War on People': Reframing 'The War on Drugs' By Addressing Racism Within American Drug Policy Through Restorative Justice and Community Collaboration," *University of Louisville Law Review* 46, 179–199.

18. Obama for America, *Change We Can Believe In: Barack Obama's Plan to Renew America's Promise* (New York: Three Rivers, 2008), 180.

19. Ibid.

20. Laura Magnani and Harmon L. Wray, *Beyond Prisons: A New Interfaith Paradigm for Our Failed Prison System* (Mineapolis, MN: Augsburg Fortress, 2006), 14–15.

21. Children's Defense Fund, *America's Cradle to Prison Pipeline*, a report published in 2007.

22. http://dpca.state.ny.us/ati_description.htm (accessed on September 1, 2008).

23. James Weldon Johnson, "Lift Every Voice and Sing," (1900) also known as the "Black National Anthem."

Selected Bibliography

Ansbro, John J., *Martin Luther King, Jr.: The Making of a Mind* (Maryknoll, NY: Orbis Books, 1982).

Asante, Molefi Kete, *The Afrocentric Idea* (Philadelphia, PA: Temple University Press, 1998).

——, *Afrocentricity* (Trenton, NJ: African World Press, 1988).

Baker, Ray Stannard, *Following the Color Line: American Negro Citizenship in the Progressive Era* (New York: Harper & Row, 1964; originally published by Doubleday, 1908).

Baldwin, Lewis, *There is a Balm in Gilead: The Cultural Roots of Martin Luther King, Jr.* (Minneapolis, MN: Augsburg Fortress, 1991).

——, *Toward the Beloved Community: Martin Luther King, Jr. and South Africa* (Cleveland: Pilgrim Press, 1995).

Berrian, Albert H., comp. *Negritude; Essays and Studies* (Hampton, VA: Hampton Institute Press, 1967).

Bishop, Jim, *The Days Of Martin Luther King, Jr.* (New York: Barnes and Noble, 1971).

Black, Andrew, "'The War on People': Reframing 'The War on Drugs' By Addressing Racism Within American Drug Policy Through Restorative Justice and Community Collaboration," *University of Louisville Law Review* 46, 179–199.

Boff, Leonardo, *Global Civilization: Challenges to Society and Christianity* (London: Equinox, 2005).

Branch, Taylor, *Parting the Waters: America in the King Years 1954–63* (New York: Simon & Schuster, 1988).

——, *Pillar of Fire: America in the King Years 1963–65* (New York: Simon & Schuster, 1998).

Brown, Michael K., Martin Carnoy, Elliott Currie, Troy Duster, David B. Oppenheimer, Marjorie M. Shultz, and David Wellman, *Whitewashing Race: The Myth of a Color-Blind Society* (Berkeley, CA: University of California Press).

Carson, Clayborne (ed.), *The Papers of Martin Luther King, Jr., Volume I: Called To Serve* (Berkeley, CA: University of California Press, 1992).

——, *The Papers of Martin Luther King, Jr., Volume II: Rediscovering Precious Values.* (Berkeley, CA: University of California Press, 1994).

————, *The Papers of Martin Luther King, Jr., Volume III: The Birth of A New Age* (Berkeley, CA: University of California Press, 1997).

Cesaire, Aimé, *Discourse on Colonialism*, trans. Joan Pinkham (New York: Monthly Review Press, 2000; originally published as an essay in 1950).

Cone, James, *Malcolm & Martin & America: A Dream or A Nightmare?* (Maryknoll, NY: Orbis, 2000).

Davis, Townsend, *Weary Feet, Rested Souls: A Guided History of the Civil Rights Movement* (New York: W.W. Norton, 1998).

Dayton, Soren, "The Obama Campaign's Tech-Savvy Revolution," Pajamasmedia.com.

Diop, Cheikh Anta, *The African Origin of Civilization: Myth or Reality*, trans. by Mercer Cook from French (Chicago, IL: Lawrence Hill Books, 1974).

————, *Anteriorite des civilisations negres: Mythe ou verite historique?* (Paris: Presence Africaine, 1967).

————, *Civilization or Barbarism: An Authentic Anthropology*, trans. Yaa-Lengi Meema Ngemi from French (Brooklyn, NY: Lawrence Hill Books, 1991).

————, *L'Afrique Noire precoloniale* [Precolonial Black Africa] (Paris, France: Presence Africaine, 1960).

————, *L' Antiquite Africaine par l'image* (Dakar: IFAN, 1976).

————, *L'Unite culturelle de l'Afrique Noire* (Paris, France: Presence Africaine, 1959).

————, *Nations negres et Culture* (Paris, France: Presence Africaine, 1954, Pocketbook edition, 1979).

————, *Parente genetique de l'egyptien pharaonique et de langues negro-africaines* (Dakar: IFAN, 1977).

Downing, Frederick L., *To See the Promised Land: The Faith Pilgrimage of Martin Luther King, Jr.* (Macon, GA: Mercer University Press, 1986).

Du Bois, William Edward Burghardt, *The Souls of Black Folk* (New York: Penguin, 1995; originally published 1903).

————, *Darkwater: Voices from Within the Veil* (New York: Schocken Books, 1969; first published in 1920).

Erskine, Noel Leo, *King Among The Theologians* (Cleveland, OH: Pilgrim Press, 1994).

Fanon, Frantz, *A Dying Colonialism*, trans. Haakon Chevalier with introd. by Adolfo Gilly (New York: Grove, 1994).

Feagin, J. R., and M. p. Sikes, *Living with Racism: The Black Middle-Class Experience* (Boston, MA: Beacon, 1994).

Finn, Julio, *Voices of Negritude: With an Anthology of Negritude Poems Translated from the French, Portuguese and Spanish* (London: Quartet, 1988).

Franklin, John Hope, *The Color Line: Legacy for the Twenty-First Century* (Columbia, MO: University of Missouri Press, 1993).

Fukuyama, Francis, *The End of History and the Last Man* (Toronto: HarperCollins Canada, 1993).

Garrow, David J., *Bearing the Cross: Martin Luther King, Jr., and the Southern Christian Leadership Conference* (New York: Vintage Books, 1986).

Gates, Henry L., and Kwame Appiah, *Africana* (New York: Basic Civitas Books, a division of Perseus Books, 1999).

Gever, Martha, Trinh T. Minh-ha, and Cornel West (eds.), *Out There: Marginalization and Contemporary Cultures* (Cambridge, MA: MIT Press, 1990).

Glissant, Edouard, *Caribbean Discourse: Selected Essay* (Charlottesville, VA: University Press of Virginia, 1999).

Gobineau, Joseph, *Essai sur l'inegalite des races humaines*, Book II, chapter VII (Google Books).

Goudzwaard, Bob, and Harry de Lange, *Beyond Poverty and Affluence: Towards a Canadian Economy of Care*, trans. and ed. Mark Vander Veenen, with forward by Maurice F. Strong (Toronto: University of Toronto Press, 1994).

————, Mark Vander Vennen, and David Van Heemst, *Hope In Troubled Times: A New Vision for Confronting Global Crises* (Grand Rapids, MI: Baker, 2007).

Hacker, Andrew, *Two Nations: Black and White, Separate, Hostile, Unequal* (New York: Scribner, 1992).

————, *Money: Who Has How Much and Why* (New York: Scribner, 1997).

Hall, Stuart, "Ethnicity: Identity and Difference," in *Radical America* (Oct.–Dec., 1989), published June 1991, 10.

————, "Notes on Deconstructing 'the Popular'," in R. Samuel (ed.) *People's History and Socialist Theory* (Boston: Routledge and Kegan Paul, 1981).

————, "Thinking the Diaspora: Home-Thoughts from Abroad," *Small Axe,* no. 6 (September 1999), 1–18.

Higginbotham, A. Leon Jr., *In the Matter of Color: Race and the American Legal Process* (New York: Oxford University Press, 1978).

Hopkins Dwight, *Heart and Head: Black Theology—Past, Present, and Future* (New York: Palgrave Macmillan for St. Martin's Press, 2002).

Hughes, Langston, *The Collected Poems of Langston Hughes* (New York: Alfred A. Knopf, 1940).

Hutchinson, Earl O., *The Assassination of the Black Male Image* (New York: Simon & Schuster, 1994).

Kelley, Robin D. G., *Race Rebels: Culture, Politics, and the Black Working Class* (New York: Free Press, 1996).

Kennedy, Randall *Sellout: The Politics of Racial Betrayal* (New York: Pantheon, 2008).

————, "Memo to Martin Luther King," editorial, *National Review* 19 (Dec. 12, 1967): 1368; *Crito* 50b.

————, *Negro History Bulletin* 31, no. 5 (May, 1968), 22.

————, *Strength To Love* (Philadelphia: Fortress, 1963).

————, *Stride Toward Freedom: The Montgomery Story* (New York: Harper & Row, 1958).

————, "The Rising Tide of Racial Consciousness," *The YMCA Magazine* (December, 1960).

————, *Where Do We Go From Here: Chaos or Community?* (New York: Harper & Row, 1967).

————, *Why We Can't Wait* (New York: Harper & Row, 1963).

King, Coretta Scott, *The Words of Martin Luther King, Jr.* (New York: New Market, 1987).

King, Martin Luther Jr., "An Autobiography of Religious Development" (Unpublished document).

————, "The Early Days," excerpts of a sermon delivered at the Mt. Pisgah Missionary Baptist Church, Chicago, IL (The King Center Archives, 27 August 1967), 9–12.

————, "The Ethical Demands of Integration," *Religion and Labor* (May, 1963), 4.

————, "Facing the Challenge of a New Age," *Phylon* 18 (April, 1957).

————, *King Papers*, Mugar Memorial Library, Boston University, Boston, Mass., n.d., circa 1950).

Lasn, Kalle, *Culture Jam: How To Reverse America's Suicidal Consumer Binge—And Why We Must* (New York: Quill, 1999).

Locke, Alain, *The New Negro*, in *Afrocentric Christianity* (New York: Atheneum, 1992), p. 22.

Long, Richard, *Negritude: Philosophy of Culture, CAAS occasional paper*, no. 7 (Atlanta, GA: Atlanta University, Atlanta Center for African-American Studies, 1971; originally published in 1927).

Magnani, Laura, and Wray, Harmon L., *Beyond Prisons: A New Interfaith Paradigm for Our Failed Prison System* (Minneapolis, MN: Augsburg Fortress, 2006).

Mansfield, Stephen, *The Faith of Barack Obama* (Nashville, TN: Thomas Nelson, 2008).

Markovitz, Irving L., *Leopold Sedar Senghor and the politics of Negritude*, 1st edit. (New York: Atheneum, 1967, originally published in 1934).

Marsh, Charles, *God's Long Summer: Stories of Faith and Civil Rights* (Princeton University Press, 1999).

Massey, D., and N. Denton, *American Apartheid* (Cambridge, MA: Harvard University Press, 1993).

McKay, Claude, "A Capitalist At Dinner," in *Selected Poems*, ed. and with an introd. by Joan R. Sherman (New York: Dover, 1999).

Mendell, David, *Obama: From Promise to Power* (New York: HarperCollins, 2007).

Michael, Colette Verger, *Negritude: An Annotated Bibliography* (West, Cornwall, CT: Locust Hill, 1988).

Miller, Claire Cain, "How Obama's Internet Campaign Changed Politics," *The New York Times*, November 7, 2008.

Mincy, Ronald B., *Nurturing Young Black Males: Challenges to Agencies, Programs, and Social Policy* (Washington, DC: Urban Institute Press, 1994).

National Research Council, *A Common Destiny: Blacks and American Society* (Washington, D.C.: National Academy Press, 1989).

Noguera, Pedro, "Reducing and Preventing Youth Violence: An Analysis of Causes and An Assessment of Successful Programs," in 1995 *Wellness Lectures* (Oakland, CA: University of California Office of the President, 1995).

Nygren, Anders, *Agape and Eros*, trans. Philip Watson (New York: Harper & Row, 1969).

Obama, Barack, *The Audacity of Hope: Thoughts on Reclaiming the American Dream* (New York: Three Rivers, 2006).

———, *Dreams from My Father: A Story of Race and Inheritance* (New York: Three Rivers, 1995).

———, "Renewing The Economy," *New York Times*, March 27, 2008.

———, "Keeping America's Promise," Janesville General Motors Assembly Plant, February 13, 2008; http://my.barackobama.com/page/community/post/samgrahamfelsen/Cmzm.

———, Keynote Address, 2004 Democratic National Convention, July 2004, http://www.americanrhetoric.com/speeches/convention2004/barack-obama2004dnc.htm.

———, "On Africa," in *Barack Obama: In His Own Words*, ed. Lisa Rogak (New York: Carroll and Graf, 2007), 6.

———, "On the Internet," in *Barack Obama: In His Own Words*, ed. Lisa Rogak (New York: Carroll and Graf, 2007), 63. This quote also appeared in a segment as "Network Neutrality," podcast, June 8, 2006.

Obama for America, *Change We Can Believe in: Barack Obama's Plan to Renew America's Promise*, with a Foreword by Barack Obama (New York: Three Rivers, 2008), 27–28.

Paris, Peter, J. *Black Leaders in Conflict: Joseph H. Jackson, Martin Luther King Jr., Malcolm X, Adam Clayton Powell Jr.* (New York: Pilgrim Press, 1978).

Roberts, J. Deotis, *Africentric Christianity: A Theological Appraisal for Ministry* (Valley Forge, PA: Judson, 2000).

———, *A Black Political Theology* (Philadelphia, PA: Westminster, 1974).

———, *Black Theology in Dialogue* (Philadelphia, PA: Westminster, 1987).

Rogak, Lisa, ed., *Barack Obama: In His Own Words* (New York: Carroll and Graf, 2007).

Sachs, Jeffrey, *The End of Poverty: Economic Possibilities for Our Time*, forward by Bono (New York: Penguin Books, 2005).

Sanders, Cheryl, ed., *Living The Intersection: Womanism and Afrocentrism in Theology* (Minneapolis, MN: Augsburg Fortress, 1995).

Schifferes, Steve, "Internet Key To Obama Victories," BBC News, June 12, 2008.

Shapiro, Norman R., comp. *Negritude; Black poetry from Africa and the Carribean*, Bilingual ed. (New York: October House, 1970)

Smith, Ervin, *The Ethics of Martin Luther King, Jr.* (New York: Edwin Mellon, 1981).

Smith, Kenneth L., and Ira G. Zepp, *Search for the Beloved Community: The Thinking of Martin Luther King, Jr.* (Valley Forge, PA: Judson, 1998).

Stirland, Sarah Lai, "The Tech of Obamamania: Online Phone Banks, Mass Texting and Blogs," *Wired.com*, February 14, 2008.

Street, Paul, *Barack Obama and the Future of American Politics* (Boulder, CO: Paradigm, 2009).

Talbott, John R., *Obamanomics: How Bottom-Up Economic Prosperity Will Replace Trickle-Down Economics* (New York: Seven Stories, 2008).

Tapscott, Karen Don, *The Digital Economy: Promise and Peril in the Age of Networked Intelligence* (New York: McGraw-Hill, 1996).

Thomas, Evans, "A Memo to Senator Obama," *Time Magazine*, June 2, 2008, 22–27.

Thoreau, Henry, "On the Duty of Civil Disobedience," *Social and Political Philosophy*, ed. John Somervill and Ronald Santoni (New York: Doubleday, 1963).

Thurman, Howard, *Jesus and the Disinherited* (Richmond, ID: Friends United, 1949), reprinted in 1981.

Wallace-Wells, Ben, "Destiny's Child," *Rolling Stone Magazine*, February 22, 2007.

Washington, James Melvin, *Frustrated Fellowship: The Black Baptist Quest for Social Power* (Macon, Georgia: Mercer University Press, 1986).

———, *A Testament of Hope: The Essential Writings and Speeches of Martin Luther King, Jr.* (HarperCollins, 1991).

West, Cornel, *The Cornel West Reader* (New York: Basic Civitas Books, 1999).

———, "The New Cultural Politics of Difference," in *Keeping the Faith: Philosophy and Race in America* (London: Routledge, 1991), 3–32.

———, *Prophesy Deliverance! An Afro-American Revolutionary Christianity* (Philadelphia: Westminster, 1982).

———, *Prophetic Fragments* (Grand Rapids, Mich.: Wm.B. Eerdmans, 1988).

———, *Prophetic Thought in Postmodern Times* (Monroe, ME: Common Courage, 1993).

———, *Race Matters* (Boston: Beacon, 1993).

Williams, John A., *The King God Didn't Save: Reflections on the Life and Death of Martin Luther King, Jr.* (New York: Coward-McCann, 1970).

William Julius Wilson, *The Declining Significance of Race: Blacks and Changing American Institutions* (Chicago, IL: University of Chicago Press, 1978).

———, "Good Kids from Bad Neighborhoods: Successful Development," in *Social Context* with D. Elliott, S. Menard, A.C. Elliott, B. Rankin and D. Huizinga (New York: Cambridge University Press, 2006).

———, "A New Agenda for America: Ghetto Poor," in *Ending Poverty in America: How to Restore the American Dream*, ed. John Edwards, Marion Crane, and Arne L. Kalleberg (New York: New Press, 2007), pp. 88–98.

———, "Social Theory and the Concept 'Underclass,'" in *Poverty and Inequality* ed. David B. Grusky and Ravi Kanbur (Palo Alto: Stanford University Press, 2005), pp. 103–116.

———, "Speaking to Publics," in *Public Sociology: Fifteen Eminent Sociologists Debate Politics and the Profession in the Twenty-first Century*, ed. Dan Clawson, Robert Zussman, Joya Misra, Naomi Gerstel, Randall Stokes, Douglas L. Anderton, and Michael Burawoy (Berkeley, CA: University of California Press, 2007), pp. 117–123.

———, "There Goes the Neighborhood: Racial, Ethnic, and Class Tensions," in *Four Chicago Neighborhoods and Their Meaning for America*, with Richard Taub (New York: Knopf, 2006).

———, *Understanding Black Adolescent Male Violence* (New York: Afrikan World Infosystems, 1992).

———, *When Work Disappears* (New York: Random House, 1996).

Winant, Howard, *The New Politics of Race: Globalism, Difference, Justice* (Minneapolis: University of Minneapolis Press, 2004).

World Health Organization Report 2008, "Primary Healthcare: Now More Than Ever," http://www.who.int/mediacentre/news/releases/2008/pr38/en/index.html.

Wright, Bruce, *Black Robes, White Justice: Why Our Legal System Doesn't Work for Blacks* (New York: Kensington, 1987; reprinted in 1993).

Index